Post-Keynesian Economics for the Future

NEW DIRECTIONS IN MODERN ECONOMICS

Series Editor: Malcolm C. Sawyer, *Professor of Economics, University of Leeds, UK*

New Directions in Modern Economics presents a challenge to orthodox economic thinking. It focuses on new ideas emanating from radical traditions including post-Keynesian, Kaleckian, neo-Ricardian and Marxian. The books in the series do not adhere rigidly to any single school of thought but attempt to present a positive alternative to the conventional wisdom.

For a full list of Edward Elgar published titles, including the titles in this series, visit our website at www.e-elgar.com.

Post-Keynesian Economics for the Future

Sustainability, Policy and Methodology

Edited by

Jesper Jespersen

Professor of Economics, Roskilde University and Adjunct Professor, Aalborg University, Denmark

Finn Olesen

Professor of Economics, Aalborg University, Denmark

Mikael Randrup Byrialsen

Associate Professor, Aalborg University, Denmark

NEW DIRECTIONS IN MODERN ECONOMICS

Cheltenham, UK • Northampton, MA, USA

© The Editors and Contributors Severally 2024

With the exception of any material published open access under a Creative Commons licence (see www.elgaronline.com), all rights are reserved and no part of this publication may be reproduced, stored in a retrieval system or transmitted in any form or by any means, electronic, mechanical or photocopying, recording, or otherwise without the prior permission of the publisher.

Chapter 2 is available for free as Open Access from the individual product page at www.elgaronline.com under a Creative Commons Attribution NonCommercial-ShareAlike 4.0 International (https://creativecommons.org/licenses/by-nc-sa/4.0/) license.

Published by
Edward Elgar Publishing Limited
The Lypiatts
15 Lansdown Road
Cheltenham
Glos GL50 2JA
UK

Edward Elgar Publishing, Inc.
William Pratt House
9 Dewey Court
Northampton
Massachusetts 01060
USA

A catalogue record for this book
is available from the British Library

Library of Congress Control Number: 2023948397

This book is available electronically in the **Elgar**online
Economics subject collection
http://dx.doi.org/10.4337/9781035307517

ISBN 978 1 0353 0750 0 (cased)
ISBN 978 1 0353 0751 7 (eBook)

Printed and bound by CPI Group (UK) Ltd, Croydon, CR0 4YY

Contents

Tables

Contributors

Mikael Randrup Byrialsen, Associate Professor, Aalborg University Business School, Denmark

Anna Maria Carabelli, Professor, Universitá del Piemonte Orientale, Italy

Etienne Espagne, Senior Climate Economist, World Bank, France

Eckhard Hein, Professor, Berlin School of Economics and Law, Germany

Andrew Jackson, Research Fellow, UK

Jesper Jespersen, Professor Emeritus, University of Roskilde, and Adjunct Professor, Aalborg University, Denmark

Thibault Laurentjoye, Assistant Professor, Aalborg University Business School, Denmark

Mogens Ove Madsen, Associate Professor, Aalborg University Business School, Denmark

Jacques Mazier, Professor Emeritus, Université Paris-Nord, France

Thi Thu Ha Nguyen, PhD Candidate, France

Finn Olesen, Professor, Aalborg University Business School, Denmark

Hamid Raza, Associate Professor, Aalborg University Business School, Denmark

Luis Reyes-Ortiz, Assistant Professor, Kedge Business School, France

Louis-Philippe Rochon, Professor, Laurentian University, Canada

Peter Skott, Professor, University of Massachusetts Amherst, USA, and Aalborg University Business School, Denmark

Geoff Tily, Senior Economist, Trades Union Congress, UK

Sebastian Valdecantos, Assistant Professor, Aalborg University Business School, Denmark

Preface and acknowledgements

In an ever changing world, there are no simple answers to complex questions. That is in general the case in most circumstances. As human beings we know that as a fact. We experience that in our daily lives. Repeatedly. As such, it should not come as a surprise to economists.

However, some economists – the mainstreamers – seem to have an enduring steadfastly capacity to see things quite differently. They tend to view economics matters as harmonious individual actions of perfection delivering the best macroeconomic outcomes possible. That is, they argue that modern economies are put on a unique path of intertemporal optimality due to the strength of the market mechanism. In their understanding, economic troublesome times, if present at all, are only of a temporary nature. Be that as it may, history and present empirical evidence tell a different story. As a fact of real life, we know that economies even in modern times most often are put in disequilibrium positions. These are the lessons learnt from the years of the Great Recession from 2008 and from the just passed Covid-19 pandemic.

Seen from an empirical perspective, there is a need for an alternative to the modern macroeconomic mainstream understanding.

And alternatives exist.

For years, heterodox economists have offered a theoretical and methodological economic universe that is in better accordance with facts of real life than that of the mainstream understanding. The present book aims to argue a strong alternative to the macroeconomic mainstream, with a post-Keynesian understanding. Therefore, in a total of 15 chapters we present various aspects of importance aiming to achieve a better understanding of how modern globally financial interdependent economies function. As such, we have chosen to focus on three important themes. Part I of the book deals with sustainable development and the usefulness of applying an approach of stock-flow consistent modelling to analyse macroeconomic problems, and Part II is devoted to important economic policy aspects including perspectives on behavioural and structuralist macroeconomics, demand-led growth and monetary policy issues. Finally, Part III of the book has its focus on methodology as it discusses some aspects of Keynes's understanding on uncertainty, presents the principle of effective demand as a useful macroeconomic framework for analyses, introduces power aspects in macroeconomics, points to a possible inspiration from the writings of Polanyi regarding economics for the future and critically highlights the modern macroeconomic quest for microfoundations of macroeconomics.

The editors would like to thank all the contributors to the book for their collaboration in preparing the chapters on the above-mentioned aspects of progressive post-Keynesian economics. Furthermore, we would like to express our gratitude to Edward Elgar Publishing, in particular Matthew Pitman and Stephanie Hartley, for their help and support throughout the process.

Finalizing the book in early spring of 2023 give us as editors an opportunity to express our respect for the unlimited inspiration and intellectual support which we have received through more than 50 years from the work of the late Victoria Chick. Throughout all her writings she has been a keen observer of macroeconomics of the real world. As such, she has been a pillar of strength and wisdom for most post-Keynesians concerning theoretical as well as methodological matters of the functioning of modern monetary economies. We salute her and bow. We honour her memory.

The editors

1. Progressive post-Keynesian economics for the future: an introduction

Jesper Jespersen, Finn Olesen and Mikael Randrup Byrialsen

INTRODUCTION

The world has changed radically in the last two decades. First, globally interdependent, in trade as well as financially, modern economies were hit hard by the recession that followed the financial crisis from 2008 onwards (see, for example, Madsen & Olesen 2016). Second came the Covid-19 pandemic which took most countries by surprise and made urgent fiscal and monetary governmental intervention necessary (Byrialsen et al. 2021). Then, in 2022, the Russian invasion of Ukraine enhanced the negative economic impact. As such, inflation has yet again become a problem that central bankers and governments must take into consideration when designing policy matters, together with aspects concerning demand-side and supply-side problems.

The economic policy reaction in Europe in general following the Great Recession was one of hesitation regarding the need for conducting expansionary fiscal policy in order to stimulate the level of effective demand. The response towards the sudden Covid-19 pandemic, however, was quite different. This time not only heterodox economists claimed that an economic strategy of swift and immediate governmental action was needed but also many more mainstream economists joined the choir of worried policy advisors, having finally seemed to have understood that demand-side aspects are crucial for the wellbeing of modern financial dependent economies. A satisfactory macroeconomic outcome with a low level of involuntary unemployment is not determined by supply-side policies only.

On the surface, it seems as if mainstreamers at least to some extent have understood what for long has been an established post-Keynesian fact, that demand-side management has an important role to play even in present-day economic policy making. Taking care of the level of effective demand is not something that only has a historical interesting dimension hinged on the experiences of the Great Depression of the 1930s. Focusing on demand-side aspects is as important as having an eye on supply-side matters.

However, one could speculate as to whether mainstreamers see the Great Recession and the Covid-19 pandemic as a genuine wake-up call for good. Do they really accept and acknowledge what was hitherto known as heterodox wisdom?[1] Have they really changed their views on what should be the content of an optimal monetary as well fiscal policy strategy? Do they really understand the need of focusing on sustainability aspects when doing macroeconomics? Do they really accept that the modern macroeconomic understanding of the New Neoclassical Synthesis with their dynamic stochastic general equilibrium (DSGE) models must undergo radical change? Do they really want to join the macroeconomic heterodoxy in a new synthesis, revolutionizing macroeconomics for decades to come? To many, perhaps most, especially heterodox-minded economists, the answers to these questions are probably a lot of 'nos'.

Therefore, now more than ever, there is an imminent need to present an alternative to the modern macroeconomic mainstream understanding. Empirical evidence has falsified many of the statements made by advocates of the New Neoclassical Synthesis. DSGE models are not that good for capturing what actually happens in modern, financially dependent, globally interlinked economies. That is, there is an important role to play for a progressive post-Keynesian agenda for the future. In a troublesome uncertain economic environment where households, firms and governments must act on imperfect knowledge where the future, as least regarding some aspects, is truly unknown, they are all bound to make mistakes in predicting the macroeconomic outcome in general to be one of less than perfection. Various macroeconomic outcomes turn out to be second best, demonstrating there is room for improvement. An outcome of perfection with full employment is perhaps out of reach, but a better second-best solution might be achieved with the right strategy for conducting economic policy. Furthermore, demand-side and supply-side problems aside, the macroeconomic agenda of modern times has an urgent need to try to cope with environmental sustainability – the clock is ticking: the green dimension must be at the very top of the political agenda. Moreover, it must be understood that the green transition cannot be successful by relying on the strength of the market mechanism alone. Private enterprise is not enough by itself. Economic policy guidance is crucial for achieving the necessary success.

As such, for many reasons, post-Keynesian advocacy is in demand. Theory and macroeconomic models have to be developed further as must strategies concerning how to conduct economic policies the right way in the short as well as in the long term. Running for Lucasian optimality is not going to do the trick. Likewise, relevant methodological considerations must be put forward as alternatives to the mainstream methodological understanding of pursuing an approach only based on a uniform mathematical modelling procedure. The benefits of using an approach of pluralism should be evident to most economists.

The present book aims to highlight the need for a focus on progressive post-Keynesian economics for the future. As such, the contents of the book are organized in three parts.

In Part I, comprised of five chapters, the book highlights various aspects of how to deal with a sustainable development that ensures a green transition, especially using a stock-flow consistent (SFC) modelling approach. This is done by presenting various policy aspects of economic models of France, Denmark and Vietnam. In Part II, further theoretical aspects of macroeconomic policies for the future are presented in a progressive post-Keynesian perspective. This part is comprised of four chapters focusing on different macroeconomic policy regimes, behavioural and structuralist perspectives on macroeconomics and monetary policy. Finally, Part III on methodology and theory, consisting of five chapters, covers aspects of Keynes's uncertainty, the principle of effective demand, power aspects in macroeconomics, the quest for microfoundations of macroeconomics and how to seek inspiration on these issues from the writings of Polanyi.

PART I: SUSTAINABLE DEVELOPMENT AND SFC MODELLING

In Chapter 2, Andrew Jackson presents a SFC, input-output model for the study of the different shocks associated with transitions to a low-carbon economy. These shocks include the introduction of a carbon tax, a change in bank financing conditions, a change in the energy sector's production processes and changes in social norms. The results of these simulations suggest that shocks that affect the real side of the economy are likely to lead to larger impacts on demand and generate larger transition risks than those that primarily affect firms' borrowing costs.

In Chapter 3, Etienne Espagne and Thi Thu Ha Nguyen use an empirical SFC model of the Vietnamese economy to analyse the economy-wide impacts of climate change by integrating various damage functions, which represent losses in agriculture production, the energy sector, total factor productivity, labour productivity and human mortality due to temperature changes. The Vietnamese government is putting climate change and sustainable development at the heart of its development policy. An assessment of climate change impacts is therefore crucial for policy planning at the macroeconomic level.

In Chapter 4, Sebastian Valdecantos addresses the tensions that the green transition entails for South American countries from a more aggregated perspective. The main contention is that given their productive structure is heavily based on primary products which in many cases bear high levels of pollution, the simultaneous attainment of economic prosperity, macroeconomic stability and environmental sustainability poses serious challenges. Considering that each of the three dimensions can be measured in diverse ways and, more specifically, taking into account that there are deep debates around what prosperity and environmental sustainability mean, the analysis proposed in this chapter should be taken as a heuristic exercise aimed at illustrating the tensions that South American countries could face in the transition toward a zero-carbon economy.

In the last chapters of this part of the book two fully estimated models for the French and the Danish economies are presented. In Chapter 5, Jacques Mazier and Luis Reyes present their SFC model of the French economy; an aggregate model with a single product, five domestic agents and the rest of the world with a complete representation of real and financial sectors in stocks and flows. The structure of the model is close to that of existing SFC models with demand-led dynamics, a Kaleckian accumulation behaviour and an indebtedness norm. The dynamic simulations on the past over the period 1996–2019 provide acceptable results. The basic variants display the usual multiplier effects and a dominant profit-led logic. The dynamics of the housing sector and the land price boom seem to work at the expense of firms' productive investment. Finally, the effects of unconventional monetary policy are evaluated: distribution of helicopter money in favour of the government to finance additional public investment or social transfers and partial cancellation of the public debt held by the central bank.

In Chapter 6, Mikael Randrup Byrialsen, Hamid Raza and Sebastian Valdecantos present their empirical SFC for the Danish economy. The behavioural equations are inspired by Post-Keynesian theory. The model is able to reproduce the actual dynamics of the key variable of the Danish economy for the period 2005–2020. In order to explore how the model reacts to a well-known shock, a permanent increase in the public expenditures is introduced. Despite the fact that both income taxes and propensity to import are quite high in Denmark, the effect of fiscal policy is able to stimulate the economic activity as well as the level of employment without producing higher inflation. However, the effect on public finances is negative, eventually limiting the size of the stimuli that the government can make.

PART II: ECONOMIC THEORY AND POLICY IMPLICATION

In Chapter 7, Eckhard Hein discusses how the Covid-19 crisis has hit the Eurozone asymmetrically and aggravated the macroeconomic imbalances, which already were present and caused by policy recommendations based on New Consensus Macroeconomics (NCM). In Hein's contribution it is demonstrated how a significant shift in the European Union demand and growth regime after the Covid-19 crisis using post-Keynesian and Kaleckian macroeconomic theories could pave the way for a stable demand-led regime targeted at full employment and stable inflation. Finally, it is assessed whether the European Union economic policy response towards the pandemic has led to fundamental changes away from NCM and towards the recommended demand-led policy mix.

Peter Skott claims in Chapter 8 that post-Keynesians have unduly questioned the relevance of behavioural economics on methodological grounds. However, according to Skott the very limited influence of behavioural economics on post-Keynesian economics is unfortunate. To him it would be a serious mistake to ignore the existing insights and empirical evidence from behavioural economics. The influence of norms and of fairness on wage formation and inflation is used to illustrate and emphasize his arguments.

With inflation back in a pan-pandemic world, Louis-Philippe Rochon's focus in Chapter 9 is on the response of central banks and monetary policy. Interest rates have been raised in an effort to tame inflation. But the efficiency of this monetary policy has been questioned theoretically and empirically. In his chapter he confronts the standard NCM understanding of the transmission mechanism of monetary policy and reveals how it lacks empirical support. Accordingly, Rochon asks the question: is this monetary policy the best way to deal with inflation, especially when it is not driven by demand forces?

In the final chapter of Part II, Thibault Laurentjoye continues the debate of causes and consequences of the present high inflation. He admits that several debates are taking place to judge whether a response based on restrictive monetary policy is relevant to address and tame inflation. He agrees with Rochon that one important debate revolves around supply- versus demand-driven arguments, which resonate with the theoretical opposition between mainstream and post-Keynesian macroeconomists. But Laurentjoye takes up a perhaps even more relevant consideration understanding the roots of inflation and in particular whether they concern goods and services, which are relatively elastic or inelastic to price variations. Using a simple model consisting of two goods, inelastic and elastic, he compares the efficacy of restrictive monetary policy against inflation driven by one or the other type of good. He finds that restrictive monetary policy works relatively as expected when inflation primarily concerns elastic goods, while it has no effect – or even a perverse effect – when inflation primarily originates from inelastic goods.

PART III: METHODOLOGY AND THEORY

In Chapter 11, Anna Maria Carabelli interpretates Keynes's understanding of uncertainty as a tragic rational dilemma, that is, as a tragic choice in terms of a Greek tragedy. In general, Keynes's uncertainty is characterized by three conditions: ignorance, low weight of argument (evidential weight) and incommensurability of probability. And it is the incommensurability condition that Carabelli discusses in the chapter. She states that the non-comparability and incommensurability of Keynes's logical probability is intrinsic, due to the nature of the material constituting his probability as the material of probability is, in general, non-homogeneous since the reasons, grounds or evidence are heterogeneous and incommensurable. Therefore, it is not possible to reduce this heterogeneity characterizing the material of Keynes's probability with the use of a common or homogeneous unit of measure, since no common unit of quantity of probability exists; nor is there any possibility of introducing tacit assumptions of atomicity and independence. As such, Carabelli offers a new perspective on Keynes's uncertainty as she considers it as an incommensurable magnitude.

In Chapter 12, Jesper Jespersen reconsiders the principle of effective demand. Paraphrasing Keynes, Jespersen argues that in the long run almost anything is possible. To analyse how this could be true we have to expand the analysis given in the *General Theory* with considerations concerning the longer run. In this perspective, there must be a focus on several structural factors and also on sustainability and the process of greening the economic system to secure 'the economic possibilities for our grandchildren' in the future. Hereby, we can expand the analysis of effective demand for the longer run by adding the role of productivity and environmental costs to the sustainability analysis. In conclusion, Jespersen paraphrases the same optimism which Keynes expressed in 1942 when looking at the severely bombed London: 'Anything we can *do*, we can afford.'

In Chapter 13, Finn Olesen addresses the impact made by Robert E. Lucas on modern macroeconomics with a special focus on the 'Lucas critique'. As one of the founding fathers of New Classical Theory, Lucas has made several important contributions. As such, his thinking had an immense impact on what later became modern mainstream macroeconomics (New Neoclassical Synthesis). This started with his 'Lucas critique', which substantially influenced how to build macroeconomic models and how to evaluate economic policies. However, much of this critique should not come as a total surprise to post-Keynesians as Keynes himself discussed many of the elements present in Lucas's 1976 article, as explained by Olesen.

Geoff Tily offers a somewhat new view on macroeconomics as an instrument of power. In Chapter 14, he argues that the *General Theory* revealed a fault line in monetary economies between the interest of wealth-owners and labour, thereby confirming the role of class interests and power in economic and societal outcomes. Empirically, the events over the past century arguably prove that operating the system in the interests of the wealthy makes the overall level of economic activity dangerously unstable. This suggests a categorical imperative to rearrange the system with the needs of labour paramount. As in the final chapter of Keynes's book, the imperative is global in substance. Despite this, seen from the perspective of Tily, Keynes handled badly the political implications of his work. As such, in this chapter, Tily attempts to do better, by translating the *General Theory* into an account of the operation of power relations and drawing out the implications for policy in the broadest terms.

Finally, arguing that post-Keynesians and others need to develop theories and policies relevant to the real world, in Chapter 15, Mogens Ove Madsen takes the writings of Karl Polanyi as a source of potential interest. Economic activity is hinged on contemporary social institutions. As such, Polanyi argues that markets cannot be understood solely through economic theory. Instead, markets are embedded in social and political logics, making it necessary for economists to take politics into account when trying to understand the economy. That is, the state has become an arena of contest between economy and democracy, between the requirements of the capitalist economic order and the social and political demands of citizens. Giving a number of examples, Madsen argues that Polanyi's understanding is helpful in dealing with current global macroeconomic challenges and might be of interest to post-Keynesians in their struggle to develop relevant economic theories for the future.

NOTE

1. As highlighted by Jespersen and Olesen (2019), among others.

REFERENCES

Byrialsen, Mikael Randrup, Olesen, Finn & Madsen, Mogens Ove (2021) 'The macroeconomic effects of Covid-19: The imperative need for a Keynesian solution', *Revue de la regulation – Capitalisme, institutions, pouviors*, 29, 1–19.

Jespersen, Jesper & Olesen, Finn (Eds) (2019) *Progressive Post-Keynesian Economics: Dealing with Reality*, Edward Elgar Publishing, Cheltenham, UK and Northampton, MA, USA.

Madsen, Mogens Ove & Olesen, Finn (Eds) (2016) *Macroeconomics after the Financial Crisis: A Post-Keynesian Perspective*, Routledge, London.

PART I

Sustainable development and SFC modelling

2. Modelling transition-related shocks in the green economy

Andrew Jackson

INTRODUCTION

Limiting global temperature increases to 2°C above pre-industrial levels will necessitate a transition away from fossil fuels and towards net-zero carbon forms of energy production.[1] While an energy technology transition is necessary to avoid the catastrophic effects of climate change, the policy, technology and behaviour changes associated with the transition process are likely to generate transition risks, including asset stranding (Grant, 2018; McGlade & Ekins, 2015; Pfeiffer et al., 2018), as well as opportunities for economic development and growth (Mountford et al., 2018). To investigate these risks and opportunities, this chapter presents a stock-flow consistent (SFC), input–output (IO) model which is used to simulate the introduction of a carbon tax, divestment campaign, change in bank-financing conditions and a change in the energy return on energy invested (EROI) in the energy sector.[2]

THE MODEL

The model[3] presented is made up of three firm sectors ('green', 'fossil fuel' and 'other'), two household sectors ('ethical' and 'normal') and one banking sector. The financial assets included in the model are equities (issued by the green, fossil fuel and other firm sectors) and deposits and loans (issued by banks). The real assets included in the model are the capital assets produced by the green, fossil fuel and other firm sectors.

The basic structure of the model is summarised by Figure 2.1. Starting with the firm sectors, the green sector produces net-zero carbon energy goods, the fossil fuel sector produces high-carbon energy goods and the other sector produces 'everything else' – i.e., all non-energy goods. Each firm sector sells its output to the household sectors and to each firm sector (this requires the inclusion of an IO model into the SFC model). The production of output requires labour (which is purchased from households), capital (which firms

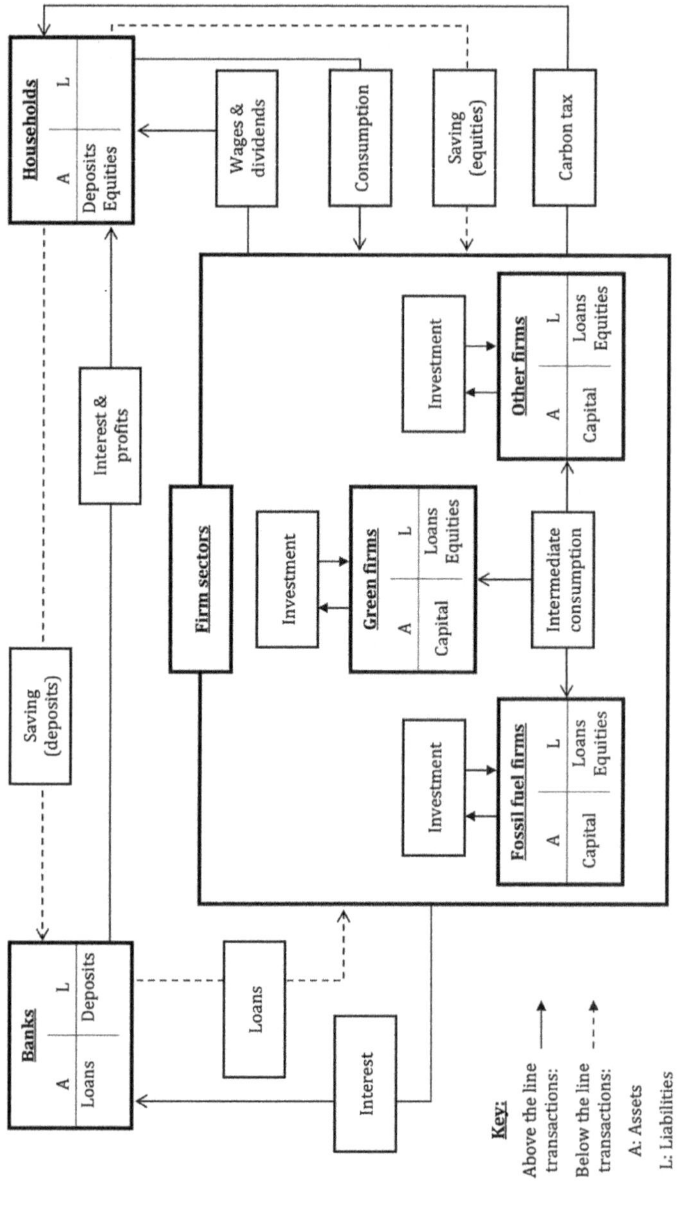

Figure 2.1 SFC IO model diagram

produce themselves) and intermediate goods. An increase in the relative price of an intermediate good leads to a reduction in the intermediate consumption of that good relative to the other two goods. Firms finance themselves through retained earnings, by borrowing from banks and by issuing equities (which are purchased by households), with the weight of each form of financing determined by its relative cost.

Turning to the household sectors, both ethical and normal households buy goods from firms (with consumption depending on relative prices), sell their labour to firms and allocate their wealth between the different equities issued by each firm sector and bank deposits (following a Tobinesque portfolio allocation approach). Although they have different names, ethical and normal households behave identically in the initial stationary state. However, in certain simulations the behaviour of a household sector may be altered – e.g., in one simulation ethical households divest from the fossil fuel sector's financial assets. In aggregate, ethical households account for 30 per cent of the total households in the initial steady state (by number, income and wealth), while normal households make up the remaining 70 per cent.

Finally, the banking sector makes loans to firms and issues deposits (which end up being held by the household sectors). Firms pay interest to banks on their loans, and banks pay interest on deposits to households. Bank profits, which are made from the spread between loan and deposit rates, are paid to households.

Although the aim of the model is to understand the theoretical impacts of various changes in market conditions that are associated with the transition to net zero, where possible the values of the parameters in the model are based on empirical estimates of these parameters for the UK economy (in 2016). When these are not available, parameter values are based on empirical estimates from other advanced economies, and when these are not available, parameter values are taken from equivalent parameters in other SFC models.[4]

SIMULATIONS

The structure of the model allows us to simulate the economic effects of various changes in market conditions that are associated with the transition to a net-zero economy. In particular, we are interested in looking at the economic impacts of: (1) the introduction of a carbon tax; (2) a divestment campaign; (3) a change in bank-financing conditions; and (4) an increase in the EROI of the green energy sector.

Each simulation is carried out under four parameter regimes. These regimes vary the values taken by two sets of parameters which determine first how sensitive households and firms are to the price of green and fossil fuel energy goods, and second how sensitive households are to the relative rate of return on financial assets. The primary motivation for varying these parameters is to investigate the extent to which the results of the various simulations are sensitive to different assumptions regarding: (1) the level of renewable and storage technology (which will influence the extent to which renewable energy can be substituted for fossil fuel energy); and (2) the sensitivity of agents to the returns on financial assets (which will be important in determining the economic impacts that are generated via financial markets). In what follows, the symbol (G^H) represents the high sensitivity to goods price regimes, the symbol (G^L) represents the low sensitivity to goods price regimes, the symbol (A^H) represents the high sensitivity to asset return regimes and the symbol (A^L) represents the low sensitivity to asset return regimes.

Market Conditions Simulation 1 (MC1): Carbon Tax on Fossil Fuel Sector Output

This simulation involves the introduction of a carbon tax on fossil fuel sector output. Starting in 2020, a carbon tax of £0.12 per unit of output is imposed on the fossil fuel sector. This tax is then increased by £0.12 a year, until it reaches £0.60 per unit of output in 2024. The tax then remains at £0.60 per unit of output from 2024 until the end of the simulation period. The value of tax is set at approximately 10 per cent of the price of a unit of fossil fuel sector output (in the initial steady state). Fossil fuel firms respond to the carbon tax by increasing their prices, to pass on the entire cost of the tax to their customers. As there is no government sector in the model, the funds raised by the carbon tax are distributed directly to each household sector, with the payments split between ethical and normal households in proportion to their size (i.e., 30 per cent of payments go to ethical households, while 70 per cent go to normal households).

The implementation of a carbon tax leads to fossil fuel prices increasing by approximately 13.3 per cent. Of the 13.3 per cent increase, approximately 10.3 percentage points can be directly attributed to the carbon tax. The other three percentage points are due to an increase in the price of the fossil fuel sector's intermediate inputs. Fossil fuel, green and other firm prices also increase because each sector uses fossil fuel goods as an input in their production processes. Overall, the carbon tax leads to an increase in the general price level (Figure 2.2a) of almost 2.5 per cent, which is around one percentage point more than the increase in the price of the other sector's goods.

One of the key features of the model is that changes in relative prices lead to changes in demand. Figures 2.2a and 2.2b illustrate how the price changes that result from a carbon tax lead to changes in the level of demand for green and fossil fuel goods. As is clear from the charts, the degree to which demand changes is highly dependent on the parameter regime in place. In the (G^L)

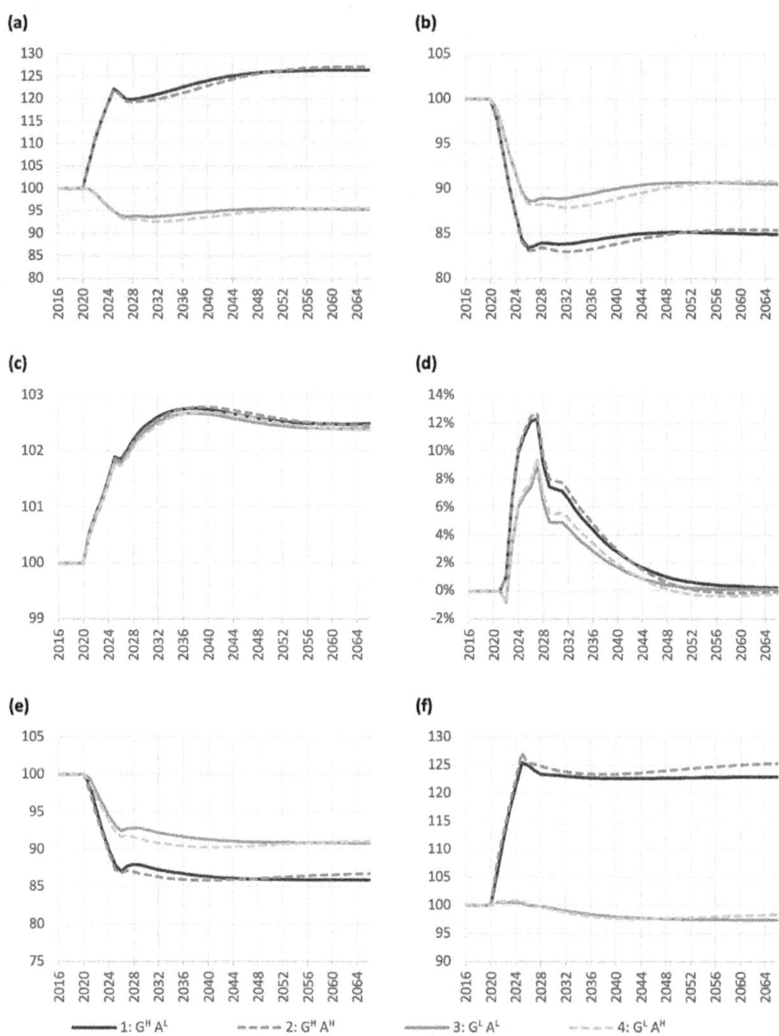

Figure 2.2 Carbon tax on fossil fuel output (MC1)

regimes, the change in relative prices leads to a fossil fuel output falling by more than green output (so that the ratio of green-to-fossil fuel output increases). Conversely, in the (G^H) regimes, the change in prices leads to a large increase in green output and a larger fall in fossil fuel output than occurs in the

(G^L) regimes. The changes in the demand for fossil fuel goods leads to fossil fuel capital being stranded (Figure 2.4). Approximately 12 per cent of fossil fuel assets are stranded in the (G^H) regimes, versus just over 8 per cent in the (G^L) regimes. The reason for the discrepancy in the degree of stranding relates to the larger reduction in fossil fuel demand in the (G^H) regimes.

Interestingly, in the (G^L) regimes, the demand for green output falls even as the relative price of green goods falls. This fall in green output is largely driven by the fall in real final demand. Real final demand decreases because the increase in prices (due to the carbon tax) causes real wealth to fall (real wealth enters into the consumption function). Thus, the increase in prices leads to a lower level of real consumption and consequently a lower level of real final demand. Thus, even as green goods become relatively cheaper, the demand for green goods is lower.

On the financial side, the fall in demand for the fossil fuel sector's goods leads to a reduction in the fossil fuel sector's return on equity and, thus, its market capitalisation (Figure 2.2e) (with the reduction in the fossil fuel sector's market capitalisation significantly larger in the G^H regimes). In the (G^H) regimes the increase in the demand for green goods leads to an increase in the green sector's return on equity and market capitalisation (Figure 2.2f). However, in (G^L) regimes the market value of the sector falls by just over 2 per cent, reflecting the small drop in the demand for green goods in these regimes.

Market Conditions Simulation 2 (MC2): Ethical Households Divestment Campaign

In this simulation, the ethical household sector divests from the fossil fuel sector's equities and invests in the green sector's equities. This simulation is intended to model a divest/invest campaign in which 30 per cent of the population (in this model the ethical household sector) decide to divest from the fossil fuel sector and instead invest their funds in financial assets issued by the renewable sector.

Starting in 2020, ethical households reduce/increase the proportion of their wealth they allocate to fossil fuel/green assets by 20 per cent each period, so that by 2024 (five years after the start of the simulation) they have completely divested from fossil fuel assets. The increase in the demand for green equities pushes up their price, while the decrease in the demand for fossil fuel equities leads to a fall in their price. These price changes lead to changes in the relative rates of return on each equity class, and these changes induce normal households to increase their purchases of fossil fuel equities and sell part of their holdings of green equities. Indeed, if ethical households are selling fossil fuel equities, then normal households must be buying fossil fuel equities. Likewise, the normal household sector must be selling green equities if the ethical household sector is buying green equities.

The divest/invest campaign thus leads to a change in each sector's equity price, market capitalisation and return on equity. The green firm sector's market capitalisation increases by between 30 and 60 per cent, whereas the fossil fuel firm sector's market capitalisation decreases by around 15 to 23 per cent (Figures 2.3a and 2.3b). The market value of each firm sector changes by more in the (A^L) regimes than in the (A^H) regimes. This is because the fall (increase) in the market capitalisation of fossil fuel (green) firms leads to an increase (a decrease) in the return on fossil fuel (green) equities, and households respond more aggressively to these changes in the (A^H) regimes. The more aggressive response prevents the market capitalisation of fossil fuel firms falling/the market capitalisation of green firms increasing as much in the (A^H) as they do in the (A^L) regimes. These changes in market capitalisation are reflected in changes in each sector's return on equity: the green firm sector's return on equity decreases by between 15 and 40 per cent, whereas the fossil fuel firm sector's return on equity increases by between 25 and 40 per cent.

The divest/invest campaign affects relative prices, and this leads to a small increase in the demand for green goods relative to the demand for fossil fuel goods. Essentially, changes to each firm sector's return on equity affects each firm sector's weighted cost of capital, and consequently each firm sector's target capital-output ratio. These changes lead to a surge in green investment (and green capital) and a fall in fossil fuel investment (and fossil fuel capital) (Figures 2.3c and 2.3d). Consequently, there is an increase in the green firm sector's capital-output ratio and capital-labour ratio, as well as a decrease in the fossil fuel firm sector's capital-output ratio and capital-labour ratio. These changes to the capital-labour ratios affect each sector's labour productivity. As labour productivity influences the number of workers firms need to produce a unit of their output, fossil fuel unit costs and prices rise while green unit costs and prices fall. The change in prices causes the demand for fossil fuel goods to fall relative to the demand for green goods by a few percentage points, even as the demand for energy goods decreases overall.

As well as leading to an overall fall in the demand for energy goods, the divest/invest campaign also leads to a fall in the output of the other sector, as well as in the overall level of final demand. The fall in final demand (and total output) comes about primarily for two reasons. First, the divest/invest campaign has an asymmetric effect on energy firms' investment expenditures (fossil fuel investment falls by more than green investment increases). Second, the divest/invest campaign leads households to slightly reduce the proportion of their wealth that they allocate to equities and increase the proportion they allocate to bank deposits. This leads to capital losses, a fall in real wealth and, consequently, a fall in real consumption.

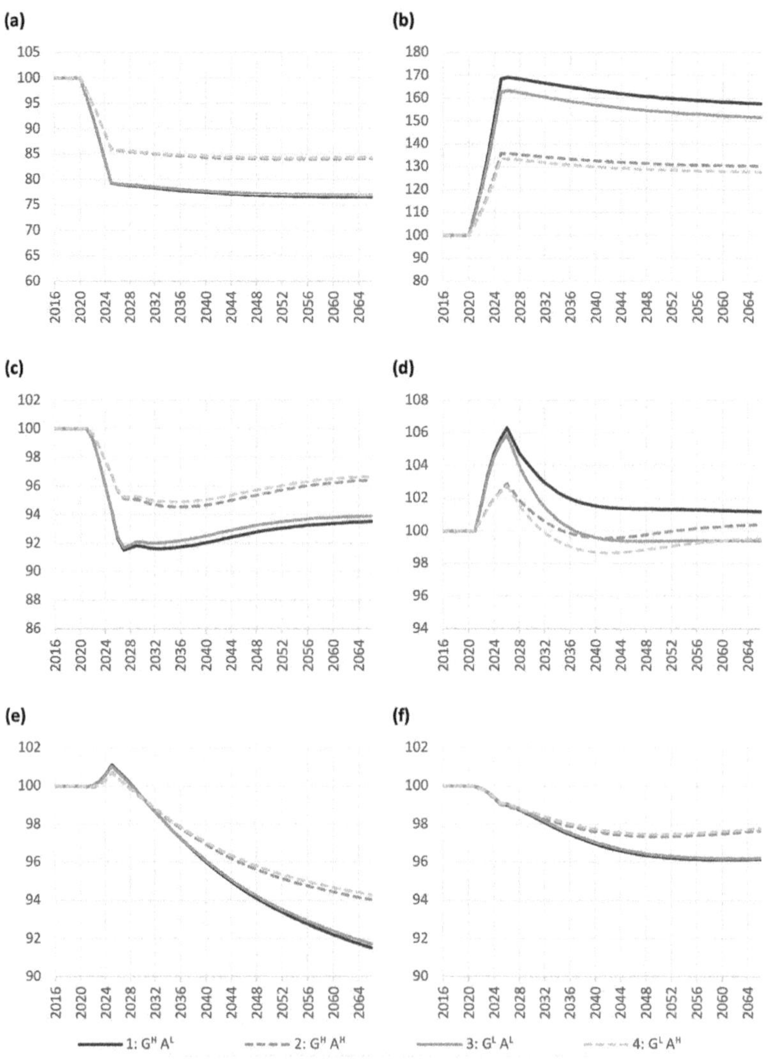

Figure 2.3 Ethical households divestment campaign (MC2)

Why does green investment fall by more than fossil fuel investment rises? As we have already seen, the divest/invest campaign leads to an increase in green investment and a decrease in fossil fuel investment. These changes are largely driven by changes to each sector's target capital-output ratio – the green sector's target capital-output ratio increases by approximately 2–2.5 per cent, while the fossil fuel sector's target capital-output ratio falls by approximately 1.5–2 per cent. However, despite the green sector's target capital-output ratio increasing by more than the fossil fuel sector's target capital-output ratio falls, the overall effect on green and fossil fuel investment (together) is negative. This is because each firm sector's investment also depends upon the higher of either the expected demand for that sector's output or the sector's actual output. Thus, while the green sector does see an increase in its target capital-output ratio, the sector's relatively small size (compared to the fossil fuel sector) means that the increase in green investment is smaller than the fall in fossil fuel investment. Hence, the overall effect on investment in the energy sector is negative.

The divest/invest campaign also causes real final demand to fall, as the campaign leads households to increase the proportion of their wealth that they place in bank deposits. This is because while the divest/invest campaign leads to an increase in the return on fossil fuel equities and a decrease in the return on green equities, the decrease in the return on green equities is larger than the increase in the return on fossil fuel equities. As a result, equities become slightly less attractive, and bank deposits become slightly more attractive. This results in households increasing the proportion of wealth they place into bank deposits. The reason the divest/invest campaign has an asymmetric effect on equity returns is again related to the green sector being smaller than the fossil fuel sector. Thus, an increase in the demand for green equities will have a proportionately larger effect on green equity prices (and, therefore, on the return on green equities) than an equivalently sized decrease in demand for fossil fuel equities.

Turning now to the impact on each household sector, the divest/invest campaign makes the ethical (divesting) households relatively worse off, and the normal households relatively better off (although both sectors end up worse off overall). To understand why this happens, recall that normal households are holding the portfolio of financial assets they want to hold as the divest/invest campaign gets under way. To induce normal households to sell green equities and buy fossil fuel equities, either the return on fossil fuel equities will have to increase or the return on green equities will have to fall. The increase/decrease in the demand for green/fossil fuel equities from the ethical household sector (with no change in demand from the normal household sector) leads to a decrease/increase in the return on green/fossil fuel equity. As the changes in demand are exogenously imposed upon the model and not the result of a change in a sector's distributed profits, ethical households are forced to buy green equities at a premium, and sell fossil fuel equities at a discount (where the discount/premium is relative to the price that would exist in the absence of the divest/invest campaign). Given this, the divest/invest campaign leads to an increase in the quantity of financial assets held by normal households and a decrease in the quantity of financial assets held by ethical households. These assets pay interest income/dividends, so that the divest/invest campaign leads to a decrease in the level of interest income/dividends received by ethical households and an increase in the level of interest income/dividends received by normal households. Ultimately, the changes in household income lead to a reduction in ethical household wealth relative to normal household wealth (Figures 2.3e and 2.3f).

As was pointed out earlier, the change in the return on fossil fuel and green equities is larger in the (A^L) regimes. As a result, in these regimes, fossil fuel firms' weighted cost of capital is higher (and investment lower), while green firms' weighted cost of capital is lower (and investment higher). These differences in investment have important implications for each sector's capital-labour ratio and level of labour productivity, which then influence relative prices and, through this channel, the level of demand for each sector's goods. As a result, fossil fuel output is lower in the (A^L) regimes than it is in the (A^H) regimes.

Market Conditions Simulation 3 (MC3): Bank Interest Rate Discrimination

In this simulation, banks increase interest rates on fossil fuel sector debt and decrease interest rates on green sector debt. The simulation is intended to help us understand what might happen if banks start to perceive the risks associated with lending to each energy sector differently.

To carry out the simulation, the exogenous parameters that control the margin on bank loans are altered, so that over a five-year period (2020–2024), the interest rate on fossil fuel loans increases by 50 per cent and the interest rate on green loans decreases by 50 per cent. The changes to interest rates leads to a fall in the output of the fossil fuel sector and an increase in the output of the green sector (Figures 2.4a and 2.4b). These changes in output happen for two reasons. First, the change in interest rates affects the weighted cost of capital of each sector, and this affects each sector's target capital-output ratio, and so each sector's level of investment. Second, the change in investment leads to a change in each sector's capital-labour ratio, and this affects each sector's labour productivity. Labour productivity determines the level of employment required by each sector to produce a unit of its output, which influences unit costs. Unit costs affect the price of each sector's output, and prices affect the relative demand for green and fossil fuel goods (albeit only by a few percentage points). The changes in demand are larger in the (G^H) regimes. In the (G^L) regimes the reduced ability of households and firms to substitute away from

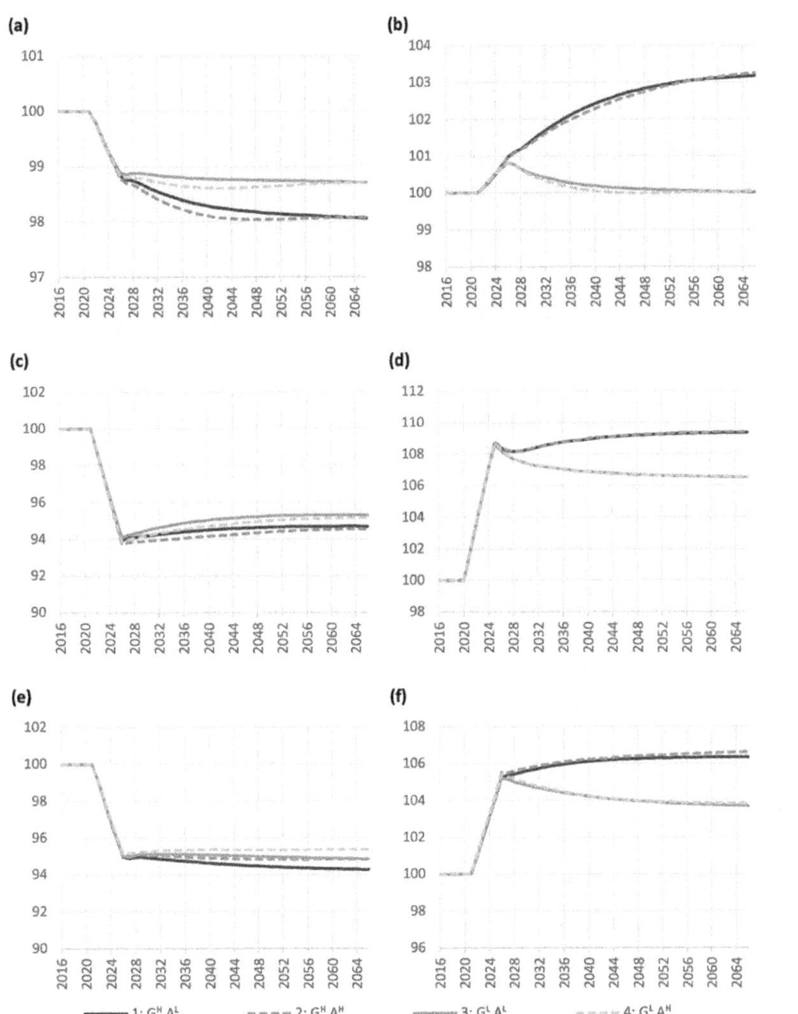

Figure 2.4 *Bank interest rate discrimination (MC3)*

higher-priced fossil fuel goods leads to a higher general price level and so a reduction in real income (and real output). This in turn leads to green sector output falling back towards its original steady state value, even as green sales increase relative to fossil fuel sales.

Financial markets are also affected by the changes in interest rates. The increase in interest rates on fossil fuel sector loans reduces the fossil fuel sector's nominal profits, while the reduction in the interest rate on green loans increases the green sector's profits (Figures 2.4c and 2.4d). The effect on profits is a result of firms setting their mark-up over wages and intermediate goods, rather than over interest payments. The increase in green profits boosts the green sector's return on equity, while the decrease in fossil fuel profits reduces the fossil fuel sector's return on equity. These changes lead households to reallocate their wealth towards green equities and away from fossil fuel equities. This leads to an increase in the price of green equities and a fall in the price of fossil fuel equities. As a result, the market capitalisation of the fossil fuel sector falls while the market capitalisation of the green sector increases (Figures 2.4e and 2.4f).

Market Conditions Simulation 4 (MC4): Increase in Green Sector Energy Return on Energy Invested

Empirical estimates of current EROIs tend to find that renewable energy generation technologies have lower EROIs than fossil fuels (Hall et al., 2014; Murphy & Hall, 2010). In this simulation, the green sector's EROI increases over a five-year period until it is equivalent to the EROI of the fossil fuel sector. This simulation is intended to show what might happen if green firms become more efficient in terms of their energy inputs. A full analysis of the economic impacts of changes in EROI during energy transitions is conducted by Jackson and Jackson (2021).

To carry out the simulation, an exogenous parameter is altered that controls the sum of the A-matrix column for green firms, so that over a five-year period (2020–2024), the quantity of goods inputs required by green firms to produce one unit of their output falls from 0.825 to 0.750. The reduction in the quantity of intermediate goods required by the green sector to produce a unit of its output leads to a reduction in green prices (as unit costs include intermediate inputs) (Figure 2.5a). This in turn leads to a fall in each firm sector's unit costs (as green energy is an input in each sector's production process), which leads to a fall in the price of each sector's goods and, therefore, further falls in unit costs and prices. The reduction in green prices relative to fossil fuel prices leads to an increase in the output of the green sector and a decrease in the output of the fossil fuel sector (Figures 2.5c and 2.5d). These variations in demand impact on investment, the capital stock and the level of employment in each firm sector. As is to be expected, the change in demand is larger in the (G^H) regimes.

The change in demand also leads to a change in the market capitalisation of each energy sector. In the (G^H) regimes, the market capitalisation of green

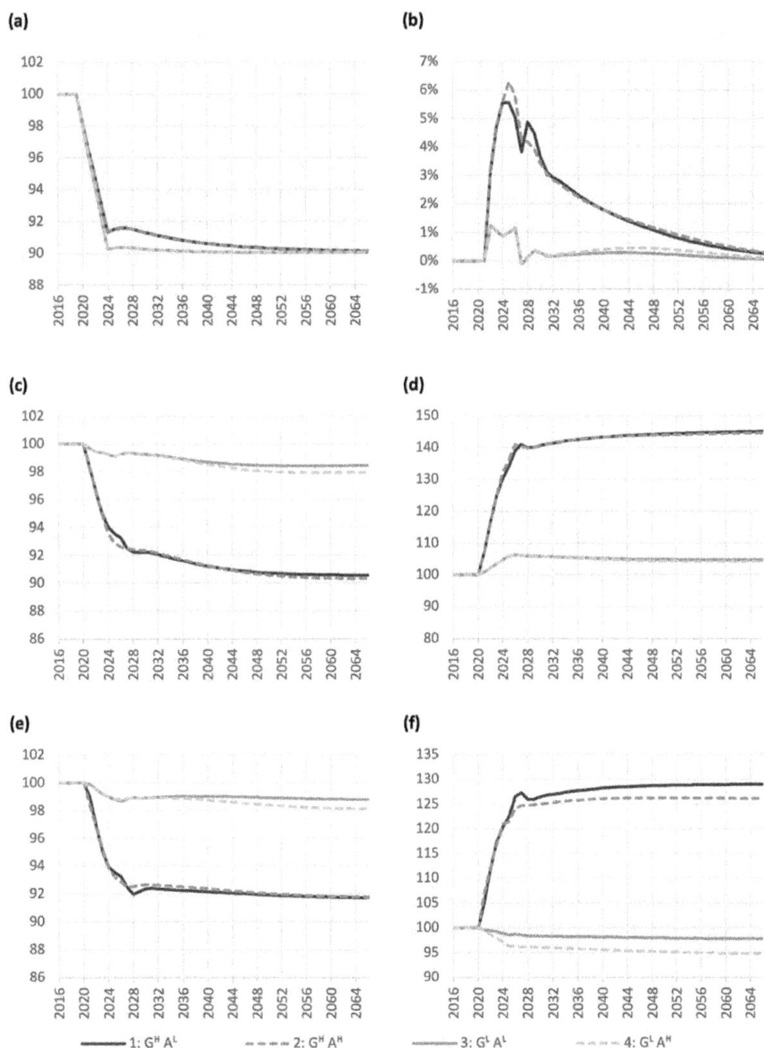

Figure 2.5 *Increase in green sector energy return on energy invested (MC4)*

firms increases (by around 25–30 per cent), while the market capitalisation of fossil fuel firms falls (by around 8 per cent) (Figures 2.5e and 2.5f). However, in the (G^L) regimes, the market capitalisation of green firms actually falls, and by more than it does for fossil fuel firms. This fall happens because the supply of green equities increases at a faster rate than the demand for green equities (as green firms issue equities to finance part of their investment expenditures). Conversely, in the (G^H) regimes, the increase in the demand for green goods leads to a larger increase in green profits and return on equity, so that the demand for green equities increases faster than the supply of green equities.

Finally, the change in demand for green and fossil fuel goods leads to a part of the fossil fuel sector's capital stock being stranded. Stranding is higher in the (G^H) regimes (peaking at around 5.5–6 per cent of fossil fuel capital assets) than it is in the (G^L) regimes (where stranding peaks at around 1 per cent of fossil fuel capital assets) (Figure 2.5b).

CONCLUSION

This chapter presented the results of four simulations that looked at changes in market conditions that may be associated with a transition to net zero. The results of the simulations contained in this chapter illustrate that different changes in market conditions will lead to different types of economic effects. Crucially, the impact of each change in market conditions depends on the assumptions we make about the sensitivity of households and firms to energy prices and returns on financial assets. In general, the regimes in which households and firms were more sensitive to goods prices tend to lead to larger changes in demand and consequently greater levels of asset stranding, while the regimes in which households are more sensitive to asset prices tend to lead to greater changes in firms' market values and therefore larger financial effects. That is, our results suggest that changes in market conditions are unlikely to have a large effect on the demand for fossil fuel versus green energy (and therefore on asset stranding) unless renewable energy becomes a close substitute for fossil fuel energy (e.g., in terms of its functionality). The results therefore support the arguments made in Paun et al. (2015), who point out that advances in technology associated with renewable energy (specifically storage technology) could lead to a significant increase in demand for renewable energy and a fall in the demand for fossil fuels.

Looking at the individual simulations, the carbon tax simulation (MC1) showed that a carbon tax can be successful in reducing the demand for fossil fuels when fossil fuel firms attempt to pass on a large proportion of the tax to their customers. Conversely, the more of the tax the firms choose to absorb the less the demand for their output is likely to fall (Jackson, 2018), albeit at the cost of a reduction in profits and a large fall in their market capitalisation.

The divest/invest simulation (MC2) showed that there is the potential for a divest/invest campaign to have a large effect on fossil fuel companies' market values (assuming enough funds are divested, and that agents are not more responsive to changes in the return on financial assets in reality than they are in the model – which they could be). However, in the simulation the divest/invest campaign did not significantly affect the demand for different types of energy or the quantity of stranded assets. One reason for this is that firms can fund themselves using other sources (e.g., bank loans, retained earnings). If instead firms were unable to fund themselves using other sources, then a divest/invest campaign could significantly affect the ability of firms to finance their investment – with potentially larger effects on output. The results of the simulation were therefore somewhat in line with the literature, which argues that the direct impacts of divestment campaigns are likely to be small (e.g., see Ansar et al. 2013).

The bank interest rate discrimination simulation (MC3) led to a moderate change in the output of green and fossil fuel firms. These changes were largely driven by changes in investment that led to lower unit costs and prices for the green firms and higher unit costs and prices for the fossil fuel firms. One reason the change in investment is larger in this simulation (compared to the equity divest/invest simulation) is that the model is calibrated so that each firm sector finances a larger proportion of their investment expenditures through banks loans (compared to equities). This simulation therefore showed that a divestment campaign is more likely to be successful in directly affecting fossil fuel firms if it targets their main source of external financing.

The EROI simulation (MC4) showed that a reduction in the energy inputs required by the renewable energy sector to produce a unit of its output could reduce the sector's unit costs and therefore its prices. A change in relative prices is shown to have a large effect on the demand for energy from different sources, as long as these energy sources can be easily substituted for each other (as then agents will be more responsive to changes in relative prices). However, if renewable and fossil fuel energy are not good substitutes for each other, the effect on demand is likely to be more limited. This of course ties in with the argument (as discussed at the beginning of this section) that improvements in storage technology will be required to increase the demand for renewable energy (Paun et al., 2015).

Taken together, the results of the simulations suggest that shocks that affect the real side of the economy are likely to lead to larger impacts on demand and generate larger transition risks than those that primarily affect firms' borrowing costs.

NOTES

1. This chapter is available for free as Open Access from the individual product page at www.elgaronline.com under the Attribution-NonCommercial-ShareAlike 4.0 International (CC BY-NC-SA 4.0) license.

2. This chapter draws heavily on Jackson (2018), especially chapter 7.
3. A full description of all the equations in the model can be found in Jackson (2018), chapter 4.
4. More information on model calibration can be found in Jackson (2018), chapter 5.

REFERENCES

Ansar, A., Caldecott, B. L., & Tilbury, J. (2013). *Stranded assets and the fossil fuel divestment campaign: What does divestment mean for the valuation of fossil fuel assets?* Smith School of Enterprise and the Environment. University of Oxford.

Grant, A. (2018). *Mind the gap: The $1.6 trillion energy transition risk.* Carbon Tracker Initiative.

Hall, C. A., Lambert, J. G., & Balogh, S. B. (2014). EROI of different fuels and the implications for society. *Energy Policy, 64*, 141–152.

Jackson, A. (2018). *A stock-flow consistent framework for the analysis of stranded assets and the transition to a low carbon economy*. PhD thesis.

Jackson, A., & Jackson, T. (2021). Modelling energy transition risk: The impact of declining energy return on investment (EROI). *Ecological Economics*, *185*, 107023.

McGlade, C., & Ekins, P. (2015). The geographical distribution of fossil fuels unused when limiting global warming to 2°C. *Nature*, *517*(7533), 187–190.

Mountford, H., Corfee-Morlot, J., McGregor, M., Banaji, F., Bhattacharya, A., Brand, J., Colenbrander, S., & Stern, N. (2018). *Unlocking the inclusive growth story of the 21st century: Accelerating climate action in urgent times*. Global Commission on Economy and Climate.

Murphy, D. J., & Hall, C. A. (2010). Year in review: EROI or energy return on (energy) invested. *Annals of the New York Academy of Sciences*, *1185*(1), 102–118.

Paun, A., Knight, Z., & Chan, W. S. (2015). *Stranded assets: What next?* HSBC Global research.

Pfeiffer, A., Hepburn, C., Vogt-Schilb, A., & Caldecott, B. (2018). Committed emissions from existing and planned power plants and asset stranding required to meet the Paris Agreement. *Environmental Research Letters*, *13*(5), 054019.

3. Economic impacts of climate change: an empirical stock-flow consistent model for Viet Nam

Etienne Espagne and Thi Thu Ha Nguyen

INTRODUCTION

With a long coastal line and abundant geological and natural diversity, Viet Nam is one of the most vulnerable countries to climate change in the Asia-Pacific region. Viet Nam was ranked 99th out of 182 countries in 2019, according to the Notre Dame University Global Adaption Index (ND-GAIN), in terms of vulnerability score. Vulnerability measures a country's exposure, sensitivity and ability to adapt to the negative impact of climate change. ND-GAIN measures the overall vulnerability by considering six life-supporting sectors: food, water, health, ecosystem service, human habitat and infrastructure. In addition, according to the Global Climate Risk Index (2021), which analyses to what extent countries and regions have been affected by impacts of weather-related loss events such as storms, floods and heatwaves, Viet Nam was ranked 13th among the most directly affected countries in the period 2000–2019.

Within the last 50 years, the temperature in Viet Nam has risen at twice the speed compared to the world's average. The average annual temperature on a nationwide scale increased by 0.78°C per decade for the period 1981–2018 (Espagne et al., 2021). According to the Report on Climate Change and Sea Level Rise scenarios for Viet Nam (IMHEN, 2021), the annual temperature in Viet Nam increased by 0.74°C for the period 1986–2018. Future global climate change scenarios are generally based on global climate model simulations for different greenhouse gas scenarios on which the Intergovernmental Panel on Climate Change assessment reports are mainly based. The average temperature in Viet Nam increases by 1.13±0.87°C under representative concentration pathway (RCP) 2.6 and by 1.9±0.81°C under RCP8.5 in the middle of the twenty-first century. At the end of the century, the temperature in Viet Nam is expected to increase by 1.34 ±1.14°C under RCP2.6 and by 4.18±1.57°C under RCP8.5.

An assessment of climate change impacts in the new reality of a net-zero transformation is crucial for policy planning at the macroeconomic level. Indeed, climate change sets out major challenges for the country, and the Vietnamese government is putting climate change and sustainable development at the heart of its development policy. Existing studies on the evaluation of climate change impacts in Viet Nam usually focus on specific sectors or regions, as shown in the different meta-analysis and sectoral assessments in the second part of this report. Few studies seek to assess the economy-wide effect of climate change. UNU-WIDER (2012) is, to our knowledge, the most recent study to evaluate climate impacts on economic growth and welfare in a dynamic computable general equilibrium model via three principal mechanisms: crop yields, hydropower production and regional road networks. This latest study provides insights into the potential macroeconomic effects of different climate scenarios from the previous Intergovernmental Panel on Climate Change report. Contrary to standard computable general equilibrium models, the macroeconomic model that we have specifically developed combines real side variables with financial balance sheet effects. This more coherent approach is key for any comprehensive macroeconomic analysis and forecast in the short term and necessary to public policies for a sound development process and macroeconomic stability in the context of globalization and financialization.

In this chapter, we propose an economy-wide assessment of the economic impacts of climate change on the Vietnamese economy as a whole, using a stock-flow consistent (SFC) model. Our chapter is organized as follows. The next section describes the integrated assessment framework, followed by an explanation of the damage functions taken into account in our assessment. The chapter then describes the macroeconomic SFC model of Viet Nam, followed by the results a conclusion with suggestions for future research.

AN INTEGRATED FRAMEWORK TO ASSESS CLIMATE IMPACTS

We propose an integrated prospective economy-wide assessment to analyse the economic impacts of climate change on Viet Nam's economy (Figure 3.1). Our methodological approach in this chapter builds on the integrated assessment approach of Hsiang et al. (2017), who attempted to assess the economic cost of climate change in the United States via a combination of multiple climate scenarios, quantitative meta-analysis of sectoral and social impacts based on existing studies and aggregation and integration within a macroeconomic model.

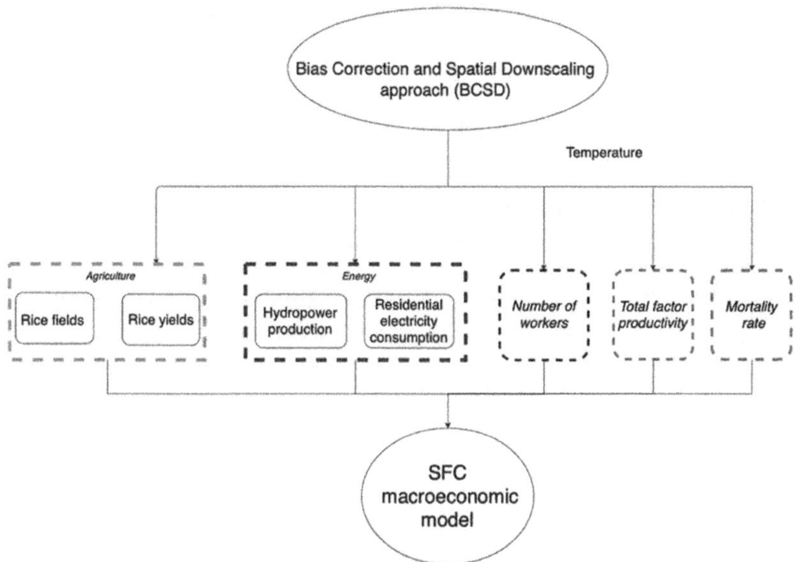

Figure 3.1 *An integrated framework to assess climate change impacts*

Our integrated assessment framework involves three main steps:

- *Valuation of direct damage*: in order to aggregate over each individual sector to obtain a total economic response to climate forcing, we first apply a monetary valuation to each individual sector, namely agriculture, energy, health, labour productivity and total factor productivity (TFP). We use the key quantitative results from Espagne et al. (2021). The choice of studies and the valuation for specific sectors is discussed below. Values are presented as a proportion of Vietnamese gross domestic product (GDP) for all direct damage.
- *Sectoral damage function calculation*: constructing sectoral damage functions requires that losses in each sector be represented as conditional on Viet Nam mean surface temperature (VNMST) change. We estimate summaries of these relationships by regressing the impact value (for all realizations) on these temperatures. As in Hsiang et al. (2017), we consider that the results are not weighted because the likelihood of states of the world is not relevant to the description of the damage function.
- *Aggregate national-level damage function*: summing different climate damage functions across the spectrum of possible temperature increases to obtain cumulative direct impacts and applying the direct damage impacts

to the stock-flow coherent macroeconomic model of Viet Nam in order to assess the intersectoral and aggregate effects.

CLIMATE DAMAGE FUNCTIONS

We include in this study several important impact channels of climate change to the economic growth of the Vietnamese economy: agriculture, energy, labour productivity, mortality and TFP. Total direct damages in each sector are valued in monetary terms, aggregated nationally and completed with a meta-analysis of selected studies. Values are presented as a proportion of Vietnamese GDP. Then, these aggregate outcomes can be indexed against the change in average temperature in the corresponding climate realization across the four RCPs.

Agriculture

Climate change has important impacts on the agricultural sector. A meta-analysis of a set of key existing studies to develop the sector-specific damage functions for agriculture (Yu et al., 2010; Deb et al., 2015; Shrestha et al., 2016; Li et al., 2017; Kontgis et al., 2018) allows deriving an average estimate of the change in rice yield as a function of temperature change.

Yu et al. (2010) first estimated the impacts of climate change on agricultural and water systems in Viet Nam based on crop simulation, hydrological simulation and river basin models. The aim of Li et al. (2017) is to assess the impact of projected climate change on rice productivity in the Indochinese Peninsula. The paper finds that the rice yield losses due to climate change (including CO^2 gains) across all of Viet Nam are expected at 5–10 per cent by 2040, with similar values under both RCPs 4.5 and 8.5. Deb et al. (2015), using AquaCrop 4.0, show future rice yield losses, under climate change and different salinity levels in irrigation water. Shrestha et al. (2016) investigated the impact of climate change on winter and summer rice yield using the AquaCrop model. They found that climate change would reduce rice yield between 1.29 and 23.05 per cent during the winter season for both scenarios and all time periods. In contrast, there was an increase in yield by expected in the summer season for the 2020s and 2050s, relative to baseline yield.

Energy

The energy sector is a crucial component in any development dynamics but is affected by climate change both in terms of energy supply and demand (Auffhammer et al., 2013; Yalew et al., 2020). The direct costs and benefits of climate-driven change in energy were assessed by including the forecasted development of the Viet Nam Power Development Plan 8 (PDP8).

On the supply side, changes in precipitation and temperature can affect energy production capacity, transmission systems or the infrastructure itself (World Bank, 2011; Ciscar and Dowling, 2014). Given the current dominant role of hydropower in total Vietnamese electricity production (37.7 per cent in 2019) despite a planned reduction to 18 per cent by 2030 and to 9 per cent by 2045 (PDP8), we study the climate impact on hydropower production. Projections indicate that the case of hydropower is more complex, as it induces an initial surplus of production (with a maximum 1°C increase in temperature) because of increased precipitation. Beyond a 2°C increase, however, there is not much change compared to the baseline without further climate change.

On the demand side, the rising temperature and weather extremes in recent years have strongly affected residential electricity demand (27 per cent of total end-use consumption in 2016). The main electricity use in households is for air conditioners, refrigerators and electric fans. The response functions are derived from the outputs of long-range energy alternatives planning in 2040 under a range of temperature scenarios. Beyond a 2°C increase in temperature, electricity demand could increase by as much as 12 per cent and more than 20 per cent above a 3°C increase.

Labor Productivity

Several studies show that heat stress can have negative impacts on human health as well as worker productivity (Kjellstrom et al., 2009; ILO, 2016, 2019; Orlov et al., 2020). Kjellstrom et al. (2012) describe how heat stress reduces work capacity leading to lower economic output in the case of South-East Asia. Dao et al. (2013) found that in Da Nang, the temperature rise has particularly affected the working conditions of low-income outdoor workers. Opitz-Stapleton et al. (2016) demonstrates that heat stress induced by climate change will increase the occupational heat exposure of workers. Kjellstrom et al. (2014) emphasize that in 2030, heat loss could represent 5.7 per cent of Viet Nam's GDP. In our case, the damage function is in terms of working hours lost. A 1°C rise in temperature is associated with a decrease of 2.5 per cent in working hours. The value of labour productivity impact is calculated by multiplying the equivalent number of workers, which is proportional to the working hours lost by GDP per worker.

Total Factor Productivity

TFP plays an important role in long-run economic growth. In Viet Nam, according to General Statistics Office data, TFP contributed 43.5 per cent to national economic growth in 2018. In addition, the approved National Assembly's resolution for Viet Nam's socio-economic development indicates that TFP is expected to contribute 45–47 per cent of GDP growth during the coming years. Several studies in the recent literature found a negative impact of climate change on TFP. Letta and Tol (2016), using macro TFP data from the Penn World Tables, examine the relationship between annual temperature shocks and TFP growth rates in the period 1960–2006. They find only a negative relationship in poor countries but indistinguishable from zero in rich countries. Dietz and Stern (2015) marginally change the DICE model of William Nordhaus and test the macroeconomic impacts when TFP is hit. Moore and Diaz (2015) test a modified DICE model, calibrated on Dell et al. (2012), and obtain increased impacts. Another theoretical study of Moyer et al. (2013) has also hypothesized a future impact of global warming on TFP growth. The value of TFP impact is calculated through their impact on GDP growth, which is then translated to changes in GDP level.

Mortality

Existing studies show negative impacts of climate change on health outcomes (e.g. physical health, mortality, infectious diseases, mental health, dietary outcomes) (Rocque et al., 2021). Regarding the effect on mortality, Gasparrini et al. (2017) investigate the projections of temperature-related excess mortality under climate change scenarios, assuming no adaptation or population changes. This study shows the negative impacts of climate change, which potentially increases mortality in most regions. Guo et al. (2018) projected excess mortality in relation to heatwaves in the future under each RCP scenario, with or without adaptation and with three population change scenarios (high variant, median variant, low variant). Another study by Vicedo-Cabrera et al. (2018) suggests that the Paris Agreement's commitment to hold warming below 2°C could prevent an increase in temperature-related mortality.

Several methods exist to value mortality damage in monetary terms, and we do not necessarily want to make a theoretical decision about them, as this should be the choice of policy-makers. As a practical solution, despite the problems on both theoretical issues of interpretation and difficult problems of measurement of the Value of Statistical Life (Ashenfelter, 2006), we use this measurement from a study of Ohno et al. (2012) evaluating diarrhoea mortality risk due to water pollution in Viet Nam. The damage function of change in mortality rate considered in our study is a function of the temperature change. Concerning the impact channel in the macroeconomic model, it is possible to consider an impact on population growth, affecting aggregate demand, the labour supply and thus economic growth.

Aggregate Direct Damages

Regarding the climate scenarios – low, intermediate, high and very high greenhouse gas emission scenarios – RCPs are considered, comprising RCP2.6, RCP4.5, RCP6.0 and RCP8.5, respectively. We use climate data projection from the GEMMES Viet Nam project. Temperature projections are estimated from the bias correction and spatial disaggregation (BCSD) (Wood et al., 2004). Global input data for the method originate from Coupled Model Intercomparison Project Phase 5 global climate models (Taylor et al., 2012).

A common set of reference years and time periods are adopted for assessing climate change impacts and potential impacts of adaptation measures: the reference period is 1997–2019, the period 1850–1900 approximates pre-industrial global surface temperature and the future reference period covers 2020–2050. The changes in temperature of each year are the difference between the projected temperature of the future reference period and the reference period.

By summing the sectoral damage functions described above, we get aggregate damages in different climate scenarios. Figure 3.2 gives us a hint of the aggregate direct damage in different RCPs, considering the uncertainty from the different climate scenarios (but not from the socio-economic side). It shows that direct damage can reach up to a 12 per cent loss in annual GDP

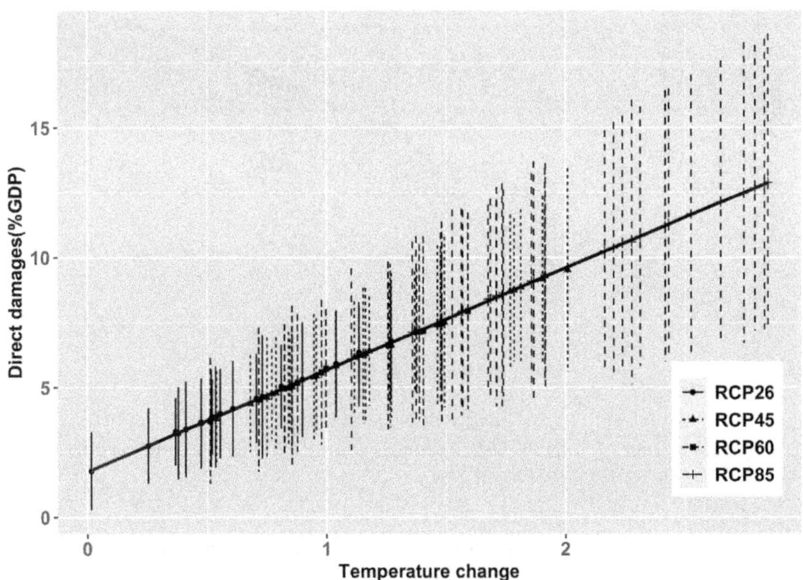

Figure 3.2 *Estimates of total direct damage under RCPs*

relative to the baseline scenario in the case of a temperature increase above 2.5°C. Remaining below a temperature increase of 1°C allows for a minimal loss of up to 6 per cent of GDP compared to the baseline scenario.

Total direct damage to the Vietnamese economy summed across different sectors as a function of VNMST changes 2020–2099 relative to 1997–2019. Dots indicate the distribution of direct damages corresponding to VNMST change in each combination of climate models and scenario projection. The dark line represents the linear regression of damage values on VNMST change.

It should be noted that this assessment considers some uncertainty on the climate side but not on the socio-economic side, where strong non-linearities in reaction to non-marginal climate changes might emerge. Some important impacts have not been considered, such as typhoon impacts, which we show independently because their dynamics in relation to climate scenarios are not yet clear. Figure 3.3 shows a breakdown of total direct damage into its sectoral components, using the mean value of climate scenarios. We found that the greatest direct damage from the increase of VNMST is the impact on labour productivity. The economic damage to agriculture is relatively small, mainly due to the Vietnamese economic restructuring in the coming years. Indeed, the agriculture share of GDP by 2045–2050 tends to decline.

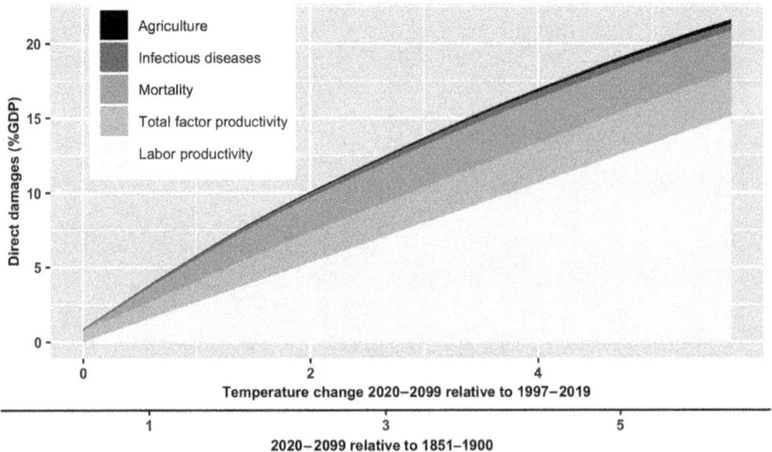

Note: The temperature of the pre-industrial period is estimated from the observation dataset and HadCRUT5 (with a coarse resolution of 5°x5°).

Figure 3.3 *Total direct damage to the Vietnamese economy by different sectors as a function of VNMST change 2020–2099 relative to 1997–2019 (contemporary climate) and 1851–1900 (pre-industrial climate)*

Given the complex relations between sectors in the economy, climate impacts cannot only be summarized by the sum of the direct impacts. These estimated damage functions will then be implemented within the empirical SFC macroeconomic model in order to assess the macroeconomic effects of different climate change scenarios.

THE MACROECONOMIC MODEL

SFC models, although marginalized during the period of the so-called great moderation, assume that financial and real variables should be integrated within the same framework and analysed as a whole in the same model. They are, therefore, best suited to address the challenges posed by the recent situation. The SFC approach relies on two main basic principles: accounting consistencies (flow consistency, stock consistency, stock-flow coherence and quadruple entry) and post-Keynesian closure/behavioural specifications explaining how economic agents determine and finance their expenditures and allocate their wealth among different non-financial and financial assets.

The accounting principles will be represented in two matrices: the balance sheet stock matrix and the flow matrix. The balance sheet represents the financial structure of the economy by displaying the tangible stocks, financial stocks and financial liabilities of each institutional sector at the end of each period. The flow matrix demonstrates the real transactions and financial flows implied from stocks of financial assets and sectoral budget constraints. To the best of our knowledge, there are not yet institutional-sector stock accounts or estimations of national wealth for the Vietnamese economy. Consequently, this model relies on the international guidelines of the system of national accounts (UN, 2009), accounting principles and uses the annual data for the period 1996–2019 from different sources to build the balance sheet and flow matrix. Following a coherent way of thinking about the macroeconomy in terms of both theory and economic policies (Arestis, 2013), the model will be divided into different blocks.

Production, Investment and Financing of Firms

In our model, for the sake of simplicity, we suppose that the economy has a single good that can be used for intermediate consumption, final consumption, exports and capital good. The economy is demand-led. The real GDP (y_t) is defined as the sum of household consumption (c_t), government current expenditures (g_t), private and public investment $(i_t^f,\ i_t^g,\ i_t^h)$, net exports $(x_t - im_t)$ and changes in inventories (i_{12_t}).

$$y_t = c_t + g_t + i_t^f + i_t^g + i_t^h + i_{12_t} + x_t - im_t \tag{3.1}$$

The demand determines production. The production decision of productive sectors is based on adaptive expectations. The expected output depends on both the expected sales (s^e) and the level of changes in inventories of the previous period ($i_{12_{t-1}}$), which represents the excess demand or the difference between supply and demand.

$$q_t^e = \gamma_q * s_t^e + (1 - \gamma_q) * i_{12_{t-1}} \tag{3.2}$$

where $(1 - \gamma_q)$ is the speed of expectations adjustment to excess demand.

Expected sales will be defined by the population growth rate (POP_{gr_t}) and the productivity growth rate (TFP_{gr_t}). We expect that the higher population and productivity growth leading to higher income per capita will increase global demand. Domestic production is calculated by the difference between total expected production (q_t^e) and total imports (im_t).

$$s_t^e = (1 + pop_{gr_t} + TFP_{gr_t}) * s_{t-1} \tag{3.3}$$

The total sales are given by:

$$s_t = c_t + g_t + i_t^f + i_t^g + i_t^h + x_t + ic_t \tag{3.4}$$

The domestic production is calculated by the difference between total expected production (q_t^e) and total imports (im_t).

$$q_t = q_t^e - im_t \tag{3.5}$$

Firms invest and accumulate physical capital by using retained profits, borrowing from banks or abroad, issuing equities or attracting foreign direct investment (Table 3A.1 in the Appendix). Climate change affects the agricultural and energy sectors via rice yields, electricity demand and the hydropower sector. They also affect firms' productivity in general via an impact on TFP.

Firms' net investment is represented as a fixed capital accumulation rate. It is modelled as a function of a constant which reflects animal spirits, the real lending rate representing the financial condition and the capacity utilization rate of capital which is proxied by the ratio of real GDP to potential GDP. A high-capacity utilization rate will lead firms to raise their capital stock by increasing investment. The cost of financing investment by bank loans has a negative impact on capital accumulation. Our investment function is similar to the one used in the SFC model for the United Kingdom by Burgess et al. (2016) or other SFC models in the literature.

$$\frac{\Delta k_t^f}{k_{t-1}^f} = \zeta_0 + \zeta_1 * \frac{y_{t-1}}{y_{t-1}^*} + \zeta_2 * (r_t - \pi_t) \tag{3.6}$$

$$k_t^f = k_{t-1}^f + i_t^f - \delta_{K_t}^f k_{t-1}^f \quad (3.7)$$

To estimate the potential GDP for the Vietnamese economy, we use the production function approach (IMF, 2019). In this approach, the production function is given as follows:

$$y_t^* = TFP_t * k_{t-1}^{\alpha} * L_t^{*\alpha} \quad (3.8)$$

where TFP_t is the TFP; L_t^* is the active population and k_{t-1}^{α} is the capital stock of the previous period; α is labour income share.

Capital stock is the sum of private and public capital.

$$k_t = k_t^f + k_t^g + k_t^h \quad (3.9)$$

In our model, we suppose that firms can finance their investment by issuing equities held by households and the rest of the world, borrowing from domestic banks or abroad and via foreign direct investment. The negative impact of climate change on firms can raise their financing need and thus increase their debt. Commercial banks impose credit rationing for firms' loans, so they decide the level of the lending amount to firms based on the loan-to-value ratio. This measures the relationship between the loan amount and the value of the assets securing the loan.

Consumption, Investment and Portfolio Choices of Households

Households use their disposable income to consume, invest and accumulate financial assets in the form of deposits, government bonds, firms' equities or other financial assets. Households can also borrow from commercial banks to meet their financing needs. Households are impacted by climate change through different channels: the number of working hours they can dedicate to firms, a decrease in productivity due to infectious diseases and the aggregate mortality rate of the population. Thus, climate change may affect households' consumption and investment decisions and their financial decisions accordingly.

Following Kalecki (1971), household consumption is partially induced and includes two components: consumption out of wages and consumption out of profits. Thus, in our model, we propose one consumption which consists of three parts. The first term corresponds to the autonomous component and the two others represent induced elements that depend on the current disposable income (including wages and household profits) and household accumulated wealth over the past.

$$\ln(c_t) = \delta_0^c + \delta_1^c * \ln\left(yd_t^h\right) - \delta_2^c * \ln\left(nw_{t-1}^h\right) \tag{3.10}$$

Crockett and Friend (1967) found that income is the most important determinant of a household's investment behaviour. In the report on household investment and accumulation surveys, the Centre for Agricultural Policy Consulting of the Institute of Policy and Strategy for Agriculture and Rural Development pointed out that income and non-financial and financial wealth accumulation had an impact on the household investment decision. Thus, our household investment is modelled as a function of their net wealth and the real interest rate, representing the borrowing cost. We expect that the higher net wealth will increase the household's investment. Following an increase in the real lending rate, households will reduce their investment.

$$\text{Ln}\left(i_t^h\right) = \eta_0^{ih} + \eta_1^{ih} * \ln\left(nw_t^h\right) + \eta_2^{ih} * \left(r_{l_{t-1}} - \pi_{t-1}\right) \tag{3.11}$$

In our model, the stock of non-financial assets should evolve according to the perpetual inventory method. It means that the stock of the current period is defined by cumulating flows of the previous period and adjusting for capital depreciation.

$$k_t^h = k_{t-1}^h + i_t^h - \delta_{K_t}^h k_{t-1}^h \tag{3.12}$$

If the household's investment is larger (less) than their savings, it represents a financing need (capacity), which is one factor driving the household's financial asset allocation. Households can hold cash, dong deposits, foreign deposits, government bonds and equities as an asset. Households can borrow from banks to finance their investment. Commercial banks impose credit rationing on the household's loan demand. The level of credit rationing depends on the debt-to-income ratio, which is calculated as the ratio of the interest payments and the new debt to the primary income.

Financial System

The Vietnamese financial system has developed since the 1990s with the transformation of the banking system from one tier to two tiers, including the State Bank of Viet Nam (SBV) as a central bank and commercial banks and the development of equity and bond markets to facilitate access to finance for firms and households in the economy.

The objectives of the SBV are inflation control, stabilization of the macroeconomy, supporting economic growth and ensuring the liquidity of credit institutions. In order to achieve these objectives, the SBV can use a set of tools, including interest rates, exchange rates, reserve requirements, open market operations and other tools depending on the macroeconomic conditions. In our model, we suppose that the central bank determines the refinancing rate as a monetary policy tool and the bank's reserves. The refinancing rate or the interest rate of credit from the central bank to commercial banks is considered one of the monetary policy tools. The refinancing rate is a function of inflation and the exchange rate.

Moreover, the interest rate of the United States impacts the interest rate of developing countries. When the Fed raises interest rates, investors tend to sell assets denominated in foreign currencies and buy dollar-denominated assets. The wider the spread between United States interest rates and interest rates in other countries, the more investors are likely to move from foreign-denominated to dollar-denominated assets. This increased demand for dollars raises the dollar exchange rate, and the currency exchange rates of other countries tend to weaken. It raises the prices of imports to those countries, pushing up inflation. A falling exchange rate can make it difficult for companies and governments to service dollar-denominated debt. To solve this problem, the central bank may decide to support their currency exchange rates by raising interest rates.

$$\Delta \ln\left(r^{cb}_{l_t}\right) = \beta_0 * \Delta \ln(xr_t) + \beta_1 * \left(r^{us}_{l_t} - r^{cb}_{l_{t-1}}\right) + \beta_2 * \left(\ln\left(r^{cb}_{l_{t-1}}\right) - \beta^l_0 - \beta^l_1 * \pi_{t-1}\right) \quad (3.13)$$

They provide advances to commercial banks. The central bank plays the role of a lender of last resort via refinancing for commercial banks.

$$\Delta LB^{cb}_t = -\Delta RES_{us_t} xr + \Delta H_t + \Delta MB^{cb}_t + \Delta GM^{cb}_t + \Delta B^{cb}_t + \Delta OTA^{cb}_t \quad (3.14)$$

The central bank intervenes in the foreign exchange market in order to respond to changes in the exchange rate. International reserves are considered as a central bank's tool to manage the exchange rate. The change in international reserves will be a function of the nominal exchange rate and the ratio between the previous level of international reserves and the nominal GDP (IMF, 2021).

$$\Delta \ln(RES_t) = \gamma_0 + \gamma_1 * \Delta \ln(xr_t) + \gamma_2 * \frac{RES_{t-2}}{Y_{t-2}} \quad (3.15)$$

In our model, commercial banks finance the economy by offering credits to firms and households. We also try to model credit rationing on firm and household loans, representing a financial constraint to the sectors. The lending rate and deposit rate are determined based on the central bank's interest rate. The lending rate will affect the sectors' investment and then impact the global demand of the economy.

$$\Delta\ln(r_{l_t}) =$$

$$\varpi_0 * \Delta\ln(r_{l_{t-1}}) + \varpi_1 * \Delta\ln\left(r^{cb}_{l_t}\right) + \varpi_2 * \ln(r_{l_{t-1}}) - \varpi^{rl}_0 - \varpi^{rl}_1 * \ln\left(r^{cb}_{l_{t-1}}\right) \tag{3.16}$$

The deposit rate depends on the lending rate.

$$\Delta\ln(r_m) = \omega_1 * \Delta\ln\left(r^l_{l_{t-1}}\right) + \omega_2 * (\ln(r_{m_{t-1}}) - \omega^{rm}_0 * \ln\left(r^l_{l_{t-1}}\right)) \tag{3.17}$$

Government

The government collects taxes, receives other transfers or payments and then consumes and invests. From 2000 to 2019, the state revenue increased by an average of 17 per cent per year. Domestic revenue accounts for the largest part of state budget revenue which contributes to the stability of government revenue. However, the Vietnamese government, adopting an expansionary countercyclical fiscal policy due to slowing economic growth in recent years, leads to a lower tax and tariff rate and then reduces the state revenue. Personal income tax is increasing, but their part in total is still moderate due to difficulties in tracking personal earnings of the private sector, and the informal sector remains important. From 2008 to the present, oil revenue has decreased due to the lower oil price and stagnant crude oil production. In terms of expenditure, the government's expenditures increased annually at roughly 17 per cent from 2000 to 2019. Current expenditures, which include expenditures on social and economic activities (education, health, society, welfare, etc.) and administration, remain the biggest part of total public spending. The state budget deficit remains at a high level, causing a rise of public debt and becoming one of the biggest macroeconomic risks facing Viet Nam. There was a huge increase in public debt in 2008 and 2012. However, since 2016, the government has improved the budget deficit with a target of under 4 per cent in the period 2016–2020. The public deficit can be financed by issuing bonds or borrowing from abroad.

Rest of the World

The external imbalances reflect the financing need of the economy to fund domestic consumption and investment through different forms of financial flows. Before 2005 and 2006, Viet Nam registered a negative current account which was mainly driven by a deficit in the trade balance. The high domestic demand was satisfied by imports. Moreover, the global financial crisis of 2007–2008 caused a reduction in world demand, which decreased Vietnamese exports and led to a bigger trade deficit. However, since 2012, the current account has become positive, resulting from a trade balance and a secondary income surplus offsetting the deficit in the primary income balance.

The volume of exports is assumed to be determined by the total volume of imports of the main commercial partners of Viet Nam, the level of domestic production and the exchange rate.

$$\Delta\ln(x_t) = \theta_0^x * \Delta\ln(im_{t-1}^{PTN}) + \theta_1^x * \Delta\ln(q_{t-1}) + \theta_2^x * \Delta\ln(\mathrm{xr}_{t-1}) \quad (3.18)$$

The volume of imports is defined by the domestic demand and the ratio between the import price and the consumption price $\left(\frac{p_{IM_{t-1}}}{p_{C_{t-1}}}\right)$. In the long run, domestic demand has a positive impact on imports. However, the fall in consumption prices relative to import prices will reduce Vietnamese imports.

The growth rate of imports is strongly determined by changes in domestic demand (3.19). There is no price effect on the growth rate of imports.

$$\ln(im_t) = \iota_0^{im} * \ln(DMD_t) + \iota_1^{im} * \ln\left(\frac{p_{IM_{t-1}}}{p_{C_{t-1}}}\right) \quad (3.19)$$

$$\Delta\ln(im_t) = \iota_0$$

$$* \Delta\ln(DMD_{t-1}) + \iota_1 * \left(\ln(im_{t-1}) - \iota_0^{im} * \ln(DMD_{t-1}) - \iota_1^{im} * \ln\left(\frac{p_{IM_{t-2}}}{p_{C_{t-2}}}\right)\right) \quad (3.20)$$

Domestic demand is the sum of intermediate consumption and final consumption.

$$DMD_t = ic_t + c_t + i_t^f + i_t^g + i_t^h + g_t \quad (3.21)$$

Integrating Damage Functions and Simulation

We integrate the damage functions into the equations that determine agriculture production, energy production, final consumption of households and the number of workers. These also enter into the equations related to population growth and TFP, which will affect the potential GDP (3.8). Table 3A.2 in the Appendix details the parameters used.

We define the effective agricultural production ($Q^*_{A_t}$):

$$Q^*_{A_t} = \left(1 - D_{AGR_t} * \gamma_{RICE}\right) * Q_{A_t} \tag{3.22}$$

where γ_{RICE} is the part of rice in agriculture; Q_{A_t} is the gricultural production of baseline scenario and D_{AGR_t} is the production loss due to climate change.

The agriculture damage function is given by:

$$D_{AGR_t} = \nu_{AGR} * \Delta T \tag{3.23}$$

Following the same modelling implication, (3.24) represents effective energy production $\left(Q^*_{E_t}\right)$ with climate change damage (D_{E_t}) on hydropower production.

$$Q^*_{E_t} = \left(1 + D_{E_t}\right) * \gamma_{HP} * Q_{E_t} \tag{3.24}$$

where γ_{HP} is the part of hydropower on the energy sector and Q_{E_t} is energy production of the baseline scenario.

$$D_{E_t} = \nu_{HPP} * \Delta T + \nu^2_{HPP} * \Delta T^2 \tag{3.25}$$

Regarding the damage on energy demand, the effective final consumption depends on the part of electricity consumption in total consumption (γ_{RE}) and climate impact (D_{RE_t}).

$$C^*_t = \left(1 + D_{RE_t}\right) * \gamma_{RE} * C_t \tag{3.26}$$

The damage function shows how the temperature change affects the residential electricity consumption of households (3.27).

$$D_{RE_t} = \nu_{RE} * \Delta T \tag{3.27}$$

We assume that climate damage affects labour productivity through the number of workers (3.28). There is a positive impact from both the demand and supply side on the number of workers. The higher level of economic activity, the higher demand for workers. The number of employed individuals depends on the size of the active population considered as the labour supply.

$$ln(NBW_t) = \left[\lambda_0 + \lambda_1 * \ln(y_{t-1}) + \lambda_2 * \ln\left(pop_{ACTIV_t}\right)\right] * \left(1 - D_{L_t}\right) \tag{3.28}$$

We define the labour productivity loss due to climate change as:

$$D_{L_t} = \nu_L * \Delta T \tag{3.29}$$

The climate impact on the mortality rate equation is represented as:

$$MORT^{*}_{GR_t} = (1 + D_{M_t}) * MORT_{GR_t} \quad (3.30)$$

where $MORT_{GR_t}$ is the mortality rate of the baseline scenario and D_{M_t} is mortality damage, which is a function of temperature change.

$$D_{M_t} = \nu_M * \Delta T \quad (3.31)$$

The equation that determines TFP is equal to:

$$TFP^{*}_{t} = (1 + D_{TFP_t}) * TFP_t \quad (3.32)$$

where TFP_t denotes TFP of the baseline scenario and D_{TFP_t} is the damage function on TFP

$$D_{TFP_t} = \nu_{TFP} * \Delta T \quad (3.33)$$

Baseline Scenario

The model simulation will generate a baseline scenario in which climate change impacts are ignored and alternative scenarios in which climate change impacts are simulated. The baseline scenario is broadly aligned with current socio-economic development trends in Viet Nam and the world.

RESULTS

Figure 3.4 shows the damages within the macroeconomic model by decade (2020s, 2030s, 2040s) in the simulation where all sectoral damages (agriculture, energy, labour productivity, TFP, mortality) are integrated simultaneously. Boxes represent the interquartile range (25th (Q1) and 75th (Q3) percentiles). The black line shows the median value and dots represent outliers (maximum = Q3 + 1.5 * – interquantile range: 25th to 75th percentile; minimum = Q1 + 1.5 * – interquantile range: 25th to 75th percentile). By the 2040s, average losses ranged between 0.7 and 10.4 per cent under RCP4.5 and between 1.7 and 12.2 per cent under RCP8.5.

Then, we consider the climate impacts when the global warming levels (GWLs) of 1.5°C and 2°C are reached for RCP8.5 in 2023 and 2039, respectively (Figure 3.5). The top graph shows the distribution of 1.5°C, 2°C and 3°C VNMST change in RCP8.5 according to the different climate models. The bottom graph represents the average macroeconomic damage relative to the baseline scenario up to 2050 in RCP8.5. The vertical green line indicates

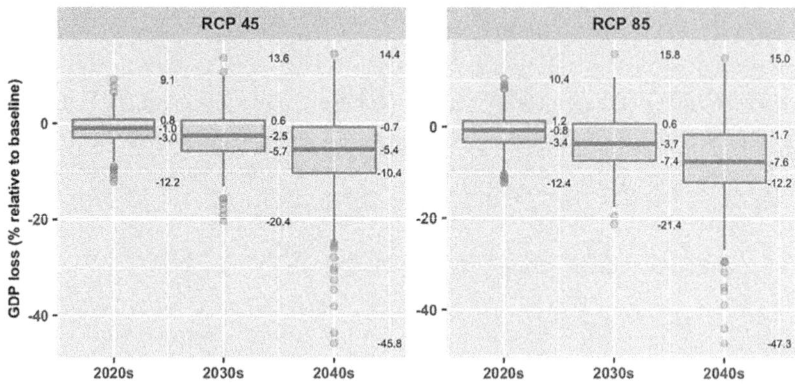

Figure 3.4 *Macroeconomic damage as a percentage of GDP loss relative to the baseline scenario*

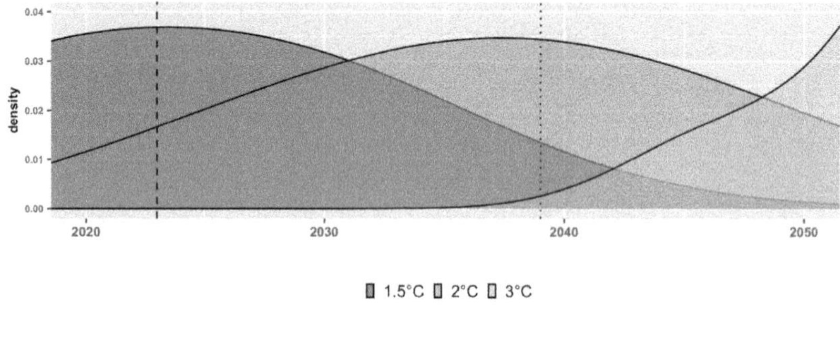

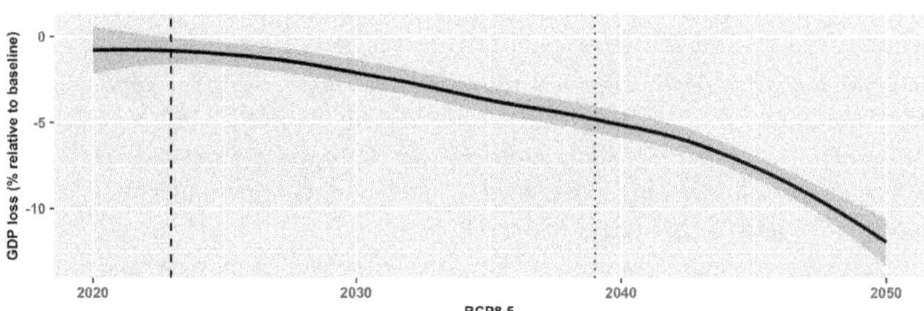

Figure 3.5 *Macroeconomic damage when the global warming levels 1.5°C and 2°C are reached for RCP8.5*

the median date when the GWL 1.5°C is reached. The red line indicates the median date when the GWL 2°C is reached. The median date for the GWL 3°C threshold appears after 2050, but there is still an increasing probability to cross it between 2040 and 2050.

We also compare macroeconomic adjusted losses with direct damage losses. Figure 3.6 shows that the direct damages of one sector in the macroeconomic model can be larger or smaller than the corresponding direct damages valuation, depending on the sector. The case of mortality is much smaller in the macroeconomic model due to the way of valuation of mortality using Value of Statistical Life. In the case of TFP, the macro impact is much larger due to the role of TFP in the model, which contributes to the production and investment decisions. Overall, the losses are larger than direct damages by around 30 per cent.

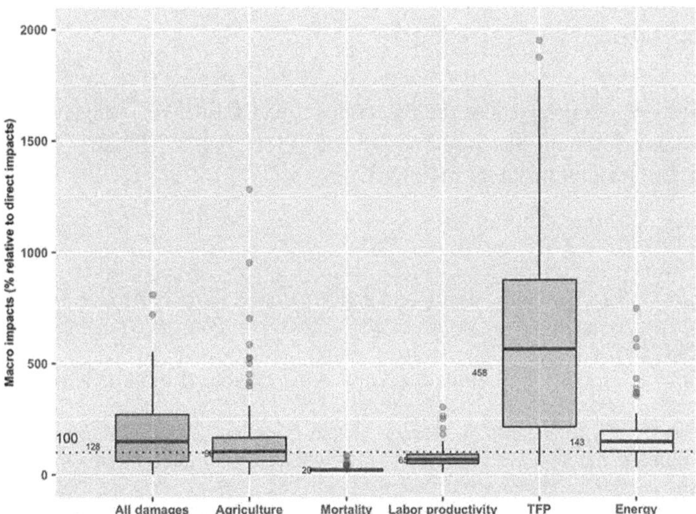

Figure 3.6 Distributions of GDP loss in the macroeconomic model compared with direct damages

CONCLUSION

Our results provide a comprehensive economy-wide assessment of the social and economic effects of climate change on the Vietnamese economy, using an integrated macroeconomic framework and empirical analyses of climate impacts and available regional and global climate models. We integrate a sectoral damage function within the SFC model of the Vietnamese economy. In that sense, growth is demand-driven, while production capacities are affected by the direct impacts of temperature increases on agriculture, energy, labour productivity and health (mortality). This estimate will certainly not be the last, as multiple known sectors of the Vietnamese economy for which no suitable studies exist have been omitted from the analysis so far. However, our approach allows for updates based on new econometric/sectoral modelling results or climate model projections.

In terms of policy implications, even if not all effects have been accounted for, the loss could prevent Viet Nam from achieving its development target, which is set at about 7 per cent GDP growth annually during 2021–2030 in order to become an industrialized country by 2045. This urges Viet Nam to pay more attention to its climate change adaptation strategy in order to improve resilience, mitigate possible negative impacts and achieve the country's development targets.

ACKNOWLEDGEMENTS

This study is integrated into the research project GEMMES Viet Nam of the French Development Agency (AFD) and Viet Nam's Ministry of Natural Resources and Environment (MONRE).

REFERENCES

Arestis, P. (2013). Economic theory and policy: A coherent post-Keynesian approach. *European Journal of Economics and Economic Policies: Intervention* 10.2, pp. 243–255.

Ashenfelter, O. (2006). Measuring the Value of a Statistical Life: Problems and prospects. *Economic Journal* 116.510, pp. 10–23.

Auffhammer, M., S. Hsiang, W. Schlenker and A. Sobel (2013). Using weather data and climate model output in economic analyses of climate change. *Review of Environmental Economics and Policy* 7.2, pp. 181–198.

Burgess, S., O. Burrows, A. Godin, S. Kinsella and S. Millard (2016). A dynamic model of financial balances for the United Kingdom. *Bank of England Staff Working Paper 614*. London: Bank of England.

Ciscar, J.-C. and P. Dowling (2014). Integrated assessment of climate impacts and adaptation in the energy sector. *Energy Economics* 46.C, pp. 531–538.

Crockett, J. and I. Friend (1967). Consumer investment behavior. *Determinants of Investment Behavior*. Cambridge, MA: National Bureau of Economic Research, pp. 15–127.

Dao, H., A.N. Do, H.P. Nguyen, T.P. Dang, V.T. Nga, R. Few and A. Winkels (2013). Heat stress and adaptive capacity of low-income outdoor workers and their families in the city of Da Nang, Vietnam. Asian Cities Climate Resilience Working Paper Series. IIED.

Deb, P., A.D. Tran and P. Udmale (2015). Assessment of the impacts of climate change and brackish irrigation water on rice productivity and evaluation of adaptation measures in Ca Mau province, Vietnam. *Theoretical and Applied Climatology* 125, pp. 641–656.

Dell, M., B. Jones and B. Olken (2012). Temperature shocks and economic growth: Evidence from the last half century. *American Economic Journal: Macroeconomics* 4.

Dietz, S. and N. Stern (2015). Endogenous growth, convexity of damage and climate risk: How Nordhaus' framework supports deep cuts in carbon emissions. *The Economic Journal* 125.

Espagne, E. et al. (2021). Climate change in Viet Nam; impacts and adaptation. A COP26 assessment report of the GEMMES Viet Nam project. Agence Française de Développement.

Gasparrini, A., Y. Guo, F. Sera, A.M. Vicedo-Cabrera, V. Huber, S. Tong et al. (2017). Projections of temperature-related excess mortality under climate change scenarios. *Lancet Planet Health*, pp. 360–367.

Global Climate Risk Index (2021). Who suffers most from extreme weather events? Weather-related loss events in 2019 and 2000–2019. Germanwatch. www.germanwatch.org/en/cri

Guo, Y., A. Gasparrini, S. Li, F. Sera, A.M. Vicedo-Cabrera, M. de Sousa Zanotti Stagliorio et al. (2018). Quantifying excess deaths related to heatwaves under climate change scenarios: A multicountry time series modelling study. *PLOS Medicine* 15, e1002629.

Hsiang, S., R. Kopp, A. Jina, J. Rising, M. Delgado, S. Mohan et al. (2017). Estimating economic damage from climate change in the United States. *Science* 356.6345, pp. 1362–1369.

ILO (2016). *Climate change and labour: Impacts of heat in the workplace*. New York: UNDP.

ILO (2019). *Working on a warmer planet: The impact of heat stress on labour productivity and decent work.* Geneva: ILO.

IMF (2019). Vietnam: Selected issues. IMF Staff Country Reports.

IMF (2021). Vietnam: 2020 Article IV Consultation – Press Release; Staff Report; and Statement by the Executive Director for Vietnam. IMF Staff Country Reports 2021/042.

IMHEN (2021). Report on climate change and sea level rise scenarios for Viet Nam. Viet Nam Institute of Meteorology, Hydrology and Climate Change.

Kalecki, M. (1971). *Selected essays on the dynamics of the capitalist economy 1933–1970*. Cambridge: Cambridge University Press.

Kjellstrom, T., I. Holmer and B. Lemke (2009). Workplace heat stress, health and productivity: An increasing challenge for low and middle-income countries during climate change. *Global Health Action* 2.

Kjellstrom, T., B. Lemke and P. Otto (2012). Mapping occupational heat exposure and effects in South-East Asia: Ongoing time trends 1980–2011 and future estimates to 2050. *Industrial Health* 51, pp. 56–67.

Kjellstrom, T., B. Lemke, M. Otto, O. Hyatt and K. Dear (2014). Occupational heat stress contribution to WHO project on 'Global assessment of the health impacts of climate change'. Technical report, Climate Chip.

Kontgis, C., A. Schneider, M. Ozdogan, C. Kucharik, P.D.T. Van, H.D. Nguyen and J. Schatz (2018). Climate change impacts on rice productivity in the Mekong River Delta. *Applied Geography* 102, pp. 71–83.

Letta, M. and R.S.J. Tol (2016). Weather, climate and total factor productivity. Working Paper Series 10216, Department of Economics, University of Sussex Business School.

Li, S., Q. Wang and J.A. Chun (2017). Impact assessment of climate change on rice productivity in the Indochinese Peninsula using a regional-scale crop model. *International Journal of Climatology* 37.

Moore, F. and D. Diaz (2015). Temperature impacts on economic growth warrant stringent mitigation policy. *Nature Climate Change* 5.

Moyer, E., M. Woolley, N. Matteson, M. Glotter and D. Weisbach (2013). Climate impacts on economic growth as drivers of uncertainty in the social cost of carbon. *SSRN Electronic Journal* 43.

Ohno, E., M. Morisugi, P. Kyophilavong and H. Sao (2012). Measurement of Value of Statistical Life by evaluating diarrhea mortality risk due to water pollution in Laos and Vietnam. 52nd Congress of the European Regional Science Association: Regions in Motion – Breaking the Path, 21–25 August, Bratislava, Slovakia.

Opitz-Stapleton, S., L. Sabbag, K. Hawley, P. Tran, L. Hoang and P.H. Nguyen (2016). Heat index trends and climate change implications for occupational heat exposure in Da Nang, Vietnam. *Climate Services* 2.

Orlov, A., J. Sillmann, K. Aunan, T. Kjellstrom and A. Aaheim (2020). Economic costs of heat-induced reductions in worker productivity due to global warming. *Global Environmental Change* 63.

Rocque, R.J., C. Beaudoin, R. Ndjaboue, L. Cameron, L. Poirier-Bergeron, R.-A. Poulin-Rheault et al. (2021). Health effects of climate change: An overview of systematic reviews. *BMJ Open* 11.6.

Shrestha, S., P. Deb and T. Bui (2016). Adaptation strategies for rice cultivation under climate change in Central Vietnam. *Mitigation and Adaptation Strategies for Global Change* 21.1, pp. 15–37.

Taylor, K., R. Stouffer and G. Meehl (2012). An overview of CMIP5 and the experiment design. *Bulletin of the American Meteorological Society* 93.4, pp. 485–498.

UN (2009). System of national accounts 2008. Technical report.

UNU-WIDER (2012). The cost of climate change in Vietnam.

Vicedo-Cabrera, A., Y. Guo, F. Sera, V. Huber, C.-F. Schleussner, D. Mitchell et al. (2018). Temperature-related mortality impacts under and beyond Paris Agreement climate change scenarios. *Climatic Change* 150.

Wood, A.W., L.R. Leung, V. Sridhar and D.P. Lettenmaier (2004). Hydrologic implications of dynamical and statistical approaches to downscaling climate model outputs. *Climatic Change* 62, pp. 189–216.

World Bank (2011). Vulnerability, risk reduction, and adaptation to climate change Vietnam. Report.

Yalew, S., M. van Vliet, D. Gernaat, F. Ludwig, A. Miara, C. Park et al. (2020). Impacts of climate change on energy systems in global and regional scenarios. *Nature Energy* 5.

Yu, B., T. Zhu, C. Breisinger and M.H. Nguyen (2010). Impacts of climate change on agriculture and policy options for adaptation: The case of Vietnam. IFPRI discussion papers 1015. International Food Policy Research Institute.

Table 3A.1 *Appendix: Theoretical balance sheet of Viet Nam*

	Firms	Central banks	Banks	Government	Households	ROW	Total
Non-financial assets	$p_K k^f$			$p_K k^g$	$p_K k^h$		$p_K k$
Inventories	$p_{K_{12}} k_{12}$						$p_{K_{12}} k_{12}$
International reserves		$RES_{us} xr$				$-RES_{us} xr$	0
Cash		$-H$			H		0
Bank reserves		$-MB^{cb}$	MB^{cb}				0
Government deposits		$-GM^{cb}$	$-GM^b$	GM			0
Dong deposits	DM^f		$-DM$		DM^h		0
Foreign deposits	$FM^f_{us} xr$			$FM^g_{us} xr$	$FM^h_{us} xr$	$-FM_{us} xr$	0
Bonds		B^{cb}	B^b	$-B$	B^h		0
Advances		LB^{cb}	$-LB^{cb}$				0
Loans	$-L^f$		L		$-L^h$		0
Foreign loans	$-FL^f_{us} xr$		$-FL^b_{us} xr$	$-FL^g_{us} xr$		$FL_{us} xr$	0
Equity	$-p_E E^f$		$-p_E E^b$		$p_E E^h$	$p_E E^r$	0
Foreign direct investment	$-p_{FDI} FDI_{us} xr$					$p_{FDI} FDI_{us} xr$	0
Other accounts receivable/payable	OTA^f	OTA^{cb}	OTA^b	OTA^g	OTA^h	OTA^r	0
Net wealth	NW^f	NW^{cb}	NW^b	NW^g	NW^h	NW^r	$p_K k + p_{K_{12}} k_{12}$

Table 3A.2 Appendix: Values of parameters estimated in damage functions

Equation	Damages	Value
3.23	Agriculture	ν_{AGR}= -6.945
3.25	Hydropower production	= 0.055;ν_{HPP}
3.27	Electricity consumption	ν_{RE} = 1.033
3.31	Mortality	ν_{M} = 4.016
3.29	Labour productivity	ν_{L}= -2.656
3.33	Total factor productivity	ν_{TFP} = −3.59

4. The tensions of the "green transition" for South American economies

Sebastian Valdecantos

INTRODUCTION

It is now widely accepted that the "green transition" is a process of structural change, where cleaner and more energy-efficient industries, both newly created and already existing ones, will gain importance in the economy, while more traditional activities (mostly those related to fossil fuels) will progressively disappear (Semieniuk et al., 2021). Even if the contribution of South American countries to global greenhouse gas emissions is low (while their share of global gross domestic product (GDP) is 4.5 percent, their share of global emissions is 3 percent), their reliance on natural resource-intensive activities entails a series of risks. This is because in most of them macroeconomic stability relies on primary commodity exports, which in many cases are related to the so-called "sunset industries," i.e., those that will be negatively affected by the series of policies that the global green transition entails.

In a recent analysis of the vulnerabilities of emerging and developing countries to the green transition, Espagne et al. (2021) break down these macroeconomic risks into three categories – external, fiscal and socio-economic exposures, each of them defining the net potential losses of foreign exchange, government revenue and employment as a result of the global move toward more sustainable ways of production and consumption. To quantify each country's exposure they rely on input–output data to see the relevance that sunset industries have in each of the three dimensions. Their analysis shows varying levels of exposure across the region. First, Bolivia and Venezuela exhibit a high exposure in all three dimensions because exports, government revenue and employment rely heavily on sunset industries. Brazil, Paraguay, Ecuador, Guyana and Suriname are more susceptible to socio-economic exposure, meaning that an important part of the employment in their economies is directly or indirectly related to sunset industries, while exports and government revenue are more diversified. Chile, Peru and Colombia, for their part, are more subject to external exposure, implying that exports are strongly related to sunset industries, while employment and government revenue are less dependent on them. According to their analysis, only Argentina and Uruguay show low levels of exposure to the green transition.

This chapter shares the concern of Espagne et al. (2021) and addresses the tensions that the green transition entails for South American countries from a more aggregated perspective. The main contention is that given that their productive structure is heavily based on primary products which in many cases bear high levels of pollution, the simultaneous attainment of economic prosperity, macroeconomic stability and environmental sustainability poses serious challenges for South American countries. In the next section we conceptually describe the nature of these tensions. Then we propose a set of indicators that help operationalize them so we can finally analyze the joint trajectories of South American countries in the last 30 years regarding these three dimensions. Considering that each of the three dimensions can be measured in diverse ways and, more specifically, taking into account that there are deep debates around what prosperity and environmental sustainability mean, the analysis proposed in this chapter should be taken as a heuristic exercise aimed at illustrating the tensions that South American countries could face in the transition toward a zero-carbon economy.

THE TENSIONS OF THE GREEN TRANSITION

The attainment of decent levels of income and need satisfaction is a well-known pending subject for South American countries. While in 2021 per capita GDP of advanced economies averaged USD 57,052 (purchasing power parity (PPP)), South America's mean per capita income totaled USD 15,726 (PPP), with Chile exhibiting the highest level (USD 24,315) and Bolivia the lowest (USD 8,424). Moreover, the region is characterized by high levels of inequality – while developed countries tend to show Gini indices below 0.3, the South American average was 0.454 in 2020, with Uruguay (0.402) and Colombia (0.542) as the least and most unequal ones, respectively. Moreover, toward the end of the 2010s the poverty rate (measured as the poverty headcount ratio at USD 3.65 a day (2017 PPP) 6.6 percent, with Colombia (13.7 percent) and Uruguay (0.5 percent) at the extremes (World Development Indicators, World Bank).

From a standard economic perspective, a necessary (albeit not sufficient) condition to increase the population's standard of living is increasing income levels, i.e., achieving higher growth rates during a sufficiently long period so that the economy catches up with advanced economies. However, as the balance of payments constrained growth literature pioneered by Thirlwall (1979) has shown, the growth rate required to catch up with advanced economies might not be feasible due to structural limitations, namely a high-income elasticity of imports and a low-income elasticity of exports, both reflecting a productive structure heavily reliant on the production and exports of low value-added primary commodities and a high technological gap with respect to the frontier. Thirlwall's arguments reinforced the earlier concerns that Prebisch (1950) and Singer (1950) highlighted in their theses on the secular declining trend in the terms of trade.

Thus, a structural limitation rests at the core of South American economies' productive configuration. Even while exports are not the main contributor to aggregate demand growth, they play a crucial role as suppliers of the foreign exchange that these economies need to maintain sufficiently high growth rates. But neither export prices nor the demand from trading partners is under the control of these countries, thereby making growth possibilities exogenous to them.

The picture gets even more dismal when the need to transition toward a low-carbon economy is incorporated into the analysis. Many export-related activities of South American countries, such as the extraction of fossil fuels, mining, livestock and agriculture, generate greenhouse gases. This implies that while attaining higher living standards requires sustained growth, and considering the strong reliance of the latter on increasing exports, the pursuit of a path along those lines would be at odds with the decarbonization of their economies. On the other hand, a firm commitment to decarbonize their economies would imply, given the current productive structure, a reduction in exports and, therefore, the imposition of a low upward limit on GDP growth rates.

The tensions that characterize South American countries' green transition can be represented in a graphical device consisting of three dimensions: prosperity, external sustainability and environmental sustainability, as shown in Figure 4.1. Prosperity is a proxy of the living standards of a country's population and was proposed by Jackson and Victor (2020) as a broader measure compared to GDP.[1] External sustainability represents the country's capacity to grow sustainably without incurring persistent balance-of-payment deficits. Environmental sustainability is the country's average carbon intensity, and how far this is from carbon neutrality.

An illustrative starting point of South American economies is represented by the dot in the bottom left of the cube, where all prosperity, environmental sustainability and external sustainability are low. The "bliss point" is given by the dot on the top right, where the three dimensions exhibit satisfactory levels denoting high prosperity combined with environmental sustainability, both being compatible with the balance-of-payments equilibrium. Given the initial conditions the bottom-left dot represents, the green transition would be characterized by a pathway along the lines shown by the long arrow. On the contrary, a failed transition would be given by dynamics such as those shown by the short arrow, where the attempt to increase prosperity (which from a standard

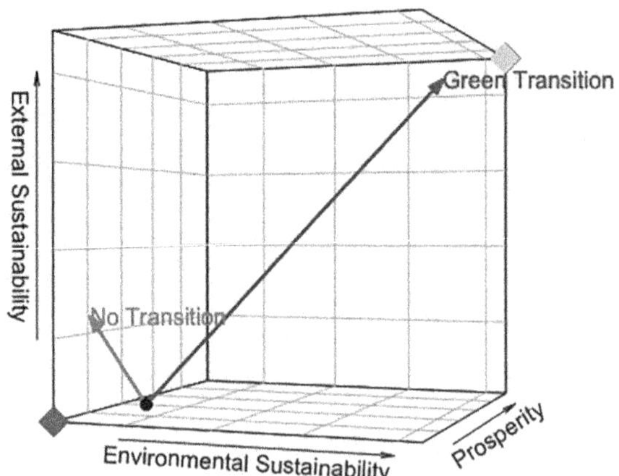

Figure 4.1 *The tensions of the green transition for South American economies*

economic perspective, in turn, requires more growth) through higher exports ends up backfiring the decarbonization of the economy. Moreover, even higher prosperity might not be attained if exports do not increase as much as needed for any exogenous reason.

OPERATIONALIZING A MEASURE OF PROSPERITY

A simplified notion of prosperity can be defined in terms of three variables: GDP per capita to account for the average income level of a country's population, the Gini index to account for how equally that income is distributed among the members of the population and the poverty rate to weigh the indicator by the number of citizens living below the standards that guarantee a decent life. Using these three indicators, prosperity (P) can be defined as follows:

$$P = \frac{Y}{POP}\left(1 - Gini\right)\left(1 - pov\right)$$

where Y is GDP in dollars at 2017 PPP levels, POP is the size of the population, $Gini$ is the Gini index and pov is the percentage of the population living with less than 3.65 USD per day. All these variables are obtained from the World Bank.

Figure 4.2 shows the prosperity index for South American countries in 2019. As a benchmark for comparative purposes we take Denmark, as it is a country at the top of the hierarchy of living standards. The prosperity index is computed using the formula presented before and then normalized with the value obtained for Denmark as 100. The values for the rest of the countries are computed as ratios from the prosperity index of Denmark. The first fact that results from the figure is the huge gap between the prosperity of South American countries and the international benchmark. Second, while the countries belonging to the "southern cone" (Chile, Argentina and Uruguay) exhibit the highest prosperity levels in the region, the countries lying in the tropics (all the rest) are lagging behind. Despite these intra-regional nuances, increasing prosperity levels is among the pending subjects for the region as a whole.

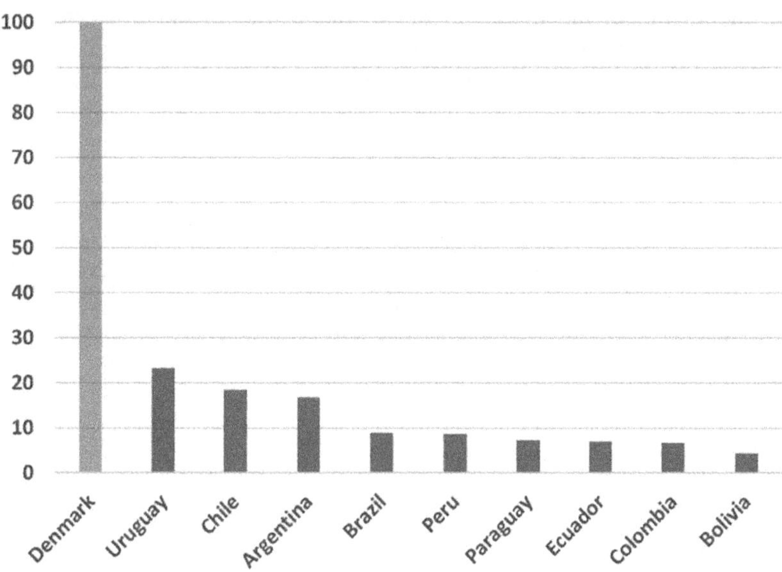

Figure 4.2 *Prosperity (2019)*

OPERATIONALIZING EXTERNAL SUSTAINABILITY

The seminal contribution of Thirlwall (1979) to the balance-of-payments constrained growth literature provides a useful tool to measure the limits that developing countries find to sustain high growth rates over time. In essence, Thirlwall showed that the long-run growth rate of an economy depends on three elements: (1) the growth rate of trading partners; (2) the income elasticity of exports; and (3) the income elasticity of imports. The higher the first two, the higher the balance-of-payments equilibrium growth rate, i.e., the maximum growth rate sustainably attainable without hitting the balance-of-payments constraint. As regards the income elasticity of imports it is known that it tends to be quite high in developing countries due to "black holes" in the productive structure. This, in turn, hampers the growth possibilities of countries specializing in the production of primary goods, as is the case of South American economies. Later, Thirlwall's contributions were extended to incorporate capital flows (Thirlwall and Hussain, 1982; Moreno Brid, 1998; Barbosa-Filho, 2001; McCombie and Thirlwall, 2004).

For simplicity we take Thirlwall's original proposal consisting of the ratio of the growth rate of real exports ($\hat{x}$) to the income elasticity of imports (π), to which we add the ratio of current account inflows to outflows, both of them measured in USD. The reason why this additional term is added is to account for the other elements of the current account, some of them temporary (like changing terms of trade or interest rates) and others structural (for instance, whether the country is a net debtor or creditor), that can define the level of the balance-of-payments constraint. Recall that the balance-of-payments equilibrium growth rate is a long-term concept, meaning that the economy can grow temporarily above that rate, eventually converging to it. The simple extension that we propose to the standard balance-of-payments equilibrium growth rate proposed by Thirlwall attempts to allow for situations where the external constraint can be relaxed due to exogenous factors, like the commodity supercycle of 2005–2013 for South American countries.

Figure 4.3 shows the external sustainability of South American countries, again, compared to an international benchmark like Denmark. As the Latin

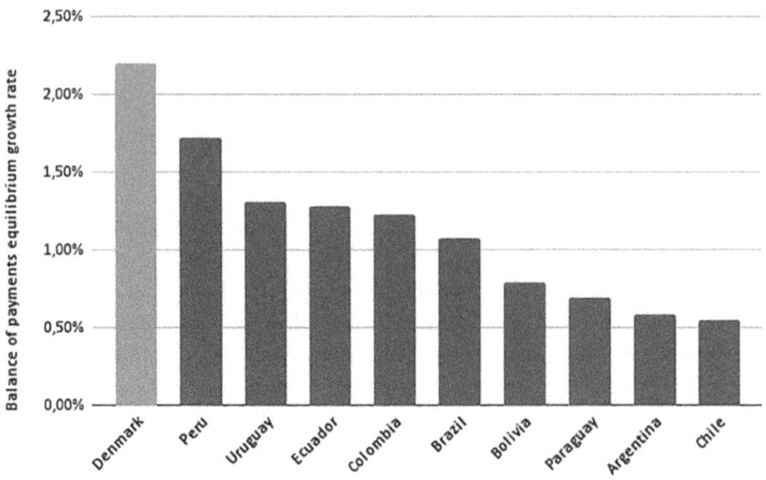

Figure 4.3 External sustainability (2019)

American structuralist school has pointed out since the mid-twentieth century, developing countries might find it hard to keep the high growth rates that a development process requires due to the constraints coming from the balance of payments. From the figures presented in Figure 4.3 it is deduced that no country in South America can sustainably grow at a rate higher than 2 percent without going into a trade deficit. Phrased differently, a high and sustained growth process would require a continuous flow of external financing that might not always be available. Although the limits imposed by the balance of payments to South American countries might not seem too different from those faced by Denmark, it should be borne in mind that for a developed country a 2 percent growth rate is considered enough (as long as the population grows a little bit less than that).

OPERATIONALIZING ENVIRONMENTAL SUSTAINABILITY

The environmental sustainability of an economy depends on a wide variety of issues, ranging from the type of industries that participate in it, the technologies they use in the production processes, the type of energy used and the degree to which the waste arising from production and consumption is recycled. Although it could be interesting to build an index of environmental sustainability capturing all these aspects, for the heuristic purposes of the analysis presented in this chapter it suffices to use the unit of greenhouse gas emissions of the total economy, i.e., the total emissions (measured in kilograms of CO^2 equivalent) divided by total output (measured in 2017 PPP USD). The information is accessible on the World Bank database.

Figure 4.4 shows the countries in the sample ordered according to their average carbon intensity. While Uruguay seems to be the one with the most sustainable production pattern, Bolivia is in the other extreme. Unlike for prosperity and external sustainability, when it comes to environmental sustainability it is not possible to conclude that the region is lagging behind the international benchmark, as there are two countries scoring better while others are not far from it. Although there is no clear-cut pattern it seems that countries with larger surfaces (Brazil and Argentina) and/or with an important extractive industry (Peru, Chile, Ecuador and Bolivia) tend to exhibit lower levels of environmental sustainability. On the other hand, the most environmentally sustainable countries, Uruguay and Paraguay, are characterized by being small in surface and not relying on extractive activities.

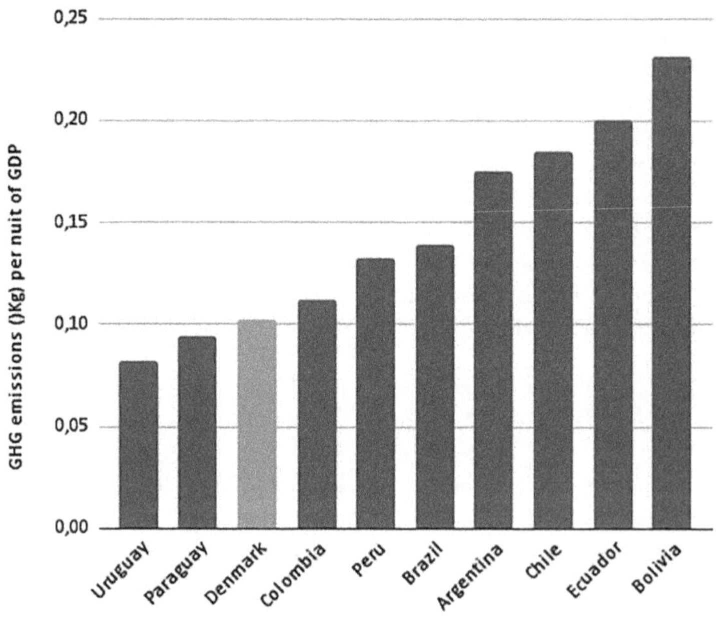

Figure 4.4 *Environmental sustainability (2019)*

TRANSITION PATHWAYS OF SOUTH AMERICAN COUNTRIES IN THE TWENTY-FIRST CENTURY

The indicators constructed for prosperity, external and environmental sustainability can be plotted in the three-dimensional space presented in Figure 4.1, to see: (1) where each country is located in each of the three dimensions; and (2) what has been the joint evolution of these three indicators across time. As mentioned at the beginning of this chapter, the best-case scenario is given by a situation where the country is located in the back-north-east vertex of the cube. As this is an unlikely position to find (mostly thinking about developing countries) a second-best situation is one where the country is moving in that direction. In that case it can be argued that the economy in question is on the "right path" and that as long as that trajectory is not interrupted it will eventually reach the "bliss point" consisting of prosperity, environmental and external sustainability.

Figure 4.5 shows the trajectories South American countries followed in the first two decades of the twenty-first century. As throughout this chapter, Denmark is also included as the international benchmark for comparability reasons. In order to make the figures for individual countries comparable, all of them are plotted using the same scale. Not surprisingly, Denmark is clearly closer to the "bliss point." South American countries, on the contrary, are closer to the front-south-west vertex, which shows the size of the challenge

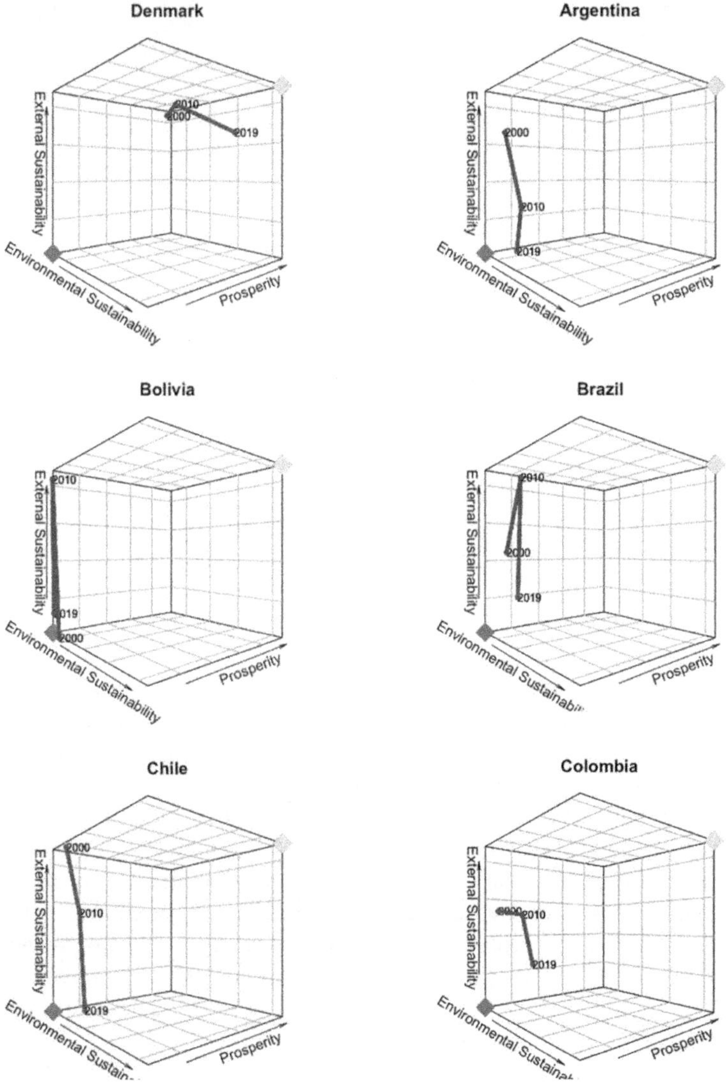

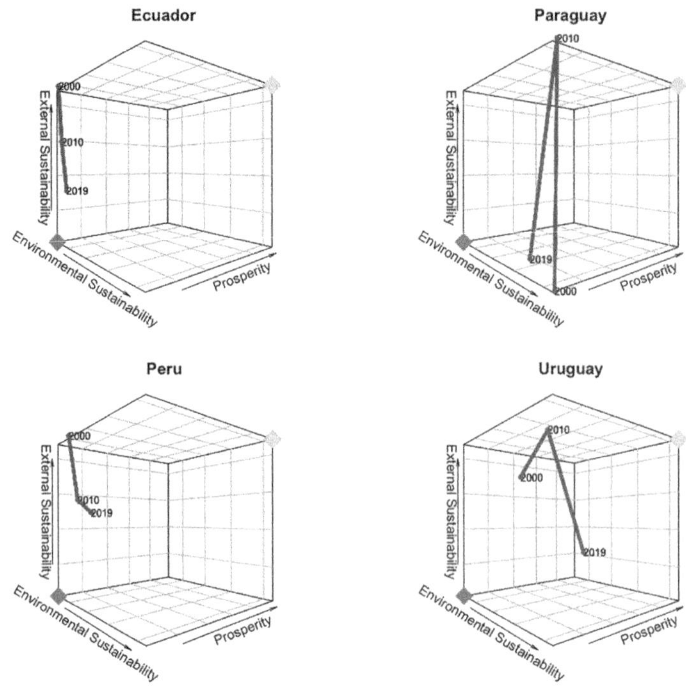

Figure 4.5 Transition pathways (2000–2019)

that entails the combination of the transition toward a zero-carbon economy with increasing levels of prosperity, without hitting the balance-of-payments constraint on the way.

When the dynamics of prosperity are analyzed Uruguay stands out as the best-performing country, not only exhibiting the highest levels of prosperity in the region but also increasing them, as the more right-ward location of the 2019 dot along the prosperity axis shows. It is also worth mentioning that Chile, Peru and Paraguay registered increases in their prosperity. However, their starting points were much lower – while in the case of Chile prosperity was mostly increased in the 2000s, Paraguay and Peru seem to have benefited most in the 2010s. An increase in prosperity was also observed in the cases of Bolivia, Colombia and Ecuador, albeit to a smaller degree. Finally, Argentina and Brazil experienced decreases in prosperity in the 2010s as a direct consequence of their respective long-lasting crises (more macroeconomics-related in the case of Argentina, while more related to political instability in Brazil).

Overall, it seems like South American countries have been improving their prosperity levels to a certain extent, though they are still far from international standards.

The dynamics of external sustainability show a different picture. A first group integrated by Argentina, Chile and Paraguay have seen a drastic decrease in their balance-of-payments equilibrium growth rates, to the extent that they were close to zero towards the end of the 2010s. While in Argentina and Chile this drop was continuous, in the case of Paraguay it seems that cyclical factors allowed for higher balance-of-payments equilibrium growth rates in the 2000s. A second group is integrated by Brazil, Colombia, Ecuador, Peru and Uruguay, where the balance-of-payments equilibrium growth rate also fell but was still allowing for some growth towards the end of the 2010s. The picture looks brighter for this group's members than the previous one because higher external sustainability implies that prosperity levels can be increased without compromising the country's macroeconomic stability. Finally, Bolivia is the only case where external sustainability improves end to end, albeit still with a low balance-of-payments equilibrium growth rate compared to what would be required to reach significantly higher prosperity levels.

In most countries of the region the evolution of environmental sustainability exhibited a slight improvement starting (and therefore ending) at a low level compared to international standards. Argentina, Brazil, Chile, Colombia, Ecuador and Peru all seem to have exhibited a trajectory along these lines. The rest of the countries, on the other hand, have shown specific patterns. Bolivia seems to be in the worst scenario, as its environmental sustainability has not only worsened but is far from the international benchmark. Paraguay, for its part, has also worsened its environmental sustainability but it is much closer to the international benchmark. Finally, Uruguay stands out (as with prosperity) as it not only improved its environmental sustainability but is also located close to the international benchmark.

The joint analysis of the end-to-end dynamics of prosperity, external and environmental sustainability shows that all countries have moved along the lines of the undesirable trajectory illustrated in Figure 4.1. While Bolivia and Paraguay moved in the sense of the arrow, implying an increase in prosperity allowed by an increase in external sustainability at the expense of environmental sustainability, the rest of the countries went in the opposite direction, showing an increase in environmental sustainability and a worsening in external sustainability. Again, a trade-off seems to be between these two dimensions. To make matters worse, in the cases of Brazil and Argentina prosperity was also reduced, signaling that factors beyond the tensions described in this chapter might have been affecting their performances.

Do these dismal results imply that a sustainable green transition, i.e., a process where a continuous increase in prosperity is made possible without hitting the balance-of-payments constraint and increasing environmental damage, is impossible? To see this we look for intervals along the trajectories where the dynamics could have been along the desired lines (as represented by the long arrow in Figure 4.1). Only two cases were found: Brazil and Uruguay in the 2000s. In both cases a simultaneous increase in prosperity, external and environmental sustainability was registered. This might have been allowed for by a combination of their relatively low carbon intensity (Uruguay much lower than Brazil) with the positive terms-of-trade effects that characterized those years, which temporarily increased GDP growth rates without necessarily leading to balance-of-payments deficits. However, it is well known that those extraordinary conditions ended in 2013. Despite the increase in commodity prices recorded in the post-Covid era, it is still uncertain whether these conditions will hold for a sufficiently long period, allowing South American countries to grow at fast rates. Even if this were the case, it would still be a challenge to harmonize the increase in prosperity levels that these higher growth rates would bring about with the goal of decarbonizing their economies.

CONCLUSIONS

We started this chapter by expressing concern about South American countries' possibilities of increasing their prosperity levels while transitioning to a zero-carbon economy. Underlying this concern is that they have a primary-good carbon-intensive export-oriented productive structure in varying degrees. As the balance-of-payments constrained growth literature has shown, laggard countries might find it hard to catch up because a sustained growth process will most likely be interrupted by an endogenously generated balance-of-payments crisis. Thus, increasing the growth rate of exports seems to be an unavoidable (though not sufficient) condition to increase prosperity levels, given their productive structure. However, the bias of the export basket toward primary goods and, in some cases, extractive activities the main drivers of exports, produces a dilemma between the need to decarbonize the economy and the stability of the balance of payments required to increase income levels sustainably.

Using very simple indicators we attempted to illustrate the dynamics of prosperity, external and environmental sustainability of South American countries in the period 2000–2019, to see whether there is descriptive evidence supporting our contention. We found that in most cases the dynamics are in line with the green transition dilemma and that only in a few cases during a specific interval (the commodity supercycle) was the performance in line with what could be dubbed a sustainable green transition. Further analysis is needed, more specifically using other indicators, to strengthen the drawn conclusions and explore alternative solutions to the problem.

NOTE

1. The sustainable prosperity index constructed by Jackson and Victor (2020) includes GDP per capita, the Gini index, hours worked, households' loan to value ratio, the government debt to GDP ratio and the unemployment rate.

REFERENCES

Barbosa-Filho, N. H. (2001). The balance of payments constraint: From balanced trade to sustainable debt. In: J. S. L. McCombie and A. P. Thirlwall (eds). *Essays on Balance of Payments Constrained Growth: Theory and Evidence*. Routledge, London.

Espagne, É., A. Godin, G. Magacho, A. Montes and D. Yilmaz (2021). Developing countries' macroeconomic exposure to the low-carbon transition. *AFD Research Papers*, 220, 1–42.

Jackson, T. and P. Victor (2020). The transition to a sustainable prosperity: A stock-flow-consistent ecological macroeconomic model for Canada. *Ecological Economics*, 177.

McCombie, J. S. L. and A. P. Thirlwall (2004). *Essays on Balance of Payments Constrained Growth: Theory and Evidence*. Routledge, London.

Moreno-Brid, J. C. (1998). On capital flows and the balance-of-payments-constrained growth model. *Journal of Post Keynesian Economics*, 21(2).

Prebisch, R. (1950). The economic development of Latin America and its principal problems. *Economic Bulletin for Latin America*, 7(1), 1–22.

Semieniuk, G., E. Campiglio, J.-F. Mercure and U. V. N. R. Edwards (2021). Low-carbon transition risks for finance. *WIREs Climate Change*, 12, e678.

Singer, H. W. (1950). U.S. foreign investment in underdeveloped areas: The distribution of gains between investing and borrowing countries. *American Economic Review, Papers and Proceedings*, 40, 473–485.

Thirlwall, A. P. (1979). The balance of payments constraint as an explanation of international growth rate differences. In: J. S. L. McCombie and A. P. Thirlwall (2004). *Essays on Balance of Payments Constrained Growth: Theory and Evidence*. Routledge, London.

Thirlwall, A. P. and M. N. Hussain (1982). The balance of payments constraint, capital flows and growth rate differences between developing countries. In: J. S. L. McCombie and A. P. Thirlwall (eds). *Essays on Balance of Payments Constrained Growth: Theory and Evidence*. Routledge, London.

5. Conventional and unconventional economic policies in an econometric SFC model of the French economy

Jacques Mazier and Luis Reyes-Ortiz

INTRODUCTION

The 2008 and Covid crises have led to increasing public debts and to the launching of unconventional economic policies. Thanks to a complete description of the balance sheets of the domestic and foreign agents, stock-flow consistent (SFC) modelling was well equipped to evaluate their economic consequences. The founding works of Godley and Lavoie (Godley, 1999; Lavoie and Godley, 2001; Godley and Lavoie, 2007) on SFC modelling were simply calibrated. Since 2005, better calibrated or econometrically based SFC models have become more frequent. The Levy model of the United States (Godley et al., 2005) was a forerunner. A first version of an econometric SFC model of the French economy based on the accumulation accounts of INSEE and on the financial accounts of the Bank of France has been presented (Mazier and Reyes, 2022a). This provides the overall structure, the main equations and the basic properties of the model.

This chapter is based on the same model with some improvements. The determinants of the structure of the interest rates are more developed. The treatment of the central bank includes the description of interests received and paid. A key equation of the model, the rate of capital accumulation of firms, has been modified in order to introduce a demand effect. Also, a provisional version of the model with an endogenous public bonds interest rate is shown at the end of the chapter. These improvements do not change fundamentally the properties of the model but some inflexions can be noticed.

The chapter is organized as follows. A second part presents the overall structure of the model and the main equations with a focus on the new ones. A third section is devoted to the simulations on the past and to basic shocks with an evaluation of the value of the multipliers of this version compared with the previous one. A fourth section analyzes some forms of unconventional or more conventional economic policies to finance public investment or social transfers. A fifth section studies the economic consequences of an imported inflationary shock and some possible policy responses. The next section gives some proposals towards endogenization of public bonds interest rate. A final part concludes.[1]

MODEL STRUCTURE AND MAIN EQUATIONS

The model is aggregate with a single product. Its structure is analogous to that of already existing national-level SFC models. Production in volume is determined by domestic and foreign demand. The general price level depends on a mark-up pricing rule and is a function of unit labor costs with an effect from demand pressures. Value added is split among the different agents depending on simple structural parameters. Its distribution between wages, profits and taxes is based on a wage-price-unemployment equation and on institutional relations. Exports and imports are analyzed for all goods and services determined by demand and relative prices. Financing methods via bank credit, bond and equity issuing, as well as financial investment behavior are described for each agent. Changes in assets and liabilities, as well as investment and changes in inventories, combined with the revaluation accounts for capital gains or losses, facilitate the transition of the accumulation accounts from one year to the next in an SFC manner. The balance sheet structure of domestic and foreign agents and the uses-resources table combined with the flow of funds can be found in Mazier and Reyes (2022a). Although not fully consistent with a post-Keynesian approach, a supply constraint is introduced, mainly for empirical reasons. This results in a simple production function that determines potential output and allows for computation of an output gap. Its impact on firms' accumulation rate and inflation appears significant and representative of demand pressure. Our focus in this chapter is on the equations that have changed from the previous version.

Firms

Non-financial firms have an accumulation rate of productive capital $\left(\frac{\Delta^{*}K_{1}^{F}}{K_{1-1}^{F}}\right)$ that depends on four variables, following a post-Keynesian logic: the share of profit in value added $\left(\frac{\Pi^{F}}{VA^{F}}\right)$ representative of firms' profitability; the output gap of the market sector representative of a demand effect; the real interest rate[2] $\left(r_{L}^{F} - \pi_{Y}\right)$ with a negative sign; and the debt structure here represented as the debt-to-own funds ratio $\left(\frac{L_{L}^{F}}{p_{E_{L}}^{F}E_{L}^{F} + WLTH^{F}}\right)$, also with a negative effect.

The output gap is defined in the model as $gap = \left(\frac{va^M - va^{pM}}{va^{pM}}\right)$, where va^M is the market sector's value added and va^{pM} the potential value added. In spite of its weaknesses this has been preferred to the capacity utilization rate, which is measured by INSEE based on firms' surveys and is limited to the manufacturing sector (www.insee.fr/en/statistiques/4636533). The two indicators are rather close (see Figure 5.1) but the stronger correlation between the accumulation rate and the output gap deserves to be highlighted. Potential value added is determined by a simple production function which is used as a pragmatic compromise in spite of its limits ($\ln\left(\frac{va^{M^*}}{N^M}\right) = 0.8 + 0.5\ln\left(\frac{K_1^M}{N^M}\right) + 0.014t - 0.01\,t_{1992-2019}$). The alternative solution in the post-Keynesian tradition would be the capacity utilization rate defined by $u = Y/Y^f$, where Y^f is full capacity output ($Y^f = K/v$) and v the potential capital output ratio. This gives $u = vY/K$. The utilization capacity rate u is closely related to a simple apparent productivity of the capital (Y/K). Figure 5.1 shows a poorer empirical correlation with this theoretical indicator.

A version without the output gap (*gap*), with a positive effect of the lagged rate of profit and a negative effect of financial profitability, was used in the previous version of the model, more in line with a Kaleckian logic. The results are not fundamentally different, as will be discussed more in detail below.

Without output gap (previous model)

$$\left(\frac{\Delta^* K_1^F}{K_{1-1}^F}\right) = 0.02 + 0.1\left(\frac{\Pi^F{}_{-1}}{p_{K_{1-1}}^F K_{1-2}^F + p_{K_{2-1}}^F K_{2-2}^F}\right) - 0.2\left(r_L^F - \pi_Y\right) - 0.01\left(r_{E_A}^F - \pi_Y\right)$$

$$-0.03\left(\frac{L_L^F}{p_{E_L}^F E_L^F + WLTH^F}\right)$$

1983–2019 (5.9) (2) (2.2) (−2.3)
(−4) $R^2 = 0.5$

With output gap (this model)

$$\left(\frac{\Delta^* K_1^F}{K_{1-1}^F}\right) = 0.08\left(\frac{\Pi^F}{VA^F}\right) + 0.3gap - 0.12\left(r_L^F - \pi_Y\right) - 0.01\left(\frac{L_L^F}{p_{E_L}^F E_L^F + WLTH^F}\right)$$

1983–2019 (17.2) (8.2) (−5.1) (−5.6) $R^2 = 0.81$

In financialized capitalism, firms tend to favor financial accumulation at the expense of productive accumulation. This translates into a financial accumulation rate that is an increasing function of the profit rate and of financial profitability of equities held, where indebtedness plays a supporting role. The change in firms' deposits and the flow of inter-firm credit are the subject of

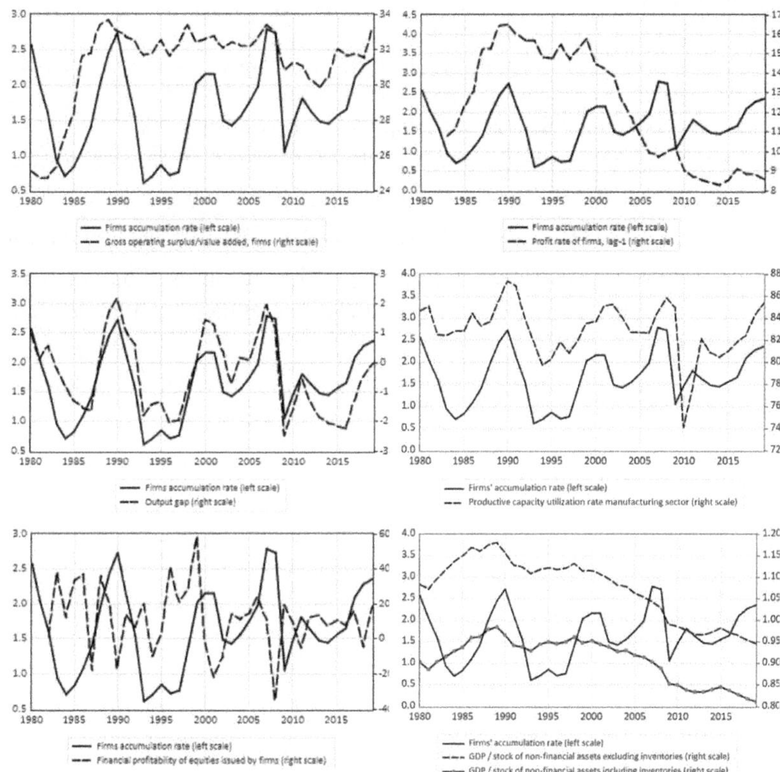

Source: Elaboration by the authors using data from INSEE (detailed accounts of agents, comptes de patrimoine, comptes nationaux annuels) and Banque de France (comptes nationaux financiers), except output gap (IMF).

Figure 5.1 Firms' accumulation rate and its determinants (1980–2019)

a simplified model in which the real 10-year interest rate (with a negative sign) and the firms' indebtedness (as a liability) intervene respectively. Firms have an indebtedness behavior. In the medium term their debt structure, as a ratio of total non-financial capital, depends positively on the profit rate and negatively on the real interest rate. More than a debt behavior, it is an indebtedness norm, which reflects a given institutional relation between firms and banks. A split between bank debt and bonds is also made. Equities issued close the firms' account.

Banque de France

Interests and dividends paid and received by Banque de France are computed according to the corresponding assets. Profits are transferred to the government as tax. Bills and coins (H) are supplied by the central bank. Central bank deposits held by the government ($D_L^{CB_G}$) are isolated as they are used to study helicopter money (HM). Foreign bonds held by the central bank ($p_{B_A}^{CB_R} B_A^{CB_R}$), public bonds ($p_{B_A}^{CB_G} \Delta^* B_A^{CB_G}$), other domestic bonds ($p_{B_A}^{CB} \Delta^* B_A^{CB}$) and refinancing ($RF^{CB}$) correspond to different forms of quantitative easing. Equities issued by the central bank ($p_{E_L}^{CB} E_L^{CB}$) are exogenous. Central bank equilibrium is the unwritten identity.

$$\Delta^* H = \Delta^* H^F + \Delta^* H^B + \Delta^* H^H + \Delta^* H^R$$

$$D_L^{CB_G} = D_A^{G_{CB}}$$

$$p_{B_A}^{CB_R} B_A^{CB_R} = \varphi_{BA}^{CB} p_Y Y$$

$$p_{B_A}^{CB_G} \Delta^* B_A^{CB_G} = \gamma_{B_A}^{CB_G} p_Y Y$$

$$p_{B_A}^{CB} \Delta^* B_A^{CB} = \gamma_{B_A}^{B} p_Y Y$$

$$\Delta^* RF^{CB} = \varphi_{RF}^{CB} p_Y Y$$

$$p_G^{CB} \Delta^* G^{CB} + \Delta TRGT2 + \Delta^* RF^{CB} + \Delta^* D_A^{CB} + p_{B_A}^{CB_G} \Delta^* B_A^{CB_G} + p_{B_A}^{CB_R} \Delta^* B_A^{CB_R}$$

$$+ p_{B_A}^{CB} \Delta^* B_A^{CB} + \Delta^* L_A^{CB}$$

$$+ p_E^{CB} \Delta^* E_A^{CB} = \Delta^* H + \Delta^* RES + \Delta^* D_L^{CB} + \Delta^* D_L^{CB_G} + p_{E_L}^{CB} \Delta^* E_L^{CB} + Adj^{CB}$$

Interest Rates and Assets' Prices

The European Central Bank (ECB) key interest rate ($r_€$) and the 10-year interest rate on public bonds (i_{10yrs}) are exogenous in this version. Proposals are made towards the end to endogenize the 10-year interest rate. Apparent (or implicit) interest rates are calculated for the various securities and are determined with simple margins with respect to the 10-year bonds interest rate or the ECB interest rate. The short-term interest rate on deposits (r_D) and the long-term interest rate on credit ($i^{LT_{cr}}$) are determined in the same manner. The price of public bonds ($p^G_{B_L}$) varies inversely with respect to that paid by the government (r^G_L). It plays a leading role in the determination of other prices of bonds such as bonds issued by firms ($p^F_{B_L}$), public bonds held by firms ($p^{F_G}_{B_A}$), private bonds held by households ($p^H_{B_A}$) or private bonds held by banks ($p^B_{B_A}$). Lastly, for each security (domestic private bonds, foreign bonds, public bonds), one price ($p^B_{B_L}$, $p^{B_R}_{B_A}$, $p^{R_G}_{B_A}$) must be obtained implicitly to guarantee flow-stock consistency by writing that the sum of the revaluation effects equals to zero.

$$r^F_A = 3.6 + 0.63\, r_€$$

$$r^H_A = 1.6 + 0.5\, r_€$$

$$r^F_L = 1.9 + 0.6\, i_{10yrs} + 0.2\, r_€$$

$$r^B_A = 0.4 + 0.5\, r^B_{A-1} + 0.4\, i_{10yrs}$$

$$r^B_L = 1.9 + 0.4\, i_{10yrs} + 0.7\, r_€$$

$$r^G_A = 2.5 + 1.6\, r_€$$

$$r^G_L = 1.1 + 0.75\, i_{10yrs} + 0.1\, r_€$$

$$r^H_L = 0.9 + 0.5\, i_{10yrs} + 0.4\, r_€$$

$$r^R_A = i_{10years} + \kappa^R_{r_A}$$

$$i^{LT_{cr}} = 0.93\, i_{10yrs}$$

$$r_D = 1.4 + 0.5\, r_€$$

$$\ln\left(p^{G}_{B_L}\right) = -0.39 + 0.1\ln\left(\frac{1}{r^{G}_{L}}\right)$$

$$\ln\left(p^{F}_{B_L}\right) = 0.8\ln\left(p^{F}_{B_{L-1}}\right) + 0.9\ln\left(p^{G}_{B_L}\right) - 0.7\ln\left(p^{G}_{B_{L-1}}\right)$$

$$p^{F_G}_{B_A} = \psi^{F_G}_{p_{BA}} p^{G}_{B_L}$$

$$p^{H}_{B_A} = \psi^{H}_{p_{BA}} p^{B}_{B_L}$$

$$\Delta\ln\left(p^{B}_{B_A}\right) = 0.2\,\Delta\ln\left(p^{B}_{B_{A-1}}\right) + 0.7\,\Delta\ln\left(p^{G}_{B_L}\right)$$

$$\Delta p^{B}_{B_L} = -\left(\frac{B^{F}_{L-1}}{B^{B}_{L-1}}\right)\Delta p^{F}_{B_L} + \sum_{i}\left(\frac{B^{i}_{A-1}}{B^{B}_{L-1}}\right)\Delta p^{i}_{B_A} \quad \text{for } i = B,\ CB,\ G,\ H,\ R$$

$$\Delta p^{B_R}_{B_A} = \left(\frac{B^{R}_{B_{L-1}}}{B^{B_R}_{B_{A-1}}}\right)\Delta p^{R}_{B_L} - \sum_{i}\left(\frac{B^{i_R}_{B_{A-1}}}{B^{B_R}_{B_{A-1}}}\right)\Delta p^{i_R}_{B_A} \quad \text{for } i = F,\ CB,\ G,\ H$$

$$\Delta p^{R_G}_{B_A} = \left(\frac{B^{G}_{L-1}}{B^{R_G}_{A-1}}\right)\Delta p^{G}_{B_L} - \sum_{i}\left(\frac{B^{i_G}_{A-1}}{B^{R_G}_{A-1}}\right)\Delta p^{i_G}_{B_A} \quad \text{for } i = F,\ B,\ CB$$

SIMULATIONS AND BASIC SHOCKS

Figure 5.2 allows for a comparison between the observed and simulated evolution of a sample of series in the model, which includes the output gap in the specification for firms' non-financial accumulation rate. The model performs rather well. The gap between the observed series and the baseline lies within reasonable limits, with a few exceptions.

We compare the multiplier effects of two model specifications, one with no output gap in firms' accumulation rate and the other that includes it. Two shocks are examined, first a permanent increase of public investment of 1 percent of gross domestic product (GDP) and second an increase of 1 percent in the growth rate of wage per worker.

The increase in public investment has a greater effect on economic growth in the short term in the model, including a demand effect in the accumulation rate of firms. This is due to the larger increase of the rate of non-financial accumulation of firms, but this accumulation boom does not last long as the output gap decreases with the increase in capital stock. In the long term the multiplier effect of the two models is similar. The evolution of the price level is

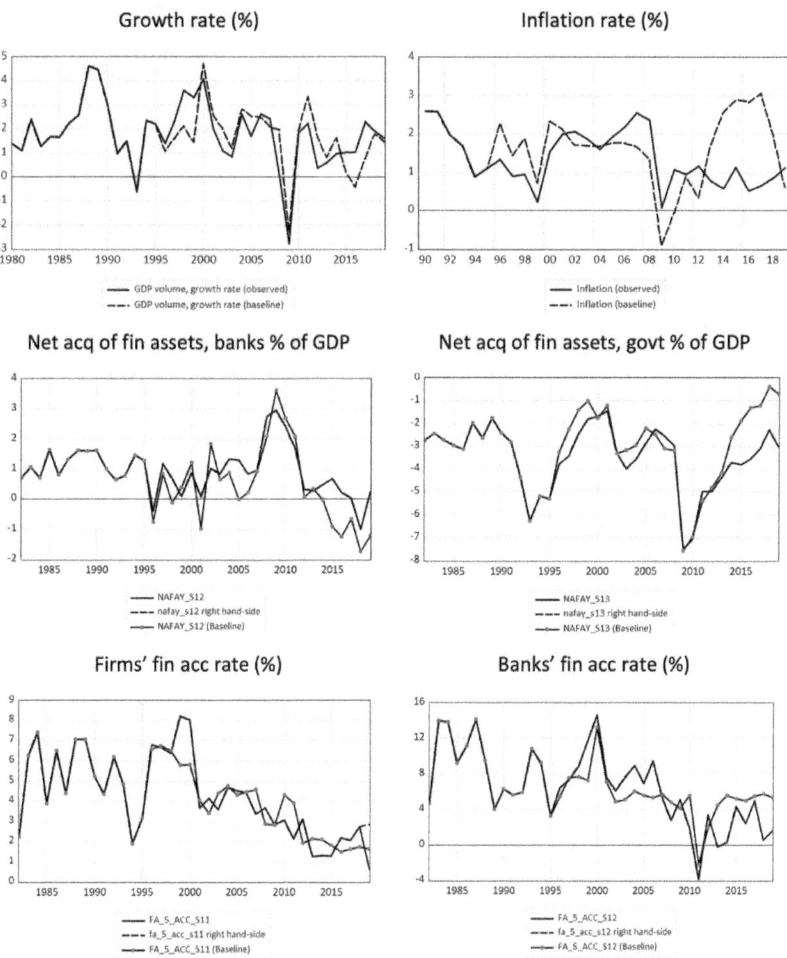

Note: Simulations start in 1996.
Source: Observed series were elaborated by the authors using data from INSEE (detailed accounts of agents, comptes de patrimoine, comptes nationaux annuels) and Banque de France (comptes nationaux financiers), except output gap (IMF). Baseline is the results of the model.

Figure 5.2 Model performance; selected series, observed versus simulated

also similar in both; it increases by about 2.5 percent after 10 years. The trade balance worsens more in 2021 in the model with the output gap effect due to the more sustained growth. Similarly, public finances worsen less and public debt increases less (Figure 5.3).

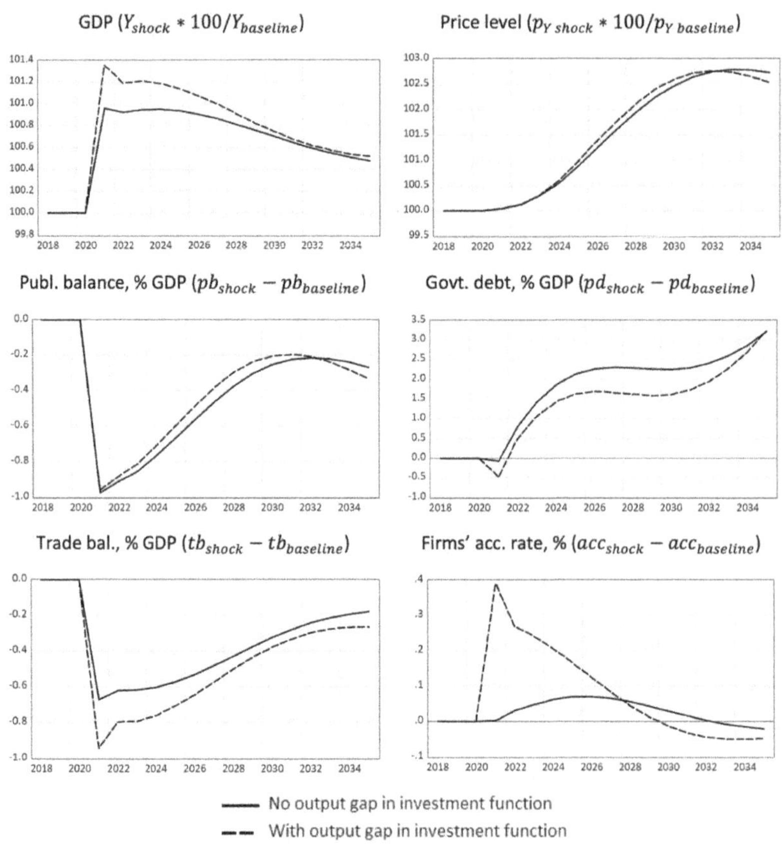

Figure 5.3 *Public investment increases permanently by 1 percent of GDP between 2021 and 2035*

A 1 percent increase in the growth rate of wage per worker has a small initial positive impact on GDP but after two years (model with output gap effect on investment) or four years (model without the gap effect) the impact of the wage increase becomes negative. This suggests that the French economy is under a moderate wage-led regime in the short term and in a profit-led regime in the longer term. The reversal is reflected also in the trade balance, which initially tends towards deficit then shifts in the opposite direction. Similarly, the public balance improves in the medium term (0.5 percent of GDP) thanks to the increase in resources, but this surplus is progressively reduced. The increase in wages induces an inflationary drift (1.8 percent in the medium term). It makes inflation rise proportionally more than it makes GDP fall in the medium term (hence, nominal GDP increases), thus reducing debt-to-GDP ratios, especially that of the government (−4 percent of GDP in the medium term). But a reversal appears in the long term. Even if differences exist between the two versions of the model, the results are rather similar and not in favor of a wage-led policy which would be reduced to a simple wage increase (Figure 5.4).

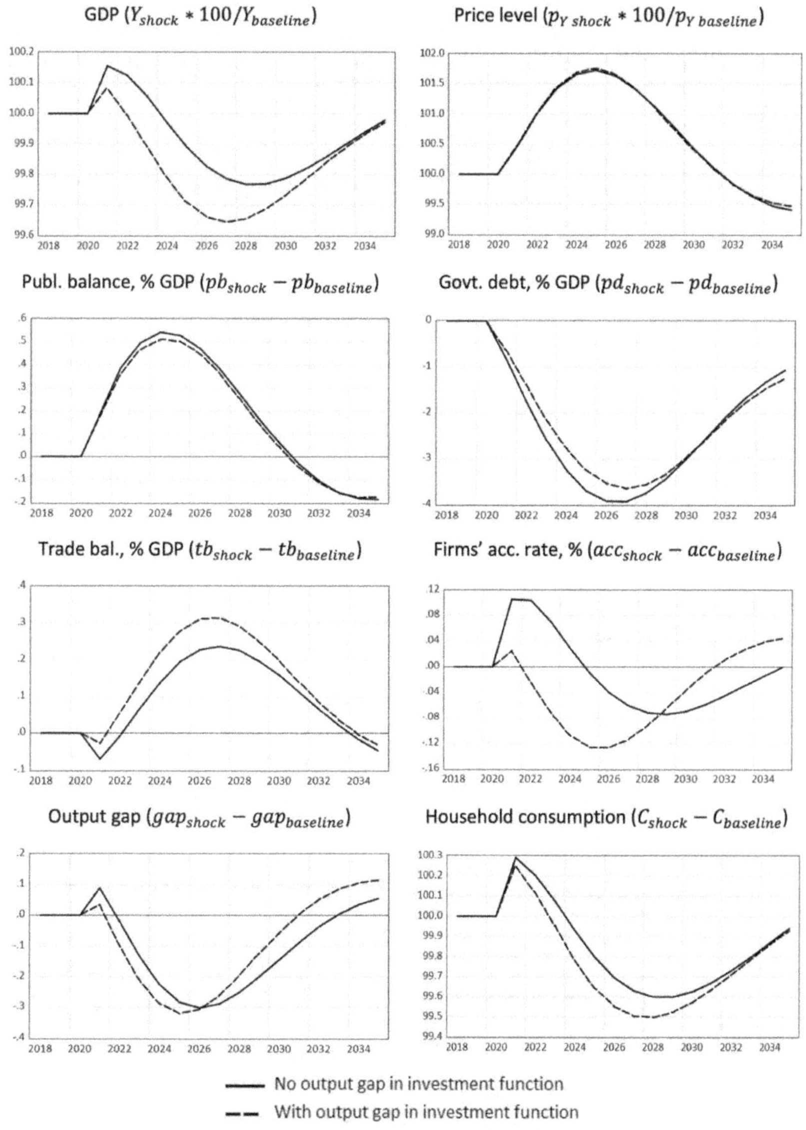

Figure 5.4 *Growth rate of wage per worker increases permanently by 1 percent between 2021 and 2035*

UNCONVENTIONAL MONETARY AND FISCAL POLICY

Various forms of unconventional economic policies can be considered: HM, public indebtedness and repurchase by the central bank, cancellation of a part of the public debt held by the central bank, recapitalization of the central bank's own funds, taxation of wealthy households and redistribution. HM can take several forms, either as a distribution of central bank money directly to households or businesses, or as a distribution to the government. If the purpose is to avoid a distribution of banknotes, one way is to assume that all households and firms have an account with the central bank. This is possible and corresponds to the project of development of central bank digital currency. Here we are only interested in the second form of HM, i.e. via the state and its account with the central bank. Two uses of HM are distinguished: one to finance public investments, the other to finance social transfers. These unconventional economic policies have been analyzed in Mazier and Reyes (2022a, 2022b).

HM to finance public investment (a permanent increase in public investment of 1 percent of GDP) leads to a recovery with a public debt falling gradually until reaching −10 percent of GDP in the long term. However, central bank financial wealth decreases by 13 percent of GDP and bank reserves increase by 12 percent of GDP. Furthermore, rest-of-the-world financial wealth increases by 11 percent of GDP which means an equivalent deterioration of the domestic net financial assets, mainly due to a decline of the trade balance induced by the loss of price competitiveness and the volume effect of the recovery. According to supporters of this policy, a central bank could continue working with negative own funds. This could be the case if the procedure is punctual and limited, but more problematic in the context of sustained policy. Financial markets could push interest rates up. The size of bank reserves would facilitate capital outflows or slippages in the securities and/or real-estate markets. In the French case, as in the case of countries in the Eurozone without a central bank properly speaking, such policy would contradict European treaties. It could only be undertaken after a series of time-consuming negotiations whose outcomes would be uncertain.

Another answer is given. As the central bank can create its own currency, its recapitalization would be easy and costless. This point can be examined with the model. Recapitalization of the central bank can be done in a simple way. The central bank issues new equities which are bought by the government thanks to a distribution of HM to the government. In the non-financial sphere (GDP and price) nothing changes. At the monetary and financial level the equities issued by the central bank are increased but the wealth of the central bank is reduced by the same amount. All in all, the own funds of the central bank (equities issued plus wealth) remain unchanged. However, two other evolutions must be noted. The government wealth is increased since the government holds the new equities issued by the central bank. For the public sector as a whole (government and central bank) this means that its wealth is constant. This gives a more positive estimate of the financial situation of the public sector. But simultaneously the bank reserves, which can be interpreted as a debt of the central bank towards the commercial banks, increase by the same amount. As has already been noted, these increasing bank reserves could facilitate capital outflows and slippages in the financial markets. Overall, the results show that the recapitalization of the central bank raises problems. It cannot be done as simply as it is sometimes said (i.e. with a "simple click").

Traditional public indebtedness to finance public investment can be combined with repurchase of public bonds by the central bank, which can be seen as an illustration of Modern Monetary Theory (Kelton, 2020). Repurchasing the public bonds by the central bank is simply described in the model by adding an add-factor in the corresponding equation. The real effects in terms of growth and inflation are similar in all cases. The deterioration of the nation's financial wealth is the same (12 percent of GDP in the long term with a permanent shock). The banks hold less public bonds and their reserves increase largely. The results appear close to the case where there is no repurchase by the central bank. Compared to the case of HM an opposition appears at the level of the financial situation of the various sectors. The financial wealth of the government improves in case of HM and decreases in case of repurchase by the central bank. Conversely, central bank financial wealth decreases in case of HM while it is stable in case of central bank repurchase. However, the impact of the repurchase of public bonds by the central bank can be underestimated in the current version, where interest rates are exogenous.

A proposal put forward by some authors (e.g. Scialom and Bridonneau, 2020) is to cancel part of the large amount of government securities held by the central bank in order to lighten budget constraints, thus providing room for maneuver to better finance the low-carbon transition. This policy can be studied in the model in a simple way. A first gap-filling variable is introduced in the flow-stock equation generating the stock of public debt held by the central bank. The same negative shock is introduced in the flow-stock equation generating the stock of total debt. Lastly, another gap-filling variable equation indicates that the cancellation concerns only public bonds. This partial cancellation of public debt held by the central bank has no effect on the real economy. Public debt falls initially but central bank wealth falls as much and remains lower than in the baseline. For supporters of this policy, the reduction of public debt would loosen the constraints and would open the way to an increase in public investment to finance the energy transition. The combination of these two measures, partial cancellation of debt and increase in public investment, leads to a sustained recovery with rising inflation. Thanks to the cancellation, public debt remains under control despite the initial increase in the public deficit. The counterpart of these evolutions is a persistent and marked deterioration of central banks' wealth. These results raise the same reservations as those formulated about HM. Insofar as the amounts of cancellation are high, it is difficult to believe that this marked deterioration of central banks' own funds can remain without consequences.

Another possible use of HM is to finance social transfers to households for a one-shot or permanent increase. The results are similar to the previous ones, a recovery and a moderate price increase. Government balance deteriorates but without rising public debt thanks to the HM distribution and recovery. The counterpart is a deterioration of central bank wealth and an increase in bank reserves. If the measure is punctual and limited in time this would not be a problem. However, it seems difficult to sustain this measure on a permanent basis as it is illustrated by a permanent distribution of HM to finance social transfers equivalent to 1 percent of GDP (Figure 5.5). Production is persistently higher with a price drift still rather moderate. Government debt in percentage of GDP decreases but central bank wealth falls dramatically and bank reserves rise considerably. Last, the rising rest-of-the-world financial wealth reflects a sharp decrease of domestic financial wealth.

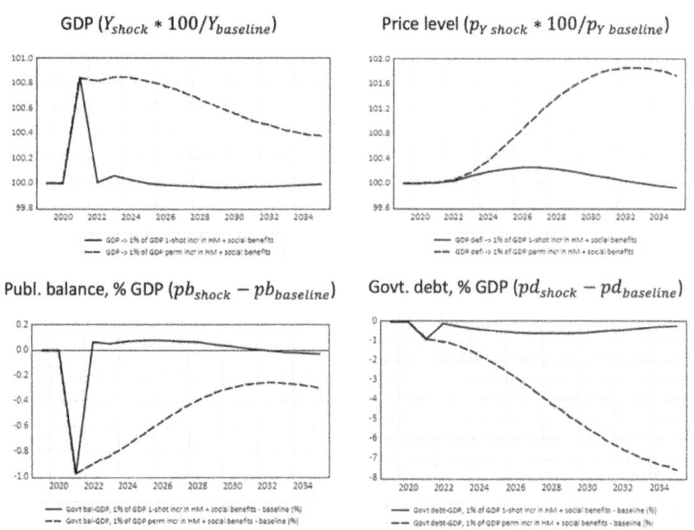

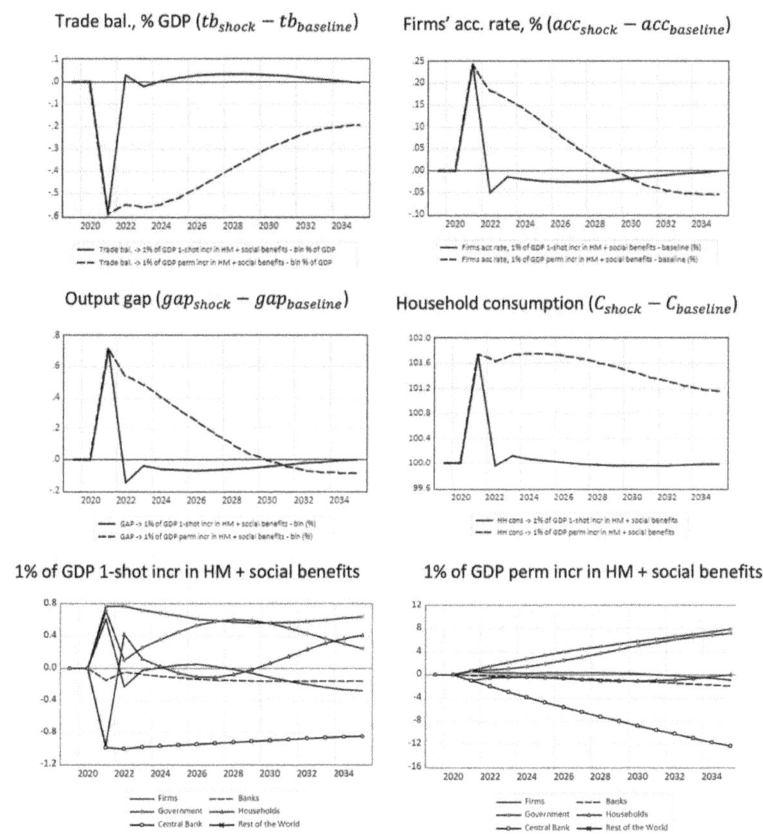

Figure 5.5 *Increase in helicopter money with social transfers 1 percent of GDP, one-off versus permanent shock*

Taxation of the Rich and Social Transfers

Last, we analyze a simple incomes policy based on taxation of the rich to finance social transfers. This policy can be justified since income inequality has increased considerably over the past four decades and the top incomes have benefited from important tax relief measures. This incomes policy can be simulated in three steps. First, we consider a one-off increase in the tax rate of households affecting all income brackets. This is characterized by an increase of 10 billion euros in (4 percent of) the income taxes paid by households (solid line in Figure 5.6). Unsurprisingly, this increase in income taxation has a negative effect on economic activity but slightly improves public finances.

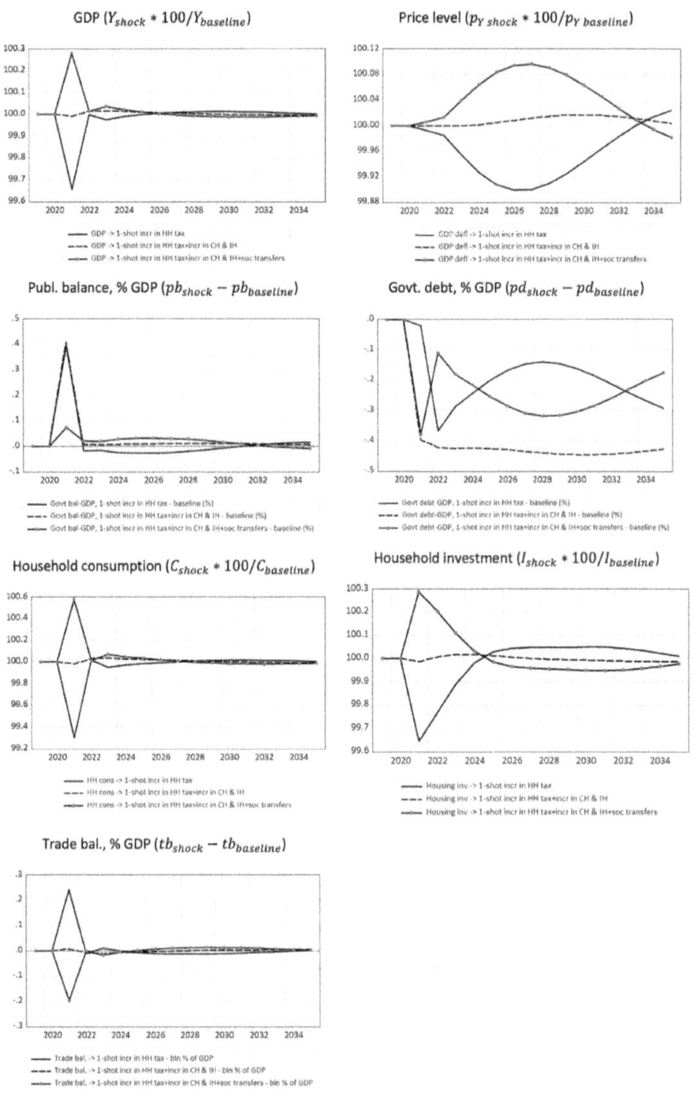

Note: Solid line = taxes on households increase by 10 billion euros (4 percent of income taxes paid by households) in 2021. Dashed line = solid line + 5.8 billion increase in household consumption in 2021 and −4.5 billion reduction in 2022 + 0.25 percent increase in growth rate of household investment in 2021 and −0.1 percent in 2022. Solid line + circles = dashed line + increase of 8.5 billion in social benefits.

Figure 5.6 Increase in rich household taxes and social transfers

Second, if the increase only concerns wealthy households, they will not reduce their expenditures but they will save less to pay taxes. This can be introduced in the model by adding to the initial shock a second one including a 0.5 percent increase in the volume of household consumption and an additional 0.32 percent in the growth rate of the volume of households' investment (0.4 percent increase in level). The result of this combined shock is clear (dashed line). Since wealthy households preserve their expenditures by saving less, the impact on economic activity is almost nil. The only impact concerns public finances which improve with a reduction of public debt. The counterpart is a reduction of households' wealth. Third, this fiscal surplus can be used to finance a new policy, for example, a transfer in favor of the low-level incomes with an increase of 8.5 billion in social benefits (solid line + circles). The global result is positive. The economic activity is more sustained with more households' consumption and investment, a slight improvement of the public finance and a reduction of income inequality.

IMPORTED INFLATIONARY SHOCK AND POSSIBLE POLICY RESPONSES

In this section we study an inflationary shock coming from the rest of the world and its impact on the French economy. This takes place via an increase in import prices but also world export prices by 5 percent. We compare this to the same shock with a few policy responses added: interest rate hike of 3 percent (to fight inflation in a traditional way), increased social transfers by 0.7 percent of GDP (to support households' income) or a 1.8 percent increase in the growth rate of wage per worker (to try to preserve the purchasing power of wages). Figure 5.7 shows the effects.

In this hypothetical scenario, in 2021 a 5 percent increase in world import prices induces imported inflation which lowers workers' purchasing power. Economic activity slows down. Imports in volume are reduced but imports in current prices increase with the increase in import prices, leading to an initial 0.8 percent of GDP trade deficit. With the economic slowdown the public balance initially worsens (−0.4 percent of GDP). After the initial inflationary shock, a reversal appears. Inflation falls. The trade balance reverses its course and remains slightly in surplus. The public balance as a share of GDP also improves. Government debt mirrors this evolution, rising by 0.5 percent in 2021 and then falling by 0.7 percent the next year. All in all, after the initial drain linked to the rise in import prices, economic activity rebounds and GDP joins the baseline scenario.

Facing this external shock, the authorities could decide to increase social transfers by 0.7 percent of GDP (column 1, dashed) in order to support households. This has indeed the desired lessening effect on the output drop,

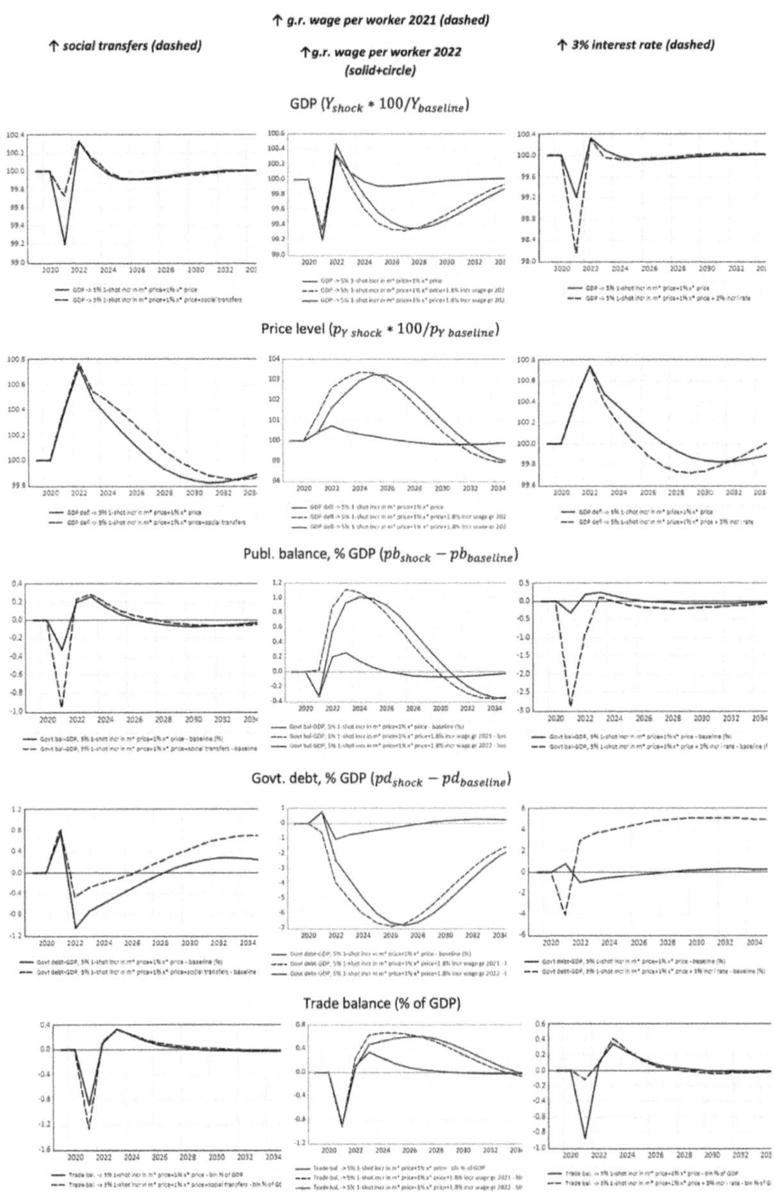

Figure 5.7 Inflationary shock (solid line) and scenarios starting in 2021 unless otherwise stated

although at the cost of (slightly) raising demand-pull inflation, worsening public finances and the trade balance. But this degradation remains limited. Fighting an imported inflationary shock through social transfers appears as a good option as long as the shock does not continue.

A second option would be to increase wages in the hope of preserving purchasing power (column 2, dashed and solid + circle). We analyze the consequences of doing so in 2021 (when the inflationary shock takes place) or the year after. The results are not fundamentally different in either case, except for the lag in the response of the series. Prices rise considerably and a wage-price spiral starts. GDP worsens due to the declining purchasing power induced by increasing inflation. In spite of the inflation drift the trade balance improves thanks to the declining demand. The only positive point of this scenario is the improvement of the public finance induced by the inflation drift. The public balance increases by more than 1 percent of GDP and the stock of government debt falls by 8 percent of GDP in 2028. Fighting an imported inflationary shock by increasing wages does not seem a good option for the workers, but the acceptance of an inflationary drift can be useful for public finances.

A third option is that the inflationary shock questions the credibility of the central bank and has to be fought by traditional monetary policy tools. A 3 percent increase in the interest rate is introduced as an illustration (column 3, dashed). The cost of this restrictive policy is high for a rather modest and delayed effect on prices. The rise in domestic prices is progressively contained, via the sharp contraction in aggregate demand (−2 percent of GDP in 2021). The public balance worsens significantly (−3.2 percent of GDP in 2021) due to the slowdown, the decrease of public resources and the rising cost of debt services. Furthermore, public debt is much higher starting in 2022 (4 percent of GDP and higher afterwards), due to the reduced activity and the more moderate prices which limit nominal GDP. This traditional contractionary monetary policy with the increase in the interest rate is not adapted to fight imported inflation that is not caused by excessive demand pressure. Its cost is high for a limited and delayed result.

TOWARDS AN ENDOGENIZATION OF THE RATE OF INTEREST

Interest rates are exogenous in the present version of the model. It seems logical to keep the ECB key interest rate ($r_{€}$) exogenous as one of the main tools for monetary policy. But the 10-year interest rate on public bonds (i_{10yrs}) could be endogenized as it is playing a leading role. Following the SFC tradition it could be determined implicitly by the balance of the public bonds market between the supply $p^{G}_{B_L} \Delta^{*} B^{G}_{L}$ coming from the government balance and the demand of public bonds by the different agents, banks $\left(p_{B_A}^{B_G}\Delta^* B_A^{B_G}\right)$, central bank $\left(p_{B_A}^{CB_G}\Delta^* B_A^{CB_G}\right)$, firms $\left(p_{B_A}^{F_G}\Delta^* B_A^{F_G}\right)$ and rest of the world $\left(p_{B_A}^{R_G}\Delta^* B_A^{R_G}\right)$.

$$p_{B_L}^{G}\Delta^* B_L^{G} = p_{B_A}^{B_G}\Delta^* B_A^{B_G} + p_{B_A}^{CB_G}\Delta^* B_A^{CB_G} + + p_{B_A}^{F_G}\Delta^* B_A^{F_G} + p_{B_A}^{R_G}\Delta^* B_A^{R_G}$$

By substituting in the previous equation the demand of public bonds by the rest of the world $\left(p_{B_A}^{R_G}\Delta^* B_A^{R_G}\right)$ and by banks $(p_{B_A}^{B_G}\Delta^* B_A^{B_G})$ and solving for i_{10yr} we obtain:

$$\left(\frac{p_{B_A}^{R_G}\Delta^* B_A^{R_G}}{p_Y Y}\right) = 0.02 + 0.78\left(i_{10yr} - i^{LT*} + \frac{\Delta NEER}{NEER_{-1}}\right)$$

$$\left(\frac{p_{B_A}^{B_G}\Delta^* B_A^{B_G}}{p_Y Y}\right) = 0.35\left(\frac{p_{B_{A-1}}^{B_G}\Delta^* B_{A-1}^{B_G}}{p_{Y-1} Y_{-1}}\right) + 0.5\left(i_{10yr} - i^{LT*} + \frac{\Delta NEER}{NEER_{-1}}\right)$$

where i^{LT*} is the weighted average long-term foreign interest rate and *NEER* is the nominal effective exchange rate.

$$i_{10yr} = \left(i^{LT*} - \frac{\Delta NEER}{NEER_{-1}}\right)$$

$$+\left(\frac{1}{1.28}\right)\left(\left(\frac{p_{B_L}^{G}\Delta^* B_L^{G} - p_{B_A}^{CB_G}\Delta^* B_A^{CB_G} - p_{B_A}^{F_G}\Delta^* B_A^{F_G}}{p_Y Y}\right) - 0.02 - 0.35\left(\frac{p_{B_{A-1}}^{B_G}\Delta^* B_{A-1}^{B_G}}{p_{Y-1} Y_{-1}}\right)\right)$$

Where the public bonds held by the central bank $p_{B_A}^{CB_G}\Delta^* B_A^{CB_G}$ are driven by quantitative easing, the public bonds held by firms $\left(p_{B_A}^{F_G}\ B_A^{F_G}\right)$ are small and simply determined in percentage of value added and public bonds issued by the government $\left(p_{B_L}^{G}\Delta^* B_L^{G}\right)$ close the government's account. According to this equation the main determinant of the 10-year interest rate on public bonds is the foreign one, after correction of the exchange rate variation $\left(i^{LT*} - \frac{\Delta NEER}{NEER_{-1}}\right)$. A larger issuance of public bonds increases the 10-year interest rate while a more active quantitative easing decreases it. Unfortunately, problems of respect of financial wealth balances appeared in solving the model with this specification.

A simpler modeling has been tested. The closure for domestic public bonds held by banks is kept as in the version where interest rates are exogenous. This allows to keep explicitly the accounting equation.

$$p_{B_A}^{B_G}\Delta^* B_A^{B_G} = p_{B_L}^{G}\Delta^* B_L^{G} - p_{B_A}^{CB_G}\Delta^* B_A^{CB_G} - p_{B_A}^{F_G}\Delta^* B_A^{F_G} - p_{B_A}^{R_G}\Delta^* B_A^{R_G}$$

The interest rate is now the solution for i_{10yr} in the (unwritten) estimated equation

$$\left(\frac{p_{B_A}^{B_G}\Delta^* B_A^{B_G}}{p_Y Y}\right) = 0.7\left(i_{10yr} - i^{LT*} + \frac{\Delta NEER}{NEER_{-1}}\right)$$

Solving the previous expression for domestic interest rate yields

$$i_{10yr} = \left(i^{LT*} - \frac{\Delta NEER}{NEER_{-1}}\right) + 1.4\left(\frac{p_{B_A}^{B_G}\Delta^* B_A^{B_G}}{p_Y Y}\right)$$

This version of the model[3] with endogenous interest rate works correctly and yields acceptable results for the simulations on the past. We can compare the multiplier effects of a permanent hypothetical increase in public investment by 1 percent of GDP starting in 2021 under three possible model specifications: *model 1* includes an exogenous interest rate and no output gap in firms' accumulation rate, *model 2* also has an exogenous interest rate and there is an output gap in firms' accumulation rate, while *model 3* includes an endogenous interest rate and the output gap in the accumulation rate (Figure 5.8).

In Figure 5.8 we observe that model 3 with endogenous interest rate displays results close to those of the models with exogenous interest rate, except for public finances which worsen more when the interest rate is endogenous (because of its slight tendency to increase following an activist fiscal policy). The evolution of the price level is very similar in the three models, which increases by about 2.5 percent after 10 years.

CONCLUSION

A new version of an econometric SFC model of the French economy has been presented, including an impact of demand pressure on firms' investment described via an output gap. The dynamic simulations on the past over the period 1996–2019 provide acceptable results. A comparison with a previous version of the model, without output gap effect on investment, has been made. The results of both models seem close.

The model has been used to study the effects of different forms of unconventional economic policies. A distribution of HM in favor of the government to finance additional public investments or social transfers has a stimulating impact without increasing public debt. However, as a counterpart, the wealth and own funds of the central bank deteriorate by an amount equivalent to the initial shock. If the intervention is not punctual and limited, this evolution could be problematic. Although the central bank can create its own currency, recapitalization of the central bank raises problems. The combination of

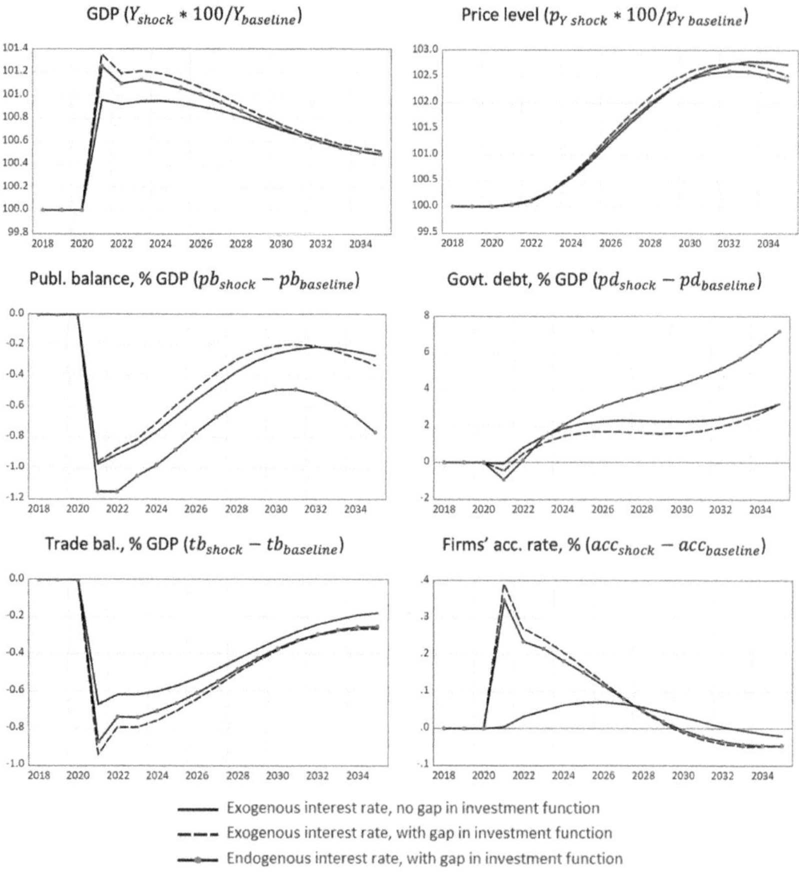

Figure 5.8 *Public investment increases permanently by 1 percent of GDP, three variants of the model*

public indebtedness and repurchase by the central bank has been described. The results seem close to the case where there is no repurchase by the central bank but the effects of the repurchase may be underestimated in a version of the model with exogenous interest rates. Partial cancellation of the public debt held by the central bank has been examined. It has, as a counterpart, a degradation of the wealth and own funds of the central bank which are too important to remain without consequences. Taxation of wealthy households to finance social transfers in favor of the bottom income brackets was simulated and provided positive results.

Imported inflationary shocks have been studied with various policy responses. Increasing social transfers to support households seems like a good option, as long as the shock does not continue. On the contrary, increasing wages in the hope of preserving purchasing power would induce an inflation drift not favorable to workers, but that could prove useful for public finances. A restrictive monetary policy with an increase in interest rates is not adapted to fight imported inflation. This would have a high cost in terms of growth and public finances for a limited and delayed result in terms of inflation.

Finally, a simple endogenization of the interest rate, based on the balance of the public bonds market, has been tested. Results seem close to the results of the model with exogenous interest rates, except for public finances which worsen more. This version of the model could be checked in more detail and improved. Furthermore, an explicit treatment of the ECB (currently integrated in the rest of the world) and a modeling of the rest of the eurozone remain to be done.

ACKNOWLEDGMENTS

Jacques Mazier acknowledges the support of the Chair Energy and Prosperity, under the aegis of La Fondation du Risque. Luis Reyes acknowledges the support of the Chair LCL Impact Finance.

NOTES

1. The complete working paper of the first version and the technical documentation are available at www.chair-energy-prosperity.org/en/research-area-2/enjeux-macroeconomique-societaux-transition-energetique-en/a-stock-flow-consistent-model-for-the-french-economy/.
2. r_L^F is the apparent (or implicit) interest rate, calculated as the ratio of interests paid by firms and the stock of indebtedness from the previous period.
3. In order to keep this version from being overly sensitive to the evolution of public bonds, the parameter 1.4 was divided by 5. Hence the actual parameter entering the equation is 0.28.

REFERENCES

Godley, W. (1999), Seven unsustainable processes: Medium term prospects and policies for the USA and the world economy, Levy Economics Institute of the Bard College.

Godley, W. and Lavoie, M. (2007), *Monetary economics*, Palgrave Macmillan.

Godley, W., Papadimitriou, D. B., Dos Santos, C. H. and Zezza, G. (2005), The US and the creditors: Can the symbiosis last? Strategic analysis, Levy Economics Institute of the Bard College.

Kelton, S. (2020), *The deficit myth: Modern Monetary Theory and how to build a better economy*, John Murray.
Lavoie, M. and Godley, W. (2001), Kaleckian growth models in a stock and flow monetary approach framework: A Kaldorian view, *Journal of Post-Keynesian Economics*, 24(2), 277–312.
Mazier, J. and Reyes, L. (2022a), A stock flow consistent model for the French economy, in M. Randrup Byrialsen, H. Raza and F. Olesen (eds), *Macro-modelling, economic policy and methodology: Economics at the edge*, Routledge.
Mazier, J. and Reyes, L. (2022b), *Unconventional monetary policy in an econometric SFC model of the French economy: Some lessons for financing the low-carbon transition*, Economie Appliquée.
Scialom, L. and Bridonneau, B. (2020), Crise économique et crise écologique: osons des décisions de rupture, *Terra Nova*, April.

6. A quarterly empirical model for the Danish economy: a stock-flow consistent approach

Mikael Randrup Byrialsen, Hamid Raza and Sebastian Valdecantos

INTRODUCTION

The situation since the Covid-19 crisis has been interesting from a macroeconomic point of view: the economic crisis due to Covid-19 was the first global economic crisis caused by a virus in a long time (Danielsson et al. 2020; Byrialsen & Raza 2021). The appropriate and timely response from policy makers in most countries mitigated the economic effects of the crisis. Even though most countries experienced milder recessions relative to those experienced in the Global Financial Crisis, the after-effects of the Covid crisis are still looming around as supply constraints and later demand recovery, in combination with high import prices, disrupted supply chains and energy prices. Once again, pressure is mounting on central banks and fiscal authorities to take steps to manage the post-Covid inflationary crisis (Raza et al. 2023). The policy makers are faced with a clear dilemma: (1) further monetary tightening to tame inflation may prolong recessions and endanger financial stability; and (2) providing a fiscal relief can further fuel inflation and increase public debt. These are genuine policy concerns which require a clear assessment of the interdependencies embedded in the global economic system. Specifically, central to both fiscal and monetary policy makers is the interaction between the real economy and the financial sector and how this interaction might play out when a particular policy is undertaken.

To support decision making to mitigate the effects of the crisis, the understanding of the interactions between the financial and real sectors has become essential. A good understanding in this regard can enable policy makers to react to early signs of unsustainable processes and take preventive measures to reduce the adverse effects of shocks, such as those experienced during the Covid-19 pandemic. The aim of this chapter is to develop a framework that coherently links the real and financial sectors of a specific economy, thereby highlighting the structural linkages through which the financial sector interacts with the real sector in a small open economy with a fixed exchange rate. The proposed framework can provide informed assessment of the interaction between the real and financial sectors. To demonstrate this feature, we carry out a simple analysis and evaluate the effects of fiscal policy in the model while using Denmark as an example.

The tradition of macroeconomic modelling in Denmark started in the early 1970s in the tradition of the work by Lawrence Klein relying on Keynesian theory (Grinderslev & Smidt 2020; Kærgård 2020; Jespersen 2022). The purpose of these models was to forecast the development of short-run fluctuations in the Danish economy, typically one to two years ahead. In 2017, the work on a new macroeconomic model, MAKRO, based on forward-looking overlapping generations and general equilibrium setup, was initiated. The motivation to switch from the traditional Keynesian structural estimated models to models including longer-run phenomena is, as mentioned in Stephensen (2020), to have a model that can be used to present a framework for evaluating the short-run effects of economic policy, create medium- and long-term projections and evaluate the consequences of policy initiatives and exogenous shocks to the economy. The modelling team describes it as a hybrid between the short-run and long-run overlapping generations models, the short-run dimension being described as a hybrid between a dynamic stochastic general equilibrium model and a structural estimated model (Stephensen et al. 2017).

While the trend in economic modelling as presented above moves towards equilibrium models, the model presented in this chapter follows the well-known stock-flow consistent (SFC) approach, where the macroeconomic system as a whole is assessed from an aggregative perspective comprising sectors with conflicting goals rather than through a microeconomic lens involving a 'representative agent' whose individual behaviour generalizes the whole economy. From a theoretical perspective, the real and the financial sectors are linked through standard accounting principles, and the dynamics of the data are explained through behavioural equations, which theoretically are predominantly inspired by post-Keynesian theory. The structure of our model is greatly influenced by a number of studies within the post-Keynesian empirical SFC tradition, including, among others, Godley and Zezza (1992), Byrialsen and Raza (2020) and Valdecantos (2022). Since the number of empirical SFC models is still very limited in the existing literature, our chapter also contributes to the literature on empirical SFC models.

The rest of the chapter is organized as follows. The second section presents the main assumptions, data and estimation strategy. The third section presents the structure of the model. The fourth section explains the results of the model followed by the conclusion.

ASSUMPTIONS, DATA AND ESTIMATION

In this section we present the main assumption behind the model as well as discussing the choice of data and estimation technique, before the description of the model.

Assumptions

Given the size and openness of the Danish economy, it is important to focus on building a model for a small open economy. The Danish currency (Krones) is pegged to the euro but is floating vis-à-vis other currencies of the world. To simplify things, we take the nominal exchange rate as exogenous in the model, since it is set by the Central Bank to keep fixed parity with the euro.

Since the Danish economy is small, we take advantage of 'small open economy assumptions', meaning that the dynamics of the Danish economy do not affect the rest of the world (RoW). Moreover, variables like the economic activity of the RoW, import prices, foreign interest rates, returns of securities and dividends on foreign assets are kept exogenous.

Being a post-Keynesian model in nature, economic activity is determined by the level of aggregate demand in the short term, medium term and long term. This means that the economy is demand-led in both the real side of the economy as well as in the financial market, where no credit constraints are introduced. Being a mature economy with a high rate of employment, however, the Danish economy is very likely to face shortages in the labour market. In order to capture the possibilities of labour shortages, we add a supply constraint in the labour market, where even small changes in the rate of unemployment affects wages and thereby prices in the model.

Regarding the dimensions of the model, we assume five institutional sectors: non-financial corporations, financial corporations, the general government, households and the RoW. It is assumed that all domestic production takes place in the non-financial sector, which also gathers the totality of imports.

To keep the complexity of the financial market at an aggregated level without losing information, the number of financial assets is aggregated to five: interest-bearing assets, debt securities, loans, equities and insurances. This level of aggregation enables a transparent link between the stock of financial assets reported in the national account with the flow of property income reported in the same accounts. Prices on assets as well as the rate of dividends and interest on individual assets are assumed to be exogenous in the model. In order to account for the varying capital gains derived from the different existing physical assets, the model distinguishes between two types of investment goods: buildings and dwellings, normally subject to a low depreciation and a more volatile price, and equipment, which is often subject to a higher depreciation and a more stable price. The sum of these two types of physical goods gives gross fixed capital formation, to which the change in inventories is added to obtain gross capital formation, which we can simply call investment.

Data

The data used in this databank are the sectoral national accounts provided by Statistics Denmark from 2005Q1 to 2020Q1. This time span was selected based on quarterly sectoral national accounts availability. The data included in the databank are non-seasonally adjusted – the seasonal adjustment is only applied to the variables that will enter an estimation of a behavioural equation.

A way to present the important flows on the real side of the economy is as a Sankey, which illustrates both the origin and the use of each transaction. All flows can be seen as an inflow in one sector and an outflow of another sector. The relative width of the flow illustrates the relative value of the transaction found in the national account for first quarter 2020, as shown in Figure 6.1.

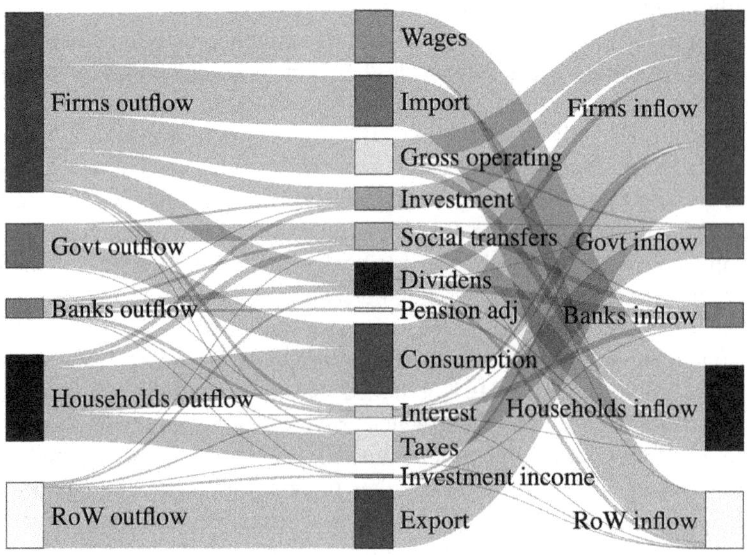

Figure 6.1 Sankey diagram of flows from 2020q1

We also visualize the balance sheets interaction through a Sankey as shown in Figure 6.2. The accumulation of financial assets follows the description of the balance sheet matrix and transaction flows matrix presented in previous sections.

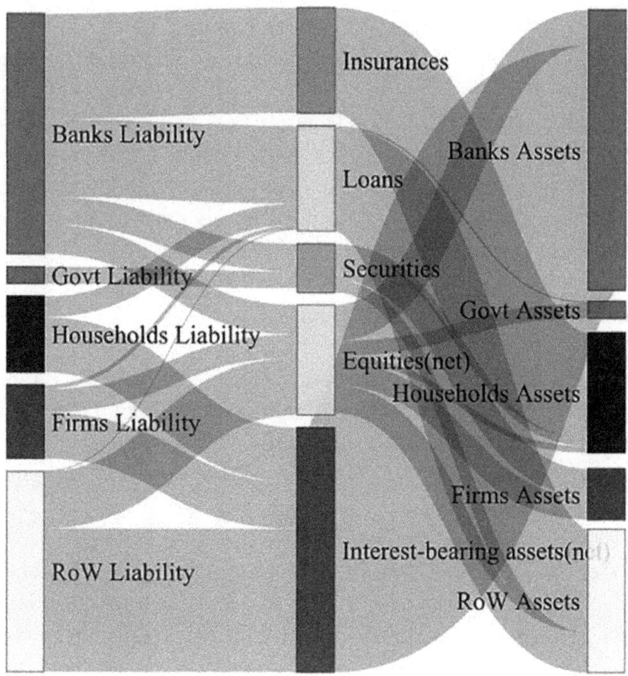

Figure 6.2 *Sankey diagram of the balance sheets transactions from 2020q1*

Estimation Strategy

After constructing the databank, we use a single equation estimation technique to obtain the parameters of each behavioural equation. While estimating the structural parameters, we also take the log of certain variables, if it is theoretically intuitive.

Since we have data with seasonal fluctuations, we remove seasonal fluctuation from our variables before estimating the behavioural equations. After de-seasonalizing the data, we test the variables for stationarity and then explore the dynamic relationship between the variables of interest. In most cases, the structural parameters are estimated using auto-regressive dynamic lag, following the technique proposed in Pesaran et al. (2001). This strategy is useful in exploring cointegrating relationships among variables, since it allows different orders of integrations.[1] We follow general-to-specific methodology where we start with a large number of lags and then drop irrelevant lags to choose a parsimonious model. In case of cointegration, we estimate the so-called error-correction version of the model. If we do not find any cointegration, we simply estimate a dynamic regression using stationary data.[2]

Even though our estimation strategy attempts to choose a functional form that attempts to best describe the data for a given dependent variable, our choice of variables in every equation is purely based on theory. Our strong reliance on theory helps us avoid model misspecifications. Moreover, we ensure that neither the sign nor the magnitude of our estimated equations are at odds with the theory. In short, we do not aim for a purely data-driven solution to the model but attempt to choose a balance between empirics and theory.

DESCRIPTION OF THE MODEL

The presentation of the model in this section will focus mostly on the behavioural equations, while the accounting identities can be found together with the full list of equations in Byrialsen et al. (2022).

Non-Financial Corporations

In this model it is assumed that all production takes place in non-financial corporations. The total production is determined by the aggregate demand.

While the production creates an income for the firms, the major expenditures for the firms are wages (*WB*) paid to households in Denmark and abroad, net indirect taxes (including taxes and subsidies on products and production) (T_t^N) to the government sector and gross operating surplus paid to the other domestic sectors of the economy. The wage bill is a product of the wage rate ($Wage_t$) and the level of employment (N_t^N), where the wage rate is assumed to be the same for Denmark and the RoW. Wages and employment are determined based on the conditions prevailing both in the labour and the goods markets.

Employment (*N*) is simply given as the ratio of real output to productivity.

The number of unemployed individuals is defined as the difference between the total labour force and the number of employed individuals.

Since most taxes paid by the firms are taxes on production, it is further assumed that the tax rate in our model is fixed, and the total amount of taxes paid by the non-financial corporations changes accordingly with variations in total production.

From an accounting perspective, the gross operating surplus $(B2_t)$ is the residual between gross domestic product (GDP) at factor prices (YF_t, which is given by $Y_t - T_t^N$) and the compensation of employees.[3] Since all net taxes on production are assumed to be a proportion of total production, GDP at factor prices can be calculated as a share of GDP at market prices.

It was previously defined that the stock of capital could be decomposed into two types of assets: buildings and dwellings, and equipment. Since these two types of capital goods can be determined by different factors (or by the same ones, but with varying effects) we define a specific behavioural equation for each. The equation is written in terms of the rate of accumulation of each asset, i.e., $\frac{I^{NFC}_{BD,t}}{K^{NFC}_{BD,t-1}}$ and $\frac{I^{NFC}_{EQUIP,t}}{K^{NFC}_{equip,t-1}}$. In line with Kalecki (1971), we define the investment function as determined by an autonomous component (a proxy of the 'animal spirits') and the profit rate, which can in turn be defined as the product of the profit share and the rate of capacity utilization. The rate of capacity utilization is constructed as the ratio of real GDP to the real stock of capital. We also extend this equation to include the cost of capital, which we measured by the interest rate on loans. Finally, in order to include an interaction between the real and the financial spheres of the economy, we add Tobin's Q as an additional determinant (we construct Tobin's Q as the ratio of the market value of the outstanding stock of equality liabilities to the nominal stock of capital).

In our estimations for the period 2005Q1–2020Q1, we do not find evidence of a relationship between the rate of accumulation of any of these two capital goods with the cost of capital, neither in the long run nor in the short run. In the case of the rate of accumulation of non-financial corporations on buildings and dwellings, we found capacity utilization to have both a short-run and long-run significant relationship. In the case of the profit share only the long-run relationship was found statistically significant. Overall, these results seem to support the Kaleckian investment function. Tobin's Q was also found significant only in the long run, its effect being much smaller than those found for the profit share and capacity utilization.

$$\Delta ln\left(\frac{i^{NFC}_{BD,t}}{K^{NFC}_{BD,t-1}}\right)$$

$$= 0.40 - 0.49 * \Delta ln\left(\frac{i^{NFC}_{BD_{t-1}}}{K^{NFC}_{BD,t-2}}\right) - 0.09 * \Delta ln(\phi_t) + 0.72 * \Delta ln(u_t) + 0.01 * \Delta$$

$$ln(q_t) - 0.40 * ln\left(\frac{i^{NFC}_{BD_{t-1}}}{K^{NFC}_{BD,t-2}}\right) + 0.40 * \Delta ln(\phi_{t-1}) + 1.04 * \Delta ln(u_{t-1}) + 0.09 * \Delta$$

$$ln(q_{t-1})$$

The long-run coefficient defining the relationship between the profit share and the rate of accumulation of buildings and dwellings is 1.01, meaning that accumulation is almost one-for-one with income distribution. As shown in the equation, the short-run effect is much lower (−0.09) and with the 'wrong' sign, though not statistically significant. Regarding the long-run relationship between accumulation and capacity utilization, the coefficient is 2.6, signalling a high sensitivity of investment to the level of activity. The short-run effect is relatively smaller (0.72). Finally, the long-run relationship between investment and Tobin's Q is estimated to be around 0.23, far below the impact of the other two determinants.

Similar results are found in the case of investment in equipment, where only a significant long-run relationship with the three explanatory variables is found. The estimated equation takes the following form:

$$\Delta ln\left(\frac{i^{NFC}_{equip,t}}{K^{NFC}_{equip,\,t-1}}\right)$$

$$= -0.01 - 0.17 * \Delta ln\left(\frac{i^{NFC}_{equip,t-1}}{K^{NFC}_{equip,\,t-2}}\right) + 0.01 * \Delta ln\,(\phi_t) + 0.32 * \Delta ln\,(u_t) - 0.24e$$

$$* \Delta ln\,(q_t) - 0.41 * ln\left(\frac{i^{NFC}_{equip,t-1}}{K^{NFC}_{equip,\,t-2}}\right) + 0.44 * ln\,(\phi_{t-1}) + 0.49 * ln\left(u_{t-1}\right)$$

$$+0.06 * ln\left(q_{t-1}\right)$$

The equation also included a dummy variable to account for a few outliers that render the residuals non-normally distributed. The implicit long-run coefficients are 1.07 for the profit share, 1.20 for the rate of capacity utilization and 0.15 for Tobin's Q, also exhibiting a higher sensitivity of investment to 'real' factors than financial ones. Not surprisingly, the short-run coefficients are smaller (though not statistically significant).

Non-financial corporations set prices following a mark-up pricing setting, where nominal unit labour costs, given by the ratio of the nominal wage and labour productivity $\left(\frac{W}{A}\right)$, and import prices (P^c_t) are the main elements determining production costs. Both the long- and short-run relationships between prices and total costs are significant and economically relevant, the coefficients being 0.72 and 0.14, respectively.

$$\Delta P^c_t = -0.18 * \Delta P^c_{t-1} - 0.19 * \Delta P^c_{t-2} + \; + 0.45 * \Delta P^c_{t-4} + \; + 0.14 *$$

$$\Delta\left(\frac{W_t}{A_t} + P^m_t\right) - 0.03 * P^c_{t-1} + 0.02 * \Delta\left(\frac{W_{t-1}}{A_{t-1}} + P^m_{t-1}\right)$$

On the financial side of the economy, the firms mainly finance their expenditures by issuing equities[4] or demanding loans. The stock of equities is modelled as a stock-flow ratio, where the stock of equities is determined by the need to finance investment.

Household Sector

The household sector receives income mainly from four sources: wages from firms (WB^H), gross operating surplus from production $B2_t^H$, net social transfers (STR^H) and capital income ($Property\ income_t^H$).

The capital income of the households originates from interest-bearing assets (IBA_{t-1}^H), securities (SEC_t^H), insurance and pensions (INS_{t-1}^H) and equities (EQ_{t-1}^H), while the outflow of capital income is determined by the stock of loans (L_{t-1}^H). The exogenous determined variables (r_A^H), (r_L^H) and ($r_{B_{t-1}}$) represent interest rates on assets, liabilities and securities, respectively. (χ_t) and (ψ_t) represent returns on equities and insurance, respectively. Social transfers received by the household sector are the sum of social contributions ($NPEN^H$) paid by the households, net benefits ($NBEN_t^H$) and other transfers (OTR^H) received by the households.

The net social benefits ($NSBEN_t^H$) are determined by the difference between social benefits received and social contribution paid by the households. An important part of the net social benefits is the adjustment of pension entitlements. The net contributions to pension schemes are determined as a function of the wages received by the households and the ratio of people above 65 years old (Ret) to the total population. The change in pension entitlements due to social contributions is obtained as a function of the wage bill and the share of retirees on total population, the first having *a priori* a positive impact and the second a negative effect. The cointegration tests suggest that there is a stable long-run relationship between these variables. The short-run relationship can therefore be expressed as follows, where $NPEN_t^H$ represents the change in pension entitlements due to social contributions:

$$\Delta ln(NPEN_t^H) = 0.092 * \Delta ln(NPEN_{t-1}^H) + 0.269 * \Delta ln(WB_t^H) - 46.166 *$$

$$\Delta ln\left(\frac{Ret_{t-1}}{Pop_{t-1}}\right) - 0.609 * ln\left(NPEN_{t-1}^H\right) + 0.363 * ln\left(WB_{t-1}^H\right) - 0.954 * ln\left(\frac{Ret_{t-1}}{Pop_{t-1}}\right)$$

Before specifying the consumption function, it is required to define how social benefits – an important component of the disposable income of lower-income households – is determined. We assume that these transfers are mainly driven by the amount of people that are outside the labour force ($Pop_t - LF_t$), and by those who belong to the labour force but are unemployed (UN_t) (and therefore receive unemployment benefits). The effect of the amount of people that are outside of the labour force seems to dominate the dynamics of social benefits, which seems a reasonable result taking into account the nature of the Danish pension system.

$$\Delta ln(NBEN_t^H) = -28.18 + 1.65 * \Delta ln(Pop_t - LF_t) + 0.001 * \Delta (UN_t) + 0.0005 *$$

$$(UN_{t-1}) - 0.77 * ln(NBEN_{t-1}^H) + 0.0004 * (UN_{t-1}) + 2.48 * ln(Pop_{t-1} - LF_{t-1})$$

Since households' behaviour can be subject to their income level, we opted to break disposable income down into two components: one given by wage income plus current transfers from the government (such as social benefits) and the other given by the gross operating surplus plus property income. Each of these two types of households is assumed to be subject to different tax rates, in line with the progressive tax system of the Danish economy.

Households' consumption is defined along the lines of the standard equations used in the SFC literature, where consumption is determined by disposable income and a wealth effect. There can eventually be an autonomous component reflecting the exogenous determinants of private consumption.

In line with the underlying economic theory, there seems to be evidence of cointegration between real consumption and both real disposable income (of upper and lower classes) and real financial wealth. The consumption function is therefore estimated using an error correction model, which takes the following form.

$$\Delta ln(c_t) = 1.60 - 0.33 * ln(c_{t-1}) + 0.11 * ln(yd1_{t-1}) + 0.06 * ln(yd2_{t-1}) + 0.03$$

$$* ln(fnw_{t-1}) + 0.06 * \Delta ln(yd1_t) + 0.06 * \Delta ln(yd1_{t-2}) + 0.09 * \Delta ln(yd2_t)$$

The long-run coefficients are 0.33, 0.18 and 0.09 for disposable income of upper classes, lower classes and real net financial wealth, respectively. The short-run dynamics of consumption seem to be driven similarly by the fluctuations of the disposable income of both types of household. Financial wealth was found to be insignificant in the estimation of short-run dynamics.

It is assumed that real wages are set based on the evolution of productivity and the rate of unemployment. As productivity rises, workers aim at a higher real wage such that their share on income is not affected. As the unemployment rate decreases, their bargaining power goes up, thereby increasing their capacity to negotiate higher real wages. The equation determining the real wage (w) takes the following form:

$$\Delta ln(w_t) = 0.13 - 0.31 * \Delta ln(ur_{t-4}) + 0.55 * \Delta ln(a_t) - 0.10 * ln(w_{t-1})$$

$$-0.15 * (ur_{t-2}) + 0.07 * ln(a_{t-1})$$

where the rate of unemployment (ur) seems to affect the real wage with some delay while the effect of real productivity (a) seems to be immediate. The long-run effect of the unemployment rate and productivity are −1.52 and 0.6, respectively, but only the former is statistically significant. In the short run, on the other hand, it is the unemployment rate (with a four-period lag) that has a statistically significant effect on the real wage.

Besides consuming goods and services, households also demand capital goods, which in this model are given by buildings and dwellings on the one hand and equipment on the other. As done previously in the estimation of non-financial corporations' investment decision, the dependent variable we work with is the rate of accumulation $\left(\frac{i^H_{BD_t}}{K^H_{BD,t-1}}\right)$. Its determinants are, *a priori*, aggregate disposable income, the relative price of dwellings with respect to construction prices $\frac{P^{BD}}{P^I}$ (to introduce a speculative determinant of this type of investment) and leverage defined as the ratio of households' debt to the value of their fixed assets $(\frac{L^H_t}{K^H_{BD,t}})$. The interest rate on loans was also included in a first specification of the equation, but results were not found to be significant. A significant long-run relationship is found between investment in buildings and dwellings, and disposable income, relative prices and households' debt, the coefficients being 3.39, −4.09 and −2.04, respectively. The short-run effects exhibit signs which are in line with economic theory, although the coefficients of prices and disposable income are not highly statistically significant.

$$\Delta ln\left(\frac{i^H_{BD_t}}{K^H_{BD,t-1}}\right)$$

$$= 0.45 - 0.39 * \Delta ln\left(\frac{i^H_{BD_{t-1}}}{K^H_{BD,t-2}}\right) - 0.43 * \Delta ln\left(\frac{i^H_{BD_{t-3}}}{K^H_{BD,t-2}}\right) + 0.62 * \Delta ln\left(\frac{P^{BD}_{t-1}}{P^I_{t-1}}\right) + 0.65$$

$$* \Delta ln\left(\frac{P^{BD}_{t-2}}{P^I_{t-2}}\right) + 0.21 * \Delta ln\left(\frac{yd^H_{t-2}}{K^H_{BD,t-3}}\right) - 0.68 * \Delta ln\left(\frac{L^H_{t-1}}{K^H_{BD,t-2}}\right) - 0.16 * ln\left(\frac{i^H_{BD_{t-1}}}{K^H_{BD,t-2}}\right)$$

$$+0.53 * \left(\frac{yd^H_{t-1}}{K^H_{BD,t-2}}\right) - 0.64 * \left(\frac{P^{BD}_{t-1}}{P^I_{t-1}}\right) - 0.32 * \left(\frac{L^H_{t-1}}{K^H_{BD,t-2}}\right)$$

In the case of households' investment in equipment, no significant long-run relationship was found. As a result, it was estimated as an auto-regressive process with an 'exogenous' component given by disposable income, the underlying intuition being that a higher disposable income will lead to an increase in the purchase of the durable goods comprised in the equipment category.

$$\Delta ln\left(\frac{i^H_{EQUIP}}{K^H_{equip,\,t-1}}\right) = -0.62 * \Delta ln\left(\frac{i^H_{EQUIP_{-1}}}{K^H_{equip,\,t-2}}\right) - 0.25 * \left(\frac{i^H_{EQUIP_{-2}}}{K^H_{equip,\,t-3}}\right) + 0.19 * \left(\frac{yd^H_{-1}}{K^H_{equip,\,t-2}}\right)$$

We now turn to explaining households' allocation of wealth in the financial markets. We begin by describing the financial balance of the households, which can be written as the difference between the accumulation of financial assets and financial liabilities.

The overall development of the financial markets in our model is primarily driven by household demand for credit (loans) and assets (interest-bearing assets, equities, insurances and securities). In our behavioural equations for the demand for equities and securities, we attempt to explain the demand for a particular stock, and then let these stocks (along with capital gains) determine the transactions of each financial asset in the model. Regarding the demand for insurance and interest-bearing assets, we explain the transactions and then determine the stock by using accounting identities. In the case of insurances, the net transaction is closely related to the income of the households and the change of pension entitlements, which is the main reason for modelling the transaction instead of the stock. In the case of interest-bearing assets, this transaction ensures the fulfilment of households' budget constraint, meaning that saving is equal to the sum of the changes in households' balance sheet. Capital gains on financial assets are assumed exogenous.

Considering that equities represent on average 90 percent of the portfolio of these two assets, we keep the demand for securities as an exogenous variable and focus on the demand for equities. The demand for equities is written as a proportion of financial assets net of insurance. When carrying out the estimation, we also net out the demand for equities (taken as a stock) from the revaluation effects, as these are not part of households' demand at the moment of making their portfolio decision (in a model in discrete time revaluation effects take place at the end of each period). The main determinants of the demand for equities are given by the interest rate on securities (r_{B_t}) and the rate of profitability of equities, this later being computed as the ratio of the sum of dividends received by households and revaluation effects to the previous stock of equities. In order to avoid problems of collinearity (given by the inclusion of revaluation effects as a component of profitability), the rate of profitability is included with a lag. The cointegration tests suggest that there is a long-run relationship between these variables, which allows us to express the demand for equities as an error correction model.

$$\Delta\left(\frac{EQ_t^H - EQ_{rv,t}^H}{EQ_{t-1}^H + SEC_{t-1}^H + IBA_{t-1}^H}\right)$$

$$= 0.07 + 6.85 * \Delta r_{B_{t-1}} + 0.16 * \Delta\left(\frac{DIV_{t-1}^H + EQ_{rv_{t-1}}^H}{EQ_{t-2}^H}\right) - 0.10$$

$$* \left(\frac{EQ_{t-1}^H - EQ_{rv,t-1}^H}{EQ_{t-2}^H + SEC_{t-2}^H + IBA_{t-2}^H}\right) - 2.14 * r_{B_{t-1}} + 0.16 * \left(\frac{DIV_{t-2}^H + EQ_{rv_{t-2}}^H}{EQ_{t-3}^H}\right)$$

Although in the short run there seems to be a positive relationship between the interest rate and the relative demand for equities, this effect is smaller compared to the one registered for the long run (which is −22.06). The convergence towards the long-run equilibrium therefore offsets the positive effect that interest rates have on the relative demand for equities in the short run. Regarding the impact of profitability, although it is almost negligible in the short run, it is positive in the long run (1.64).

Regarding households' liabilities, their demand for loans is expressed as loan transaction to disposable income. The main determinants for households' loan transactions are the interest rate on loans, the ratio of households' investment to disposable income and the stock of outstanding debt to income ratio – considering that most of the credit is taken to purchase dwellings. These relationships can also be expressed by means of an error correction model, which takes the following form:

$$\Delta\left(\frac{L_{tr,t}^H}{YD_t^H}\right) = 1.27 + 0.13 * \Delta\left(\frac{L_{tr_{t-2}}^H}{YD_{t-2}^H}\right) - 26.26 * \Delta r_{L_t} + 0.26 * \Delta\, ln\left(\frac{i_{BD_{t-3}}^H}{yd_{t-3}^H}\right)$$

$$-0.72 * \left(\frac{L_{tr_{t-1}}^H}{YD_{t-1}^H}\right) - 0.49 * \left(\frac{L_{t-2}^H}{YD_{t-2}^H}\right)$$

The only relevant long-run relationship that we found is the one linking the demand for loans and the debt-to-income ratio, the coefficient being −0.68. The short-run coefficients were all found significant and with the correct sign.

Financial Sector

The financial sector in this model is the main provider of credit in the economy, which means that capital income plays a major role for the savings of the financial sector. The financial corporations' interactions with all other sectors that involve transactions for the purpose of acquiring interest-bearing stocks are captured through interest-bearing asset transactions ($IBATR^F$).

Regarding the transaction of securities for the financial corporations, the sector engages in transactions with both the domestic market and the RoW.

In this version of the model, it is assumed that all international trade in securities involves the financial corporations, where the foreign demand for securities is being met by the domestic financial sector.

For the domestic transactions of securities, the financial corporations use this asset as a residual for all other transactions to ensure the fulfilment of the budget constraint of the financial sectors.

The stock of loans is determined by the demand for credit from the rest of the economy: the stock of equities ($EQTR_t^F$) is modelled as a residual of the demand for equities from the other sectors. Finally, the overall development in $INSTR^F$ is mainly explained by household contributions to pensions, as discussed earlier.[5]

Government Sector

The Danish economy is characterized by having a welfare state with a very active government. Public expenditures are mostly financed through taxes. The total tax revenue received by the government is equal to the taxes paid by all other sectors.

A major expenditure for the government sector is social transfers. Net social transfers paid by the government sector are equal to the sum of net social transfers received by the other sectors.

On the financial side of the economy, the government is assumed to finance its deficit through issuing securities as well as a reduction in the stock of interest-bearing assets.

Rest of the World

In 1982 Denmark decided to peg the Danish krone to the Deutschmark, which later was replaced by a peg to the euro. For this reason, the exchange rate is assumed to be fixed in this model. Denmark is characterized as a small open economy, which a high degree of interaction with the RoW.

Focusing on the trade balance, exports are modelled following a traditional Armington model (1969), where the quantity of exported goods is a function of both the level of activity of trading partners and the real exchange rate. In order to estimate exports, we constructed a variable containing the weighted average of the GDP of Denmark's ten main trading partners.[6] A similar process was followed to build the real exchange rate.[7] Supply effects are simply included by adding real GDP as an additional independent variable. In order to avoid simultaneity problems, this real GDP will enter regressions with a lag. In the case of exports, the evidence seems to show that the real exchange rate is not significant in the long run. The relation takes the following form:

$$\Delta ln(x_t) = 0.60 + 1.43 * \Delta ln(y_{t-4}^{TP}) - 0.49 * \Delta ln(rer_t) - 0.49 * ln(x_{t-1})$$

$$+0.37 * ln(y_{t-1}^{TP})$$

Besides showing a strong effect of trading partners' activity on Danish exports in the short run, this estimation suggests that there is also a significant long-run relationship, the coefficient being 0.76. An increase in the real exchange rate (i.e., an appreciation) has a negative impact on exports, but this effect is only found to be significant in the short run.

The estimation of imports is based on the standard import function. Cointegration tests suggest that there is a long-run relationship between Danish imports and real GDP, the long-run coefficient being around 1.84. The estimated equation takes the following functional form:

$$\Delta ln(m_t) = -3.79 - 0.12 * \Delta ln(m_{t-2}) + 0.30 * \Delta ln(rer_{t-1}) + 0.41 * \Delta ln(rer_{t-3})$$

$$+1.30 * \Delta ln(y_t) - 0.32 * ln(m_{t-1}) + 0.59 * ln(y_{t-1})$$

The sign of the coefficients suggests that in the short run imports are quite responsive to changes in domestic demand, and much less sensitive to movements in the real exchange rate. The speed of convergence towards the long-run equilibrium is slightly lower (32 per cent) than observed in the case of exports (49 per cent). Import prices (P_t^m) are expressed in domestic currency assuming a fixed exchange rate of 1. Export prices (P_t^x) are kept exogenous in the current version of the model. The current account balance from a Danish perspective can be seen as the mirror of the net lending for the RoW.

VALIDATION OF THE MODEL

In this section, we will look at the performance of the model by both comparing the results from the simulations with actual data for the period under observation and by running a standard shock and investigating how the model responds to this shock.

In Figures 6.3–6.5, we compare the results from the simulation with the actual data for real GDP and level of employment.

As seen in the left panel of Figure 6.3, the model seems to capture the dynamics of real economic activity quite well. In particular, the model explains the medium- to long-run tendency of the data well even though there are some divergences in some quarters. The model, however, seems to overshoot the economic activity in the period from 2011 to 2016.

In order to analyse the behaviour of the model, we propose a simple shock consisting of a permanent 2 per cent increase in public expenditure starting from 2010. From the left panel of Figure 6.4, the shock produces a positive effect on real income, which is expected since public expenditure is one of the main components of aggregate demand. Following the standard Keynesian multiplier, other components of aggregated demand are affected by the increase in public expenditure. The public stimuli increase the total income in the economy, which increases both the level of consumption (due to higher disposable income) and the level of investment (due to higher capacity utilization) following the standard multiplier effect. With a given labour productivity, the level of employment also increases due to the increase in the demand for labour, which in this dynamic model creates increases in wages and prices. Since the size of the labour force is unaffected by a shock to public expenditure, the shock produces an immediate drop in the rate of unemployment (see the right panel of Figure 6.4). All three domestic demand components (consumption, investment and public expenditures) therefore contribute to the overall increase in the economic activity.

Due to the fact that Denmark is assumed to be a small open economy, the change in the level of economic activity in Denmark doesn't affect the economic activity in the RoW, as discussed earlier. Exports are therefore only affected negatively to a smaller degree, because of the increase in the relative prices between consumption prices in Denmark and prices abroad, which are determined as exogenous in the model. Finally, since imports depend on domestic activity this leakage via import reduces the multiplier. The level of imports increases due to the shock, which reduces the overall positive effect of the shock on the economic activity.

As presented in the text above, the effect of a permanent increase in the public expenditures is as expected according to standard Keynesian theory. Despite the fact that the leakages from the multiplier in Denmark, like income tax and the propensity to import, are quite high, our results suggest that using fiscal policy to stimulate economic activity seems to be effective for the Danish economy, meaning that the multiplier is larger than 1. This result contrasts with the mainstream conclusion stating that fiscal policy has no long-run effects on aggregate demand and that the multiplier effect tends to be 0, while the main consequence of expansionary fiscal policies is an increase in infla-

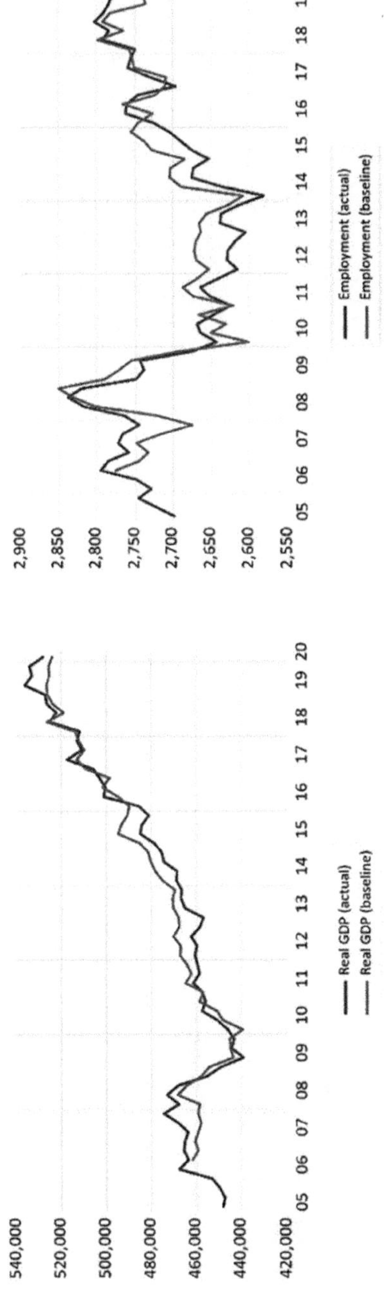

Figure 6.3 *Real GDP and employment, actual versus baseline model*

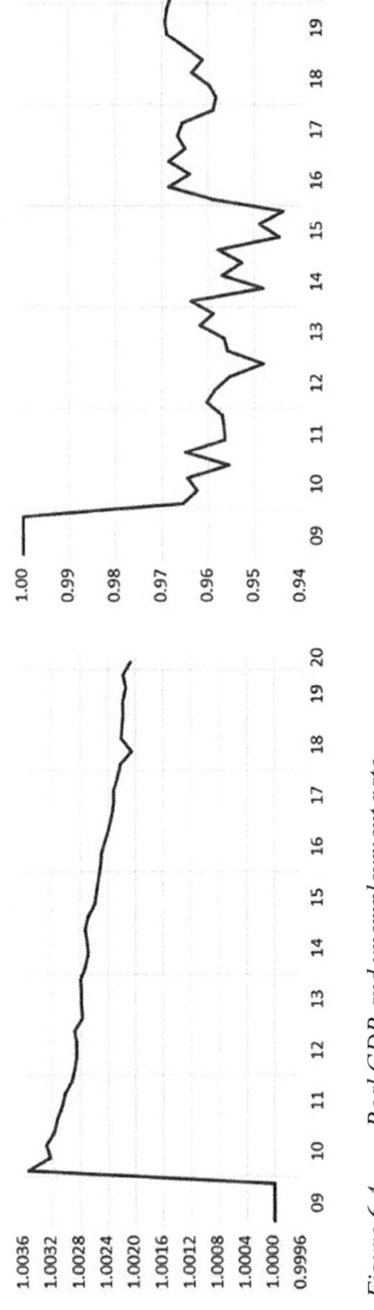

Figure 6.4 Real GDP and unemployment rate

tion. As can be seen in the left panel of Figure 6.5, the impact of a permanent level effect on public spending and the increase in aggregate demand only seem to lead to a very small increase in the rate of inflation. What is observed, on the other hand, is a slight deterioration of the budget balance of the government. Thus, all other variables being constant, the government's capacity to launch an expansionary fiscal policy would eventually be more constrained by funding possibilities than by the potential inflationary effects. This simple simulation therefore provides an example of how an empirical SFC model can be used to fine-tune macroeconomic policies and evaluate their effects across the economy so that both direct effects and also by-products are considered.

CONCLUSION

In this chapter we present our quarterly model for the Danish economy, which enables an understanding of the interactions between the financial and real sectors of the Danish economy. The model is built using available quarterly data from the sectoral national account for the period 2005–2020. In this model the economy is divided into five institutional sectors: non-financial corporations, financial corporations, government, households and the RoW. From the balance sheet perspective, we aggregate the number of financial assets into five financial assets, while two types of physical goods are represented in the model. The model seems to be able to reproduce the actual dynamics of the key variable of the Danish economy for the period 2005–2020 in a fairly accurate way. In order to explore how the model reacts to a well-known shock, we introduce a permanent increase in the public expenditures of 2 per cent.

The effect of a permanent increase in the public expenditures is as expected according to standard Keynesian theory, which means that both private consumption and investment increases as a result of the shock. At the same time, exports are affected negatively due to the fact that domestic prices increase more than prices in the RoW, which are unaffected by the shock. Import is also increased due to the overall increase in domestic activity, which reduces the overall effect of the shock. Finally, despite the fact that both income taxes and propensity to import are quite high in Denmark, the effect of fiscal policy seems to be able to stimulate the economic activity as well as the level of employment. Unlike the mainstream models, the expansionary fiscal policy does not seem to produce higher inflation. However, the effect on public finances is negative, eventually limiting the size of the stimuli that the government can make.

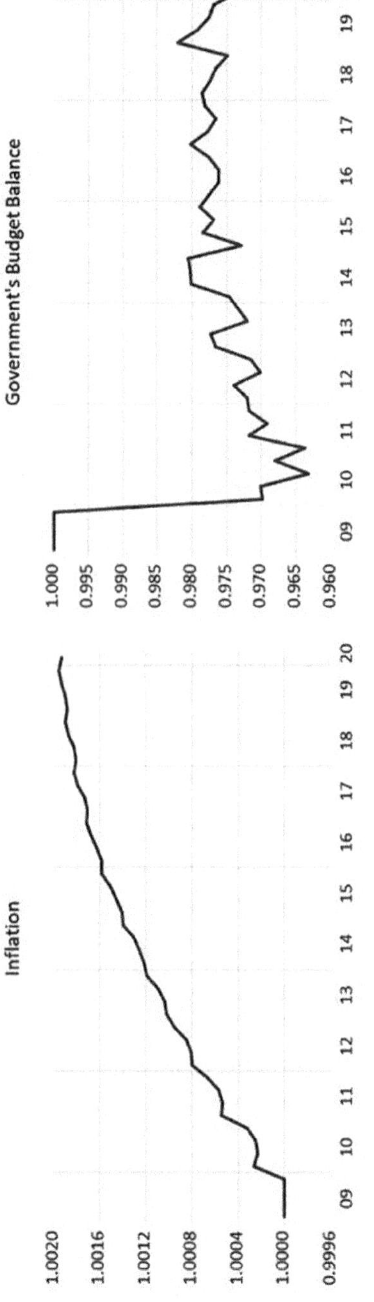

Figure 6.5 *Inflation and budget balance*

NOTES

1. This estimation technique is not very restrictive. The limitation of this approach is that it is not valid for variables that are I(2) – integrated of order 2. We did not find any variable to be I(2), hence, the estimation technique was useful and was employed in most cases.
2. The estimated parameters for the behavioural equations can be found in sections 3.1–3.5. The complete output from the estimations is presented in Byrialsen et al. (2022).
3. Since all production is assumed to take place in the same sector, any distribution of the gross operating surplus cannot be determined within the model. Since the flows of this surplus provide an important income for all sectors, the distribution of this flow is kept exogenous for financial corporations, households and the government sector, while the surplus for the non-financial corporation sector is a residual. For the government sector, however, the gross operating surplus is equal to the consumption of fixed capital, so it is endogenous.
4. The expenditures are also to a smaller degree financed by issuing securities by the firms. This, however, is kept exogenous in the current version of the model.
5. NPENTRW (net transaction of pension funds to the rest of the world) is exogenous in our model. It is a very small proportion of the total transaction.
6. Each country's real GDP was converted into United States dollars and weighted by its share on the Danish export basket.
7. The real exchange rate index was built as the weighted average of the bilateral real exchange rate, which was in turn computed using consumer price indices and nominal exchange rates.

REFERENCES

Armington, P. S. (1969). A theory of demand for products distinguished by place of production. *Staff Papers*, *16*(1), 159–178.

Byrialsen, M. R., & Raza, H. (2020). An empirical stock-flow consistent macroeconomic model for Denmark. *Levy Economics Institute, Working Papers Series*.

Byrialsen, M. R., & Raza, H. (2021). Assessing the macroeconomic effects of Covid-19 in an empirical SFC model for Denmark. *International Journal of Political Economy*, *50*(4), 318–350.

Byrialsen, M. R., Raza, H., & Valdecantos, S. (2022). *QMDE: A Quarterly Empirical Model for the Danish Economy* (No. 79-2022). IMK at the Hans Boeckler Foundation, Macroeconomic Policy Institute.

Danielsson, J., Macrae, R., Vayanos, D., & Zigrand, J. (2020). The Coronavirus crisis is no 2008. *VoxEU*, 26 March.

Godley, W., & Zezza, G. (1992). A simple stock flow model of the Danish economy. In H. Brink (Ed.), *Themes in Modern Macroeconomics*. Palgrave/Macmillan.

Grinderslev, D., & Smidt, J. (2020). Fremskrivninger og modelbrug i De Økonomiske Råds sekretariat. *Samfundsøkonomen*, *2*, 55–63.

Jespersen, J. (2022). Samfundsøkonomiske modeller og prognoser: Hvad har økonomer bidraget med? Slagmark, *84*, 59–81.

Kærgård, N. (2020). Finansministeriet og makroøkonomiske regnemodeller: Et historisk rids. *Samfundsøkonomen*, *2*, 31–40.

Kalecki, M. (1971). *Selected Essays on the Dynamics of the Capitalist Economy, 1933–1940*. Cambridge University Press.

Pesaran, M. H., Shin, Y., & Smith, R. J. (2001). Bounds testing approaches to the analysis of level relationships. *Journal of Applied Econometrics*, *16*(3), 289–326.

Raza, H., Laurentjoye, T., Byrialsen, M. R., & Valdecantos, S. (2023). Inflation and the role of macroeconomic policies: A model for the case of Denmark. *Structural Change and Economic Dynamics*, *67*, 32–43.

Stephensen, P. (2020). Den nye makroøkonomiske model MAKRO. *Samfundsøkonomen*, *2*, 64–71.

Stephensen, P., Ejarque, J., Høegh, G., Kronborg, A., & Bonde, M. (2017). The new Danish macroeconomic model MAKRO. *Working Paper*. No. 1. MAKRO.

Valdecantos, S. (2022). Endogenous exchange rates in empirical stock-flow consistent models for peripheral economies: An illustration from the case of Argentina. *Journal of Post Keynesian Economics*. DOI: 10.1080/01603477.2022.2103827

PART II

Economic theory and policy implication

7. Demand-led growth and macroeconomic policy regimes in the Eurozone: implications for post-pandemic economic policies

Eckhard Hein

INTRODUCTION

The Covid-19 Crisis starting in 2020 has hit the Eurozone asymmetrically, while it was still in a fragile situation due to insufficient recovery from the Global Financial Crisis, the Great Recession and the Eurozone Crisis. The Eurozone Crisis and stagnation before the Covid-19 Crisis had revealed the severe problems of its economic policy institutions and the economic policy model based on New Consensus Macroeconomics (NCM). First, in 'normal' times, there was no mechanism that prevented rising current account imbalances and divergence among member states. Second, in the Great Recession and the Eurozone crisis, it became clear that nominal interest rate policies of the European Central Bank (ECB) were insufficient to stabilise aggregate demand and economic activity. Third, and the main reason for the Eurozone Crisis, the role of the ECB as a 'lender of last resort', not only for the banking sector but also for member state governments, was unclear at the beginning of the crisis and has only partly been remedied since then. In this contribution we will briefly review the shift in Eurozone demand and growth regimes after the Eurozone crisis and we will then turn to the role of the macroeconomic policy regime for demand and growth regimes and regime shifts. For this purpose, we use a post-Keynesian macroeconomic policy mix as the benchmark for generating, or at least contributing to, a non-inflationary full employment 'domestic demand-led regime' (DDL). Finally, we review the European Union (EU) policy responses towards the Covid-19 Crisis in order to assess whether the previously dominating policy regime based on the NCM has been overcome, whether the fundamental problems of Eurozone macroeconomic policy making have been tackled and whether the now prevailing policies have come closer to the policy regime advocated by post-Keynesians.

DEMAND AND GROWTH REGIMES AND MACROECONOMIC POLICY REGIMES IN THE EUROZONE

Demand and Growth Regimes Before and After the 2007–2009 Crises

Finance-dominated capitalism since the 1980s, characterised by rising income inequalities, falling wage shares and weak investment in the capital stock, has generated two extreme demand and growth regimes, which allowed for flourishing demand and high profits – and thus for 'profits without investment' regimes (Hein 2012).[1] On the one side, we had the 'debt-led private demand boom' (DLPD) regime, relying on credit-financed consumption and real-estate demand in particular, and generating current account deficits. On the other side, we have seen the 'export-led mercantilist' (ELM) regime, relying on rising net exports and thus generating current account surpluses. In between these two regimes, a 'weakly export-led' (WEL) regime with either current account surpluses but negative growth contributions of net exports or with current account deficits but with positive growth contributions of net exports, and a DDL regime relying on income-financed private demand and, in several cases, on debt-financed government demand have been distinguished.

Before the Global Financial Crisis and the Great Recession, within the Eurozone the current account surpluses of the ELM countries were roughly balanced by the current account deficits of the DLPD boom countries, such that the (core) Eurozone (EA-12) displayed the features of a DDL regime (Table 7.1). However, this has changed in the period after the Global Financial Crisis and the Great Recession, when, in the course of the Eurozone crisis and after, several previously DLPD countries turned ELM (or WEL), while the pre-crises ELM countries kept their regimes. The core Eurozone thus also turned towards a post-crises ELM regime.

With these shifts in regimes, the (core) Eurozone has externalised its pre-crises internal current account imbalances and has become a current account surplus region, free-riding on demand created in the rest of the world – and thus contributing to persistent global current account imbalances (Akcay et al. 2022). Furthermore, this shift in the EA-12 regime has been associated with a particularly weak recovery of the Eurozone from the 2007–2009 crises in international comparison, with the Unites States as a reference (Figure 7.1). This recovery of the developed capitalist world has been particularly weak in historical comparison, and has triggered a renewed debate on secular stagnation in orthodox economics (Gordon 2015; Summers 2014, 2015) and on stagnation policy in heterodox economics (Hein 2016, 2018). The recovery of the core Eurozone has not only been much weaker than that of the United States,

Table 7.1 *Shift of demand and growth regimes in the Eurozone according to five studies*

		Post 2007–2009 crisis			
		Debt-led private demand (boom)	**Domestic demand-led with high public-sector deficits**	**Weakly export-led**	**Export-led mercantilist**
Pre-2007–2009 crisis	**Debt-led private demand (boom)**			Greece[a, d, e] Portugal[e] Slovakia[e] Spain[e]	Estonia[a, b, e] Ireland[d, e] Latvia[b] Spain[c, d]
	Domestic demand-led		France[a, c, d, e]	Italy[a, e] Portugal[a, d]	EA-12[c, d] Italy[d]
	Weakly export-led				Slovenia[e]
	Export-led mercantilist		Finland[d, e]	Austria[e] Belgium[d]	Austria[d] Belgium[e] Germany[a, c, d, e] Luxembourg[e] Netherlands[d, e]

Source: [a] Dodig et al. (2016), 2001–2008, 2008–2014; [b] Dünhaupt and Hein (2019), 1995–2008, 2009–2016; [c] Hein (2019), 1999–2007, 2008–2016; [d] Hein and Martschin (2020), 2001–2009, 2010–2019; [e] Hein et al. (2021), 2000–2008, 2009–2016.

and has thus contributed to global stagnation tendencies, it has also been highly asymmetric. Focussing on the four big Eurozone economies, Germany has performed much better in comparison to Spain and particularly Italy, while France has remained close but slightly above the EA-12 average.

The Role of the Macroeconomic Policy Regimes for Demand and Growth Regimes and Regime Shifts

In an attempt to understand the drivers of the demand and growth regimes and the respective changes, Hein and Martschin (2021) have linked the demand and growth regimes for the four big Eurozone countries, France, Germany, Italy and Spain, with the post-Keynesian notion of macroeconomic policy regimes, developed and applied in the early 2000s (Fritsche et al. 2005; Hein and Truger 2005, 2009; Herr and Kazandziska 2011). The concept of a macroeconomic policy regime has been used to assess international and intertemporal comparative differences in macroeconomic performances of countries or regions. It describes the set of monetary, fiscal and wage or income policies, as

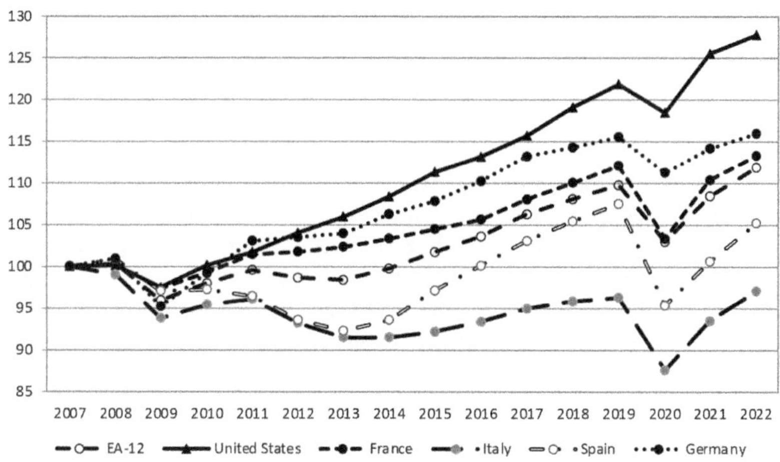

Note: 2007 = 100.
Source: Based on European Commission (2022a).

Figure 7.1 *Real GDP in Spain, Germany, France, Italy, the EA-12 and the United States, 2007–2022*

well as their coordination and interaction, against the institutional background of a specific economy, including the degree of openness and the exchange rate regime. This concept supposes that macroeconomic policies have not only short-run effects on economic performance, as in the NCM, but also have a long-run impact on output, income, employment, inflation, distribution and growth, as in the post-Keynesian macroeconomic and distribution and growth models (Hein 2014, 2023).

The benchmark supporting a stable DDL regime is derived from the post-Keynesian macroeconomic policy mix supporting non-inflationary full employment with roughly balanced current accounts, as presented by Arestis (2013), Hein (2023, ch. 6) and Hein and Stockhammer (2010). It is supposed that deviations from this benchmark should contribute to moving to the long-run unstable DLPD boom or ELM regimes and should thus have detrimental long-run effects on macroeconomic performance with regard to income, employment, inflation, distribution and growth, as well as financial stability.

For assessing the effect of monetary policies of the central bank, the focus is on the relationship between long-term real interest rates and real GDP growth. Monetary policy conducive to employment and growth, and to a stable DDL regime, should target a nominal long-term interest rate (i) slightly above the rate of inflation $(\hat{p})$ but below nominal GDP growth $(\hat{Y}^n)$, or a slightly positive real rate of interest $(i_r = i - \hat{p})$ below real GDP growth $(\hat{Y} = \hat{Y}^n - \hat{p})$:

$$\hat{p} < i < \hat{Y}^n \Leftrightarrow 0 \leq i_r \leq \hat{Y} \tag{7.1}$$

Of course, it is acknowledged that central banks cannot directly control long-term real interest rates in the credit or financial markets at any point in time, but only control short-term nominal money market rates. Nevertheless, the use of this and other tools, like open-market operations in financial markets in the context of quantitative easing, will have an impact on long-term nominal rates and, taking into account some persistence in inflation trends, also on long-term real rates beyond the short run. However, this impact might be asymmetric, since raising short-term rates will always drive up long-term rates, whereas lowering short-term rates might not be able to bring long-term rates down in a deep and persistent recession with rising risk assessments and liquidity preference of financial and non-financial actors. That is why short- and long-term real interest rates are also considered. Since the four countries under examination are members of the Eurozone, it is further taken into account that the ECB controls the short-term nominal interest rate for the Eurozone as a whole. Different inflation rates between countries might already mean different short- and long-term real interest rates. The differentials in the latter are then also affected by country-specific differentials in long-term nominal rates, in particular since the start of the Eurozone crisis in 2010 (De Grauwe 2012; Hein 2013/2014, 2018).

For wage policy, it is checked whether unit labour costs have contributed to nominal stability and grown at the target rate of inflation, which for our four countries is the target rate for the Eurozone as a whole. This means that nominal wages (w) should rise according to the sum of long-run trend growth of labour productivity $(\hat{y})$ in the national economy plus the target rate of inflation for the Eurozone as a whole $(\hat{p}^T)$, so that nominal unit labour costs $(nulc = w/y)$ grow at the target rate of inflation:

$$\hat{w} = \hat{y} + \hat{p}^T \Leftrightarrow \hat{w} - \hat{y} = \hat{p}^T \tag{7.2}$$

Furthermore, it is taken into account that rising or falling nominal unit labour cost growth will not proportionally affect the rate of inflation because of incomplete pass-through. Therefore, also changes in functional income distribution, i.e. in the labour income share, are considered. For the assessment of the effects of wage policies via functional income distribution, it is taken into account that aggregate demand in all four countries examined has been estimated to be wage-led (Hein 2014, ch. 7; Onaran and Obst 2016).

For fiscal policy, it has to be examined whether government expenditure policies (for given tax rates) are aimed at stabilising the employment rate at some non-inflationary level:

$$G_r = G_{r0} + G_{r1}(e^T - e),\ G_{r0} \geq 0,\ G_{r1} > 0, \tag{7.3}$$

with G_r for governments' real expenditure, G_{r0} as the expenditure level to reach a target employment rate e^Tassociated with non-inflationary full employment, and G_{r1} as the reaction coefficient towards deviations of the employment rate from the target rate. For a given average tax rate, this kind of functional finance fiscal policy makes government deficits and debt endogenous. Hein and Martschin (2021) use the changes of the cyclically adjusted budget balance-potential GDP ratio (CBR) of the government and relate this to the change in the output gap to assess the short-run discretionary responsiveness of fiscal policies. They are thus not directly examining equation (7.3) and do not identify potential output with the target full employment level of output, because of the well-known empirical measurement problems and endogeneity features of potential output (Heimberger and Kapeller 2017). Therefore, they do not look at the levels of CBRs and output gaps but only at the annual changes. If output gaps and CBRs move in the same direction, fiscal policies are counter-cyclical, lowering (increasing) structural deficits or increasing (lowering) structural surpluses in an economic upswing (downswing). If output gaps and CBRs move in opposite directions, fiscal policies are pro-cyclical; governments are lowering (increasing) structural deficits or increasing (lowering) structural surpluses in an economic downswing (upswing). Furthermore, the share of public investment in GDP as an indicator for the growth orientation of fiscal policies is considered.

Finally, Hein and Martschin (2021) also consider the open economy conditions, since they will have an impact on the effectiveness of domestic macroeconomic policies, on the one hand, and will also directly affect the demand and growth regime, on the other. They look at the degree of openness measured by export and import shares of GDP, and the development of price competitiveness, measured by real effective exchange rates. To take into account non-price competitiveness, the Observatory of Economic Complexity index (OEC 2020) is considered.

We briefly summarise Hein and Martschin's (2021) main findings for each country (Table 7.2). Spain's macroeconomic policy regime in the period 2001–2009 has contributed to the emergence of the DLPD regime in this period. The extremely low real interest rates and easy access to credit stimulated deficit-financed corporate investment and private household real-estate investment and consumption, the latter in the face of falling wage shares. Fiscal policy followed a more counter-cyclical stance on average and high public investment-GDP ratios supported private investment through crowding-in effects. As a result of these developments, large private-sector deficits occurred and private consumption and investment became the main drivers of growth, while housing and asset price bubbles swelled. The downside of this trend was Spain's loss of international price competitiveness. Combined with low non-price competitiveness and the economy's comparatively high growth rates, this led to negative growth contributions of net exports and a worsening current account.

The strong shift in Spain's macroeconomic policy regime over the second period has contributed to the shift of the demand and growth regime towards ELM. After the financial crisis, Spanish households and corporations had to reduce financial liabilities and deleveraged heavily. Tightening credit standards, rising real long-term interest rates and falling labour income shares dampened private domestic demand in the wage-led Spanish economy. Pro-cyclical fiscal austerity measures when the Eurozone crisis started squeezed domestic demand further. Net exports, and in particular exports, thus became the only growth driver, benefiting from the improved international price competitiveness caused by wage moderation and higher growth in foreign economies, while non-price-competitiveness remained low.

The macroeconomic policy regime of Germany also contributed considerably to its ELM demand and growth regime in the period 2001–2009. A restrictive monetary policy stance, pro-cyclical restrictive fiscal policies and weak public investment constrained domestic demand, which was further curbed by deflationary wage policies leading to decreasing labour income shares in a wage-led economy. Depressed domestic demand, together with improved international price competitiveness and, in particular, high non-price competitiveness, left growth being exclusively driven by external demand. This resulted in current account surpluses and external sector deficits associated with this ELM regime, generating only mediocre growth in international comparison.

The gradual change in the German macroeconomic policy regime in the second period had an impact on the demand and growth regime, without changing its ELM nature. However, the ELM regime became less extreme. The shift to expansionary monetary conditions as well as a rise in the labour income share fostered private investment and consumption demand, making them the main drivers of Germany's more favourable growth performance over the second period. Growth contributions of net exports declined but remained positive, so that export and current account surpluses continued to rise. Relatively dynamic private domestic and foreign demand allowed for fiscal consolidation as reflected by decreasing public-sector deficits. This was reinforced by the introduction of the 'debt brake' that limited federal budget expenditures (Detzer and Hein 2016). Therefore, although changes within the

Table 7.2 *Macroeconomic policy regimes and demand and growth regimes in Spain, Germany, France and Italy for the periods 2001–2009 and 2010–2019*

	Spain		**Germany**		**France**		**Italy**	
	2001–2009	**2010–2019**	**2001–2009**	**2010–2019**	**2001–2009**	**2010–2019**	**2001–2009**	**2010–2019**
Monetary policy stance	+	–	–	+	–	+	–	–
Wage policy stance	–	–	–	+	+/–	–/+	–	–/+
Fiscal policy stance	+	–	+/–	–	+	–/+	–	–
Open economy conditions	–	+	0/+	0/+	–/0	0	–/0	0
Demand and growth regime	Debt-led private demand boom	Export-led mercantilist	Export-led mercantilist	Export-led mercantilist	Domestic demand-led	Domestic demand-led	Domestic demand-led	Export-led mercantilist

Note: +: expansionary stance; –: contractionary stance; 0: neutral stance. *Monetary policy*: +: negative real long-term interest rate-real GDP growth differential; –: positive real long-term interest rate-real GDP growth differential. *Wage policy*: +: nominal unit labour cost growth close to ECB inflation target and rising labour income share; –: nominal unit labour cost growth far away from ECB inflation target and falling labour income share; –/+: nominal unit labour cost growth far away from ECB inflation target and rising labour income share; +/–: nominal unit labour cost close to ECB inflation target and falling labour income share. *Fiscal policy*: +: counter-cyclical in many years, high public investment-GDP ratio; –: pro-cyclical in many years, low public investment-GDP ratio; +/–: counter-cyclical in many years, low public investment-GDP ratio; –/+: pro-cyclical in many years, high public investment-GDP ratio. *Open economy conditions*: +: real depreciation; –: real appreciation, with low non-price competitiveness (complexity index); –/0: real appreciation, with intermediate non-price competitiveness (complexity index); 0/+: small real appreciation, with high non-price competitiveness (complexity index); 0: small real depreciation, with intermediate non-price competitiveness (complexity index).
Source: Based on Hein and Martschin (2021, p. 515).

German macroeconomic policy regime towards the stimulation of domestic demand occurred, they were not strong enough to reverse the ELM demand and growth regime.

The macroeconomic policy regime in France provided the grounds for the French DDL regime in the first period. Growth was driven by domestic demand, and mainly by private consumption, as enabled by a roughly stable labour income share in a wage-led economy. Wage policies also contributed to generating inflation at the target rate. Public expenditures contributed positively to growth, too, by an on-average rather counter-cyclical fiscal policy stance and, in particular, high public investment. Consequently, the financial surpluses of the private sector were almost completely absorbed by corresponding public-sector deficits.

The French demand and growth regime was not considerably altered from 2001–2009 to 2010–2019 and remained DDL. The macroeconomic policy regime contributed to this with an on-average expansionary monetary policy stance and a slightly rising labour income share in a wage-led economy, both of which were favourable to private domestic demand. High public investments supported domestic demand whereas pro-cyclical fiscal policies were partly contractionary.

The Italian macroeconomic policy regime in the first period was very restrictive and contributed to a stagnating DDL regime. Demand was exclusively driven by private household consumption which, in the traditional bank-based Italian financial system, did not increase beyond current income levels (Gabbi et al. 2016), and by government consumption. Investment was constrained by low growth expectations and high real interest rates. Price-sensitive Italian exports, with only intermediate non-price competitiveness, suffered from real exchange rate appreciation, leading to falling net exports.

The Italian macroeconomic policy regime remained highly restrictive in the crises and post-crises period and enforced the shift in the demand and growth regime, from stagnant DDL to stagnant ELM. High real long-term interest rates and restrictive monetary conditions, pro-cyclical fiscal policies in two recessions and severe cuts of public investment constrained domestic demand in the face of stagnating household income over the whole period. Together with the improvement of international price competitiveness, this made net exports the only rising component of aggregate demand, leading to export and current account surpluses in this period and making Italy a stagnating ELM economy.

These comparative country case studies show that the macroeconomic policy regime had an important impact on the emerging type of demand and growth regime and the changes in regimes after the 2007–2009 crises. An improvement of economic performance of the Eurozone and a development towards a non-inflationary full employment DDL regime would thus require a shift in the macroeconomic policy regime of the Eurozone member countries – and thus of the Eurozone as a whole – towards the post-Keynesian benchmark outlined in this section. Overcoming internal current account imbalances would also require to improve non-price competitiveness and thus the income elasticities of exports of the Eurozone periphery countries, which requires active industrial and regional policies. Such a policy regime shift would also mean overcoming the severe problems of the Eurozone economic policy institutions and the economic policy model based on the NCM, as pointed out in the introduction of our contribution.

THE RESPONSE TOWARDS THE COVID-19 CRISIS – A SHIFT IN THE EUROZONE/EU MACROECONOMIC POLICY REGIME?

When the Covid-19 pandemic hit in 2020, we saw strong responses of fiscal policies in the EU and the Eurozone. The strict budgetary rules of the Stability and Growth Pact were temporarily suspended and discretionary fiscal expansion of more than 3.5 per cent of EU GDP was implemented at national and EU levels, associated with liquidity guarantees of more than 25 per cent of EU GDP (European Commission 2020a). Together with automatic stabilisers, the overall fiscal support in 2020 amounted to 8 per cent of EU GDP, as compared to only 1.5 per cent in 2009 in the Great Recession (Ferreiro and Serrano 2021). However, discretionary measures were much smaller in those countries that started with high deficits and high debt.[2] With these measures, government deficits in the Eurozone increased to more than 7 per cent of GDP in 2020 and 2021, while the government debt-GDP ratio for the Eurozone exceeded 100 per cent in 2021, with considerable differences among member countries (European Commission 2021a). Furthermore, new assistant schemes, like the EU funding for short-term work schemes, SURE (Support to mitigate Unemployment Risk in an Emergency), were implemented (European Commission 2021b) and existing institutions were targeted towards fighting the crisis, like the European Stability Mechanism pandemic crisis support and the European Investment Bank financing for business (European Commission 2020b).

Most importantly, however, with the Next Generation EU (NGEU) programme, for the first time, the EU decided to issue debt. The NGEU is a €806.9 billion temporary recovery instrument (European Commission 2021a). The major part is the Recovery and Resilience Facility, in the context of which the European Commission issues debt to help member states implement reforms and investments that are in line with the EU's priorities. The allocation of funds is not according to the size of member countries but focus on their needs. The Recovery and Resilience Facility makes available €723.8 billion to member states, with €385.8 billion as loans and €338 billion as grants. Over a period of seven years (2021–2027) this amounts to 0.8 per cent of EU GDP per year. The target of this programme is to contribute to climate neutrality by 2050 and to the digital transition of the EU member states. Repayment of debt issued by the European Commission is envisioned from future EU budgets or by the member states concerned, by 2058 at the latest. With the NGEU programme, the Multiannual Financial Framework 2021–2027 is increased from €1.211 trillion to €2.018 trillion, which means that the annual EU budget rises to roughly 1.9 per cent of annual EU GDP – still not very impressive. However, the focus of the budget will shift away from common agricultural policies, which will shrink from 60 per cent of the budget in the early 1990s to 30 per cent, and move towards the new priorities with respect to climate change and digitalisation, covering another 30 per cent of the budget, and the economic, social and territorial cohesion funds with also roughly 30 per cent.

Expansionary fiscal policies have been supported by ECB monetary policies. The ECB kept its interest rates at the historically low levels of −0.5 per cent for the deposit facility, zero per cent for the main refinancing rate and 0.25 per cent for the marginal lending facility. Only as a response towards rising inflation rates in 2022 did the ECB start to raise rates. As a response to the Covid 19 Crisis, the ECB Council on 30 April 2020 (ECB 2020) created new Pandemic Emergency Longer-Term Refinancing Operations, with collateral easing measures and interest rates 25 basis points below the average rate applied in the Eurosystem's main refinancing operations, in order to subsidise banks. Interest rates on all targeted longer-term refinancing operations were also reduced by 25 basis points to −0.5 per cent from June 2020 to June 2021. Furthermore, unconventional monetary policies were extended by the introduction of a Pandemic Emergency Purchase Programme, with a volume of €1.85 trillion, while the asset purchase programmes already in existence were continued.

Furthermore, in July 2021, the ECB revised its monetary policy strategy (ECB 2021). Apart from including owner-occupied housing costs in the calculation of the harmonised index of consumer prices, the ECB announced that it considers the 2 per cent inflation target in the medium term to be a symmetric target. It was also clarified that the effective lower bound for the interest rate may require inflation above target for a certain period of time. The medium-term orientation of monetary policies was thus underlined. It was confirmed that the main instruments of the ECB are the policy interest rates, complemented by forward guidance, asset purchases and long-term refinancing operations, and that inflation risks are assessed based on economic and monetary/financial analysis, as already announced in its revision of the monetary policy strategy in 2003. Furthermore, the ECB announced its support of the EU's climate goals in the context of its monetary policy, making use of risk assessments, corporate-sector asset purchases and collateral policies.

In the area of wage or income policies, the European Council's (2022) new minimum wage directive may indicate a change in the attitude towards wage policies of the EU institutions (Müller and Schulten 2022). While in the past the focus had been on the deregulation of the labour market, reduction of minimum wages and on activation policies, in order to bring down the non-accelerating inflation rate of unemployment (NAIRU) in the EU, in line with the NCM, the new directive aims at strengthening collective bargaining and trade union power. Minimum wage policies in member countries should be focussed on enabling workers a decent standard of living, fighting in-work poverty and reducing wage inequality. Minimum wages should thus target 60 per cent of the gross median wage and 50 per cent of the gross average wage. The directive also stresses the importance of collective bargaining in ensuring adequate minimum wages. This could be a first step towards improving wage bargaining coordination within the EU and Eurozone – as a precondition for wage policies to come up to its stabilising role indicated in the previous section.

Summing up, in the Covid-19 crisis we have seen important changes in the stances of EU and Eurozone macroeconomic policies. Monetary policies of the ECB have been expansionary, new unconventional programmes have kept long-term interest low and the ECB has changed its monetary policy strategy towards medium-term symmetric inflation targeting. However, the ECB has not included low long-term interest into its targets and does not yet unconditionally guarantee the public debt of Eurozone member countries. Fiscal policy responses towards the crisis have been very expansionary, both at national and European levels. For the first time, common debt has been introduced at the EU level, and the EU budget has almost doubled. However, the share of this budget in EU GDP is still very low, common debt is meant to be temporary and debt repayment is envisaged in the long run. Currently, the EU is reviewing its economic governance structure. While a full return to the tight fiscal rules of the Stability and Growth Pact will be unlikely, permanent leeway at the national level to apply functional finance-type fiscal policies seems to be even more unlikely. This is the implication from the recent suggestions of the European Commission (2022b) for a reform of the EU economic governance framework. On the one hand, fiscal policy coordination should get a more medium-run orientation, focussing in particular on government non-cyclical expenditure paths, the focus on balanced or in-surplus structural government budget balances is abandoned and the policy priority is shifted towards public investment. On the other hand, however, the 3 per cent ceiling for the member countries' government deficit-GDP ratios and the 60 per cent maximum government debt-GDP ratios remain intact, debt reduction is thus still given priority and the endogeneity of GDP growth with respect to government expenditures remains ignored.

The increase in the EU budget has been associated with a shift in priorities towards climate change and digitalisation, and together with the cohesion funds this is now more than 60 per cent of the EU budget. Whether this is sufficient to improve non-price competitiveness of the catching-up member countries and to avoid future current account imbalances within the Eurozone must be doubted, given the small share of the EU budget in EU GDP. Wage and income policies and wage-bargaining coordination have not seen any significant improvements in the course of the Covid-19 crisis, but the European Council's minimum wage directive may indicate a future change in attitude towards wage policies.

CONCLUSIONS

In order to assess the macroeconomic policy responses towards the Covid-19 crisis in the Eurozone, we first reviewed the shift in Eurozone demand and growth regimes after the Eurozone crisis and linked these with the macroeconomic policy regime. For this purpose, we used a post-Keynesian macroeconomic policy mix as the benchmark for generating, or at least contributing to, a non-inflationary full employment DDL regime. We have shown that the macroeconomic policy regimes in the big four member countries, France, Germany, Italy and Spain, have contributed considerably to the ELM demand and growth regime of the Eurozone as a whole. Against this background, we have reviewed the EU policy responses towards the Covid-19 crisis in order to assess whether the previously dominating policy regime based on the NCM and generating an ELM demand and growth regime in the Eurozone has been overcome, whether the fundamental problems of Eurozone macroeconomic policy making have been tackled and whether the now prevailing policies have come closer to the policy regime advocated by post-Keynesians.

We have shown that the Covid-19 crisis has triggered a further move away from the NCM economic policy mix in the Eurozone.[3] However, the changes still seem to be insufficient to overcome the structural problems of the Eurozone, the lack of policies to prevent regional imbalances, the lack of sufficient fiscal policy space to deal with deep recessions and long-run aggregate demand failures and the lack of an unconditional lender of last resort for member state governments. Furthermore, the changes so far have been insufficient to change the Eurozone demand and growth regime, which seems to remain ELM for the near future (European Commission 2021c, p. 34) – and thus remains a major burden for global economic stability.

NOTES

1. This section draws on Hein and Martschin (2020, 2021).
2. See Ferreiro and Serrano (2021) for an evaluation, and Canelli et al. (2021) with more detailed studies on Italy and Nikiforos (2022) on Greece.
3. See Dullien (2022) for a review of Eurozone institutional reforms after the Global Financial Crisis, the Great Recession and the Eurozone Crisis.

REFERENCES

Akcay, Ü., Hein, E. and Jungmann, B. (2022), 'Financialisation and macroeconomic regimes in emerging capitalist economies before and after the Great Recession', *International Journal of Political Economy*, 51(2), 77–100.

Arestis, P. (2013), 'Economic theory and policy: A coherent post-Keynesian approach', *European Journal of Economics and Economic Policies: Intervention*, 10(2), 243–255.

Canelli, R., Fontana, G., Realfonzo, R. and Veronese Passarella, M. (2021), 'Are EU policies effective to tackle the Covid-19 crisis? The case of Italy', *Review of Political Economy*, 33(3), 432–461.

De Grauwe, P. (2012), 'The governance of a fragile Eurozone', *Australian Economic Review*, 45(3), 255–268.

Detzer, D. and Hein, E. (2016), 'Financialisation and the crises in the export-led mercantilist German economy', in E. Hein, D. Detzer and N. Dodig (eds), *Financialisation and the Financial and Economic Crises: Country Studies*, Cheltenham, UK and Northampton, MA, USA: Edward Elgar Publishing.

Dodig, N., Hein, E. and Detzer, D. (2016), 'Financialisation and the financial and economic crises: Theoretical framework and empirical analysis for 15 countries', in E. Hein, D. Detzer and N. Dodig (eds), *Financialisation and the Financial and Economic Crises: Country Studies*, Cheltenham, UK and Northampton, MA, USA: Edward Elgar Publishing.

Dullien, S. (2022), 'Ten years on, two crises later: Evaluating EMU institutional reforms since 2010', *International Journal of Political Economy*, 51(1), 5–17.

Dünhaupt, P. and Hein, E. (2019), 'Financialisation, distribution, and macroeconomic regimes before and after the crisis: A post-Keynesian view on Denmark, Estonia, and Latvia', *Journal of Baltic Studies*, 50(4), 435–465.

ECB (European Central Bank) (2020), 'Monetary policy decisions', Press release, 30 April, www.ecb.europa.eu/press/pr/date/2020/html/ecb.mp200430~1eaa128265.en.html

ECB (European Central Bank) (2021), 'The ECB's monetary policy strategy statement', 8 July, www.ecb.europa.eu/home/search/review/pdf/ecb.strategyreview_monpol_strategy_statement.en.pdf

European Commission (2020a), 'European economic forecast, spring 2020', Brussels: European Commission, https://ec.europa.eu/info/business-economy-euro/economic-performance-and-forecasts/economic-forecasts/spring-2020-economic-forecast-deep-and-uneven-recession-uncertain-recovery_en

European Commission (2020b), 'Jobs and economy during the Coronavirus pandemic', Brussels: European Commission, https://ec.europa.eu/info/live-work-travel-eu/health/coronavirus-response/jobs-and-economy-during-coronavirus-pandemic_en

European Commission (2021a), 'Recovering from the Coronavirus', https://ec.europa.eu/info/business-economy-euro/recovery-coronavirus_en

European Commission (2021b), 'The European instrument for temporary Support to mitigate Unemployment Risks in an Emergency (SURE)', Brussels: European Commission, https://ec.europa.eu/info/business-economy-euro/economic-and-fiscal-policy-coordination/financial-assistance-eu/funding-mechanisms-and-facilities/sure_en

European Commission (2021c), 'European economic forecast, autumn', Brussels: European Commission.

European Commission (2022a), 'Annual macro-economic database', Brussel: European Commission, https://economy-finance.ec.europa.eu/economic-research-and-databases/economic-databases/ameco-database_en

European Commission (2022b), 'Communication on orientations for a reform of the EU economic governance framework', Brussels, 9 November, COM(2022) 583 final.

European Council (2022), 'Adequate minimum wages in the EU', Brussels: European Council, www.consilium.europa.eu/en/policies/adequate-minimum-wages/

Ferreiro, J. and Serrano, F. (2021), 'The Covid health crisis and the fiscal and monetary policies in the Euro Area', *International Journal of Political Economy*, 50(3), 212–225.

Fritsche, U., Heine, M., Herr, H., Horn, G. and Kaiser, C. (2005), 'Macroeconomic regime and economic development: The case of the USA', in E. Hein, T. Niechoj, T. Schulten and A. Truger (eds), *Macroeconomic Policy Coordination in Europe and the Role of the Trade Unions*, Brussels: ETUI.

Gabbi, G., Ticci, E. and Vozzella, P. (2016), 'The transmission channels between the financial and the real sectors in Italy and the crisis', in E. Hein, D. Detzer and N. Dodig (eds), *Financialisation and the Financial and Economic Crises: Country Studies*, Cheltenham, UK and Northampton, MA, USA: Edward Elgar Publishing.

Gordon, R. J. (2015), 'Secular stagnation: A supply side view', *American Economic Review: Papers and Proceedings*, 105(5), 54–59.

Heimberger, P. and Kapeller, J. (2017), 'The performativity of potential output: Pro-cyclicality and path dependency in coordinating European fiscal policies', *Review of International Political Economy*, 24(5), 904–928.

Hein, E. (2012), *The Macroeconomics of Finance-Dominated Capitalism – and Its Crisis*, Cheltenham, UK and Northampton, MA, USA: Edward Elgar Publishing.

Hein, E. (2013/2014), 'The crisis of finance-dominated capitalism in the euro area, deficiencies in the economic policy architecture and deflationary stagnation policies', *Journal of Post Keynesian Economics*, 36(2), 325–354.

Hein, E. (2014), *Distribution and Growth after Keynes: A Post-Keynesian Guide*, Cheltenham, UK and Northampton, MA, USA: Edward Elgar Publishing.

Hein, E. (2016), 'Secular stagnation or stagnation policy? Steindl after Summers', *PSL Quarterly Review*, 69(276), 3–47.

Hein, E. (2018), 'Stagnation policy in the Eurozone and economic policy alternatives: A Steindlian/neo-Kaleckian perspective', *Wirtschaft und Gesellschaft*, 44(3), 315–348.

Hein, E. (2019), 'Financialisation and tendencies towards stagnation: The role of macroeconomic regime changes in the course of and after the financial and economic crisis 2007–9', *Cambridge Journal of Economics*, 43(4), 975–999.

Hein, E. (2023), *Macroeconomics after Kalecki and Keynes: Post-Keynesian Foundation*, Cheltenham, UK and Northampton, MA, USA: Edward Elgar Publishing.

Hein, E. and Martschin, J. (2020), 'The Eurozone in crisis: A Kaleckian macroeconomic regime and policy perspective', *Review of Political Economy*, 32(4), 563–588.

Hein, E. and Martschin, J. (2021), 'Demand and growth regimes in finance-dominated capitalism and the role of the macroeconomic policy regime: A post-Keynesian comparative study on France, Germany, Italy and Spain before and after the Great Financial Crisis and the Great Recession', *Review of Evolutionary Political Economy*, 2(3), 493–527.

Hein, E. and Stockhammer, E. (2010), 'Macroeconomic policy mix, employment and inflation in a post-Keynesian alternative to the New Consensus model', *Review of Political Economy*, 22(3), 317–354.

Hein, E. and Truger, A. (2005), 'What ever happened to Germany? Is the decline of the former European key currency country caused by structural sclerosis or by macroeconomic mismanagement?', *International Review of Applied Economics*, 19(1), 3–28.

Hein, E. and Truger, A. (2009), 'How to fight (or not to fight) a slowdown', *Challenge*, 52(2), 52–75.

Hein, E., Paternesi Meloni, W. and Tridico, P. (2021), 'Welfare models and demand-led growth regimes before and after the financial and economic crisis', *Review of International Political Economy*, 28(5), 1196–1223.

Herr, H. and Kazandziska, M. (2011), *Macroeconomic Policy Regimes in Western Industrial countries*, London: Routledge.

Müller, T. and Schulten, T. (2022), 'Minimum-wages directive: History in the making', *Social Europe*, 1 July, https://socialeurope.eu/minimum-wages-directive-history-in-the-making

Nikiforos, M. (2022), 'Crisis, austerity, and fiscal expenditure in Greece: Recent experience and future prospects in the post-Covid-19 era', *European Journal of Economics and Economic Policies: Intervention*, 19(2), 186–203.

OEC (2020), Observatory of Economic Complexity index, https://oec.world/en

Onaran, Ö. and Obst, T. (2016), 'Wage-led growth in the EU15 member-states: The effects of income distribution on growth, investment, trade balance and inflation', *Cambridge Journal of Economics*, 40(6), 1517–1551.

Summers, L. A. (2014), 'US economic prospects: Secular stagnation, hysteresis, and the zero lower bound', *Business Economics*, 49(2), 65–73.

Summers, L. A. (2015), 'Demand side secular stagnation', *American Economic Review: Papers and Proceedings*, 105(5), 60–65.

8. Phillips curves, behavioral economics and post-Keynesian macroeconomics

Peter Skott

INTRODUCTION

Having noted the limited impact of behavioral economics on the post-Keynesian literature, Jefferson and King (2010–2011) identify two obstacles to engagement between post-Keynesians and behavioral economics: a tendency among some post-Keynesians to "rely excessively on key authorities, such as Keynes and Kalecki, and on established texts" and, more importantly, "the close association between some forms of behavioral economics and mainstream analysis," including an emphasis on constrained optimization (p. 229). Thus, from a post-Keynesian perspective, the interesting strands of behavioral economics are to be found mainly in the "old behavioral economics" which is seen as less focused on optimization. But even this school, they argue, may not have adequately "recognized or prioritized uncertainty" in its analysis (p. 230). Overall, they suggest, there is "scope for successful engagement between behavioral and Post Keynesian economics if it is based on explicitly stated common ground, defined in terms of methodology" (p. 211).

These reservations with respect to behavioral economics and its relevance for post-Keynesian economics appear to be widespread. They are echoed, for instance, in Lavoie's highly acclaimed text on post-Keynesian economics (Lavoie 2014), which discusses microeconomic behavior in some detail. Like Jefferson and King, Lavoie emphasizes methodological differences between post-Keynesians and behavioral economists, faulting "new behavioral economics" for its failure to "go beyond the cognitive illusions view" and for merely documenting systematic deviations from an insane standard of perfect rationality (p. 86).[1] He notes that many behavioral economists see their findings as relatively minor refinements of orthodox theory, but points to greater affinity between post-Keynesians and "old behavioral economics," as exemplified by Herbert Simon.

It is undoubtedly correct that many contributors to behavioral economics view their work as providing refinements to traditional models of optimization.

Moreover, the use that has been made so far of behavioral economics in macroeconomic theory has been disappointing, often amounting to the addition of a few behavioral elements to models that are otherwise quite orthodox. The obvious example is dynamic stochastic general equilibrium models, where behavioral elements have been introduced to overcome striking empirical failures. The introduction of habit formation and "hand-to-mouth" households, for instance, have been used to improve the fit of the consumption part of the models while retaining the centrality of optimizing representative agents.

One may also have reservations with respect to the (rather limited) literature on behavioral macroeconomics that attempts a more drastic break with orthodoxy. But these reservations, I shall argue, do not render irrelevant the findings of behavioral economics for attempts to develop convincing alternatives to the prevailing orthodoxy. Nor does the importance of behavioral findings depend on whether behavioral economists themselves claim adherence to mainstream or post-Keynesian paradigms (or as may sometimes be the case, feel agnostic about the broader implications of their findings).

All macroeconomic models contain relations that describe the aggregate outcomes of the behavior of numerous decision makers. The decisions are made within a structural and institutional setting, but it would be a serious mistake to ignore evidence about systematic behavioral patterns at the microeconomic level. The findings of behavioral economics can and should be used to mount a strong critique of mainstream theories but also, more importantly, as inputs in the further development and strengthening of post-Keynesian theory.

This chapter uses wage formation as the main example to illustrate the argument. The chapter begins by outlining the dominant post-Keynesian positions on wage setting and inflation before turning to behavioral contributions that complement and, in some cases, question these positions. It then discusses post-Keynesian uses of old behavioral economics. The final section offers a few concluding comments.

INFLATION AND PHILLIPS CURVES

Post-Keynesian Positions

Distributional conflict is the recurrent theme in post-Keynesian writings on inflation. Workers have wage targets, while firms have profit targets that translate into implied targets for real wages. If the targets are mutually inconsistent, the result is inflation: workers demand and get nominal wage increases, and firms respond by raising prices. Post-Keynesian texts, including Hein (2014), Lavoie (2014) and Blecker and Setterfield (2019), present variations of this model.

Simple versions of the model treat the targets as exogenous and, abstracting from technical change and assuming constant labor productivity, equations (8.1)–(8.2) represent a typical specification of wage and price inflation:

$$\hat{w} = \alpha(\omega_w - \omega) \tag{8.1}$$

$$\pi = \hat{p} = \beta(\omega - \omega_f) \tag{8.2}$$

where ω, ω_w and ω_f denote the actual real wage and workers' and firms' target real wage, respectively; w, p and π are the money wage, price and rate of price inflation and a "hat" over a variable denotes proportional growth rate.

Equations (8.1)–(8.2) imply that the real wage follows a differential equation,

$$\hat{\omega} = \hat{w} - \pi = \alpha\left(\omega_w - \omega\right) - \beta\left(\omega - \omega_f\right) = \alpha\omega_w + \beta\omega_f - \left(\alpha + \beta\right)\omega$$

This dynamic equation for the real wage has a unique, stable stationary solution,

$$\omega \rightarrow \omega^* = \frac{\alpha\omega_w + \beta\omega_f}{\alpha + \beta} \tag{8.3}$$

Substituting this solution into equation (8.2), the inflation rate also converges to a stationary value:

$$\pi \rightarrow \pi^* = \frac{\alpha\beta}{\alpha + \beta}(\omega_w - \omega_f) \tag{8.4}$$

Long-run inflation is the consequence of distributional conflict, with the inflation rate determined by the difference between the two wage targets (a difference often referred to as the aspiration gap).

The model can be modified by introducing a constant rate of labor-saving technical change. Specifying targets in terms of the share (rather than the wage rate), this version generates convergence to a stationary solution for the wage share.

Another straightforward extension of the basic model allows a dependence of the wage targets on current conditions in the labor and goods market. Thus, it seems likely that workers' target will be increasing in the employment rate, while firms' target may depend on the utilization rate of capital. If employment and utilization evolve endogenously over time, the dynamics of the system can become complicated. But stationary solutions still satisfy equations

(8.3)–(8.4), the only difference being that the two targets now depend on the stationary values of employment and utilization.

Conflicting claims – modeled as wage-setting and price-setting equations along the lines of (8.1)–(8.2) – are perfectly consistent with mainstream macroeconomics. Indeed, Blanchard's (2021) text on intermediate macroeconomics uses this framework in its analysis of inflation and Phillips curves, focusing on the limiting case where firms achieve their target (corresponding to $\beta \rightarrow \infty$). Crucially, however, Blanchard adds inflation expectations as an influence on wage formation; from the perspective of mainstream theory, expected price inflation influence wage inflation, while expected wage inflation may influence price inflation. Formally,

$$\widehat{w} = \alpha_0(\omega_w - \omega) + \alpha_1 \pi^e \tag{8.5}$$

$$\pi = \beta_0(\omega - \omega_f) + \beta_1 \widehat{w}^e \tag{8.6}$$

The equations have been cast here in terms of inflation expectations, but the analysis and conclusions are unchanged if it is "experienced inflation" or formal indexation rather than expected inflation that enters the equations.

Post-Keynesian models have considered this extension with the conditions that $\alpha_1 \leq 1, \beta_1 \leq 1$ and $\alpha_1 \beta_1 < 1$. These parameter restrictions ensure that the model still produces a finite stationary inflation rate, even when the aspiration gap is positive (when workers' target wage exceeds firms' target):

$$\omega^* = \frac{\alpha_0(1-\beta_1)}{\alpha_0(1-\beta_1)+\beta_0(1-\alpha_1)}\omega_w + \frac{\beta_0(1-\alpha_1)}{\alpha_0(1-\beta_1)+\beta_0(1-\alpha_1)}\omega_f \tag{8.7}$$

$$\pi^* = \frac{\alpha_0\beta_0}{\alpha_0(1-\beta_1)+\beta_0(1-\alpha_1)}(\omega_w - \omega_f) \tag{8.8}$$

If $\alpha_1 = \beta_1 = 1$ and $\omega_w > \omega_f$, however, there are no stationary solutions: the numerator on the right-hand side of equation (8.8) is positive, while the denominator equals 0. Putting it differently, if workers' wage target is an increasing function of the employment rate and firms' target is constant, the model produces a "natural rate of unemployment."[2] The employment rate, which influences workers' wage target, has to adjust so as to eliminate the aspiration gap. The post-Keynesian parameter restrictions exclude this mainstream implication of the model.

Some post-Keynesian models go further, imposing conditions on the shape of the relation between the employment rate of workers' wage target. Thus, it is often assumed that the function describing workers' target real wage has a flat segment

$$\omega_w = f(e) \;; f' = 0 \text{ for } e_1 < e < e_2 \;; \quad f'(e) > e \text{ for } 0 < e_1 \text{ or } e > e_2$$

If firms' target is constant, this restriction on the relation between employment and wage targets implies that the price Phillips curve will also have a flat segment: variations in employment between e_1 and e_2 leave the inflation rate unchanged. In support of a flat segment, it is argued that coordinated wage bargaining makes workers' target wage rate insensitive to variations in the employment, while constant markups and labor productivity ensure that there will be no pressure on prices from variations in utilization rates within a wide interval.[3]

Most post-Keynesian discussions of inflation and Phillips curves, finally, include broader comments and observations: labor market institutions and norms of fairness are seen as having a strong influence on wage targets, and the degree of distributional conflict and aspiration gap may be path dependent. Lavoie's analysis of inflation, for instance, concludes by the summary statement: "In the post-Keynesian view of inflation, price inflation is explained mainly by historical and cultural features, tied to the size and strength of the aspiration gap, which itself may have been affected by the past evolution of aggregate demand" (Lavoie 2014, p. 573).

Behavioral Economics, Wage Setting and Fairness Norms

George Akerlof has addressed the implications of a behavioral approach for several macroeconomically important issues, including wage setting and unemployment. His analysis has mainly focused on wage norms and the observation that workers react to wages that are seen as unfair. If workers are unionized, the obvious reaction – demanding an increase – may be backed by threats of collective action, including strikes or work-to-rule campaigns. Non-unionized workers do not have the same options, but unfair treatment still has consequences for the firm; increased labor turnover can raise hiring and training costs, while lower levels of effort can reduce productivity and affect the quality of output.[4]

Akerlof and Yellen (1990) formalized this argument and also provided evidence from different fields, including psychology, sociology and personnel management, in support of the underlying mechanism. Their formal model shows that if firms have to pay fair wages, the result can be unemployment. The mathematical model, however, was essentially like any other efficiency wage model of unemployment. If wages influence effort, labor market equilibrium may be associated with unemployment: there are unemployed, qualified workers who would want to work at the prevailing wage.[5]

Post-Keynesians could point out, correctly, that although fairness-based unemployment is involuntary from the perspective of individual workers, it has nothing to do with aggregate demand deficiencies and Keynesian involuntary unemployment. They can also object that wages are set in nominal terms and that expected price inflation may affect wage inflation less than one-for-one. Furthermore, neither the importance of fairness in wage setting nor the role of relative-wage norms is new. In the General Theory, Keynes identified relative-wage concerns as a source of nominal wage stickiness (a stickiness that should be welcomed because without it the economic system was likely to become violently unstable), and post-Keynesians have themselves discussed fairness as an important factor in wage determination.

These objections have merit, but Keynes's narrow and sketchy discussion of how relative-wage concerns can lead to nominal-wage stickiness clearly does not exhaust the issue. It also leaves unanswered questions. What is so special about a fall in nominal wages? If workers were to expect a 10 percent rise in the general wage level, it would seem that a relative-wage concern should lead them to reject wage offers below 10 percent; there would be stickiness of nominal wage inflation, not nominal wages. The behavioral literature, moreover, suggests that although Keynes was right about the negative effects of wage cuts on worker morale and productivity, the main source of stickiness may be slightly different. In a survey of business people, labor leaders, business consultants and counselors of unemployed people, Bewley (1998) finds that workers' own previous money wage represents an important reference point for perceived fairness, with cuts in money wages therefore having adverse effects on morale and productivity.

Bewley's finding is supported by other behavioral evidence. Citing research from cognitive psychology, Shafir et al. (1997) report that when evaluating options, decision makers often entertain multiple representations contemporaneously and that framing effects (the choice of representation) can affect the decision. When this happens, decisions reflect a mixture of the assessments associated with the different representations, the relative salience of the representations determining their weights in this mixture. Applying these findings of framing effects and multiple representations to economics, decision makers, they argue, are influenced by both nominal and real variables. Nominal assessments, which are much simpler, become more salient and are weighted more heavily when inflation is low; high inflation rates, conversely, tilt decision makers toward real assessments.

A behavioral explanation of nominal wage stickiness follows if this perspective is combined with the well-documented presence of loss aversion (people perceiving losses relative to a reference point as more severe than equivalent gains relative to the reference point).[6] Akerlof et al. (1996) show how downward money wage stickiness (not surprisingly) generates a downward-sloping long-run Phillips curve. More surprising, perhaps, the behavioral findings can lead to more complex outcomes.

Nominal representations are salient when inflation is low but lose salience when inflation rates are high. One would therefore expect nominal representations to dominate wage setting when inflation is low, while real representations dominate for high inflation. The shift in relative salience of the two representations implies that the long-run Phillips curve may be neither vertical (as suggested by the natural rate hypothesis) nor monotonically downward sloping (as suggested by Akerlof et al. 1996).

His terminology was different, but Rowthorn (1977) anticipated this more complicated outcome. There may be an inflation threshold, he argued, above which wage setters rely on real representations; below the threshold, by contrast, they ignore inflation. As a result, the long-run Phillips curve may have a vertical segment at a "natural unemployment rate" at which inflation can take any value above the threshold. For inflation rates below the threshold, by contrast, the curve becomes downward sloping, with a minimum sustainable unemployment rate that is below the natural rate (see Figure 8.1).[7]

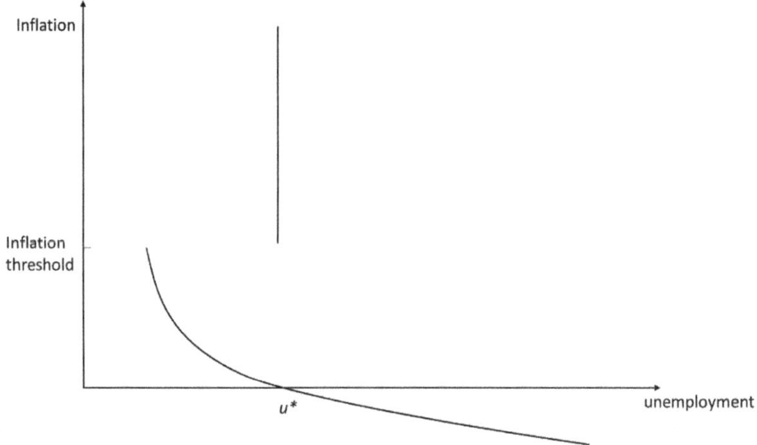

Figure 8.1 *Long-run Phillips curve in the Rowthorn model*

Moving beyond the question of wage stickiness, the role of fairness norms in wage setting invites other observations. Although predetermined in the short run, norms evolve over time. Persistent violations of a norm gradually undermine its power, while an outcome that has been sustained for prolonged periods can gain the status of a social norm. In the words of Hicks (1975, p. 65), if a system of wages is well established, it "has the sanction of custom. It then becomes what is expected; and (admittedly on a low level of fairness) what is expected is fair." Other economists have made similar comments about dependent wage norms, but it is reassuring to see these insights confirmed by more systematic findings in the psychological and behavioral literature (e.g. Kahneman et al. 1986).

As a simple formalization, assume that workers' target real wage is linear in the employment rate

$$\omega_w = a + be \tag{8.9}$$

The gradual adjustment of norms towards outcomes can be captured in a simple way by letting the term a change in response to deviations of actual from fair wages,

$$\dot{a} = \mu(\omega - \omega_w) \tag{8.10}$$

The dynamics of the nominal wage are still given by equation (what infl1) and, for simplicity, inflation expectations are adaptive,

$$\dot{\pi}^e = \lambda(\pi - \pi^e) \tag{8.11}$$

Keeping it simple, the markup is taken to be constant, and the real wage equals firms' target:

$$\omega = \omega_f = \bar{\omega}_f \tag{8.12}$$

Hence,

$$\pi = \hat{w} \tag{8.13}$$

Using equations (8.5) and (8.9)–(8.13), we have

$$\dot{a} = \mu\left(\omega_f - a - be\right) \tag{8.14}$$

$$\dot{\pi}^e = \lambda\left(1 - \alpha_1\right)\pi^e + \lambda\alpha_0\left(a + be - \omega_f\right) \tag{8.15}$$

In the "post-Keynesian case" with $\alpha_1 < 1$, the dynamic system (8.14)–(8.15) has a unique, stable stationary solution for any given value of the employment rate:

$$a^* = w_f - be \tag{8.16}$$

$$\pi^* = \pi^{e*} = 0 \tag{8.17}$$

Equation (8.17) shows that in this version of the conflicting claims theory, the long-run Phillips curve becomes horizontal, and not only that: the inflation rate converges to 0 for any rate of employment.

Matters are qualitatively different if $\alpha_1 = 1$. Equation (8.14) is unaffected, but equation (8.15) simplifies, and the change in expected inflation becomes proportional to the change in workers' wage aspirations as described by the value of a. Formally, using equations (8.5), (8.9)–(8.11) and (8.14), we have

$$\pi^e = \lambda \alpha_0 \left(a + be - \omega_f\right) = -\frac{\lambda \alpha_0}{\mu} \dot{a} \tag{8.18}$$

Both a and π^e now become stationary if $a = \omega_f - be$. The model still produces convergence to a stationary point, and the expression for a^* is unchanged. The stationary value of a depends on the employment rate, and this dependence now carries over to inflation. A change Δe in the employment rate induces a long-run change in a ($\Delta a^* = -b\Delta e$) and, using equation (8.18), it follows that

$$\Delta \pi^* = \Delta \pi^{e*} = -\frac{\lambda \alpha_0}{\mu} \Delta a^* = \frac{\lambda \alpha_0 b}{\mu} \Delta e \tag{8.19}$$

Equation (8.19) produces neither the post-Keynesian result (associated with $\alpha_1 < 1$ and $\mu > 0$) nor a mainstream natural rate of unemployment (associated with $\alpha_1 = 1$ and $\mu = 0$). A permanent increase in aggregate demand and employment raises the long-run inflation rate but by a finite amount. In the absence of stochastic shocks, this particular specification produces a stable, downward-sloping, linear Phillips curve.

Equations (8.14)–(8.15) also imply the presence of inflation hysteresis: a positive shock to the initial values of the state variables a or π^e will have no effect on the stationary solution for a, but the stationary solution for π^e (and therefore also the stationary solution for actual inflation π) will increase. If policy makers pursue a fixed inflation target, the positive shock will be offset by contractionary policy and a decline in the stationary solution for the employment rate; inflation hysteresis will be transformed into employment hysteresis; Skott (2005, 2023, ch. 6) analyzes these issues in greater detail.[8]

DISCUSSION

There are clear similarities between the post-Keynesian view and the behavioral story. In both cases, the story is one of conflicting claims; there is an emphasis on social norms and conventions; the natural rate hypothesis is rejected.

But there are also differences. The post-Keynesian analysis, first, imposes conditions on the pass-through from past to current inflation, rejecting not only propositions of a well-defined natural rate of unemployment, but also ruling out the possibility that the long-run Phillips curve may become vertical at high inflation rates. Is it reasonable to impose these post-Keynesian parameter restrictions on the rate of pass-through? If inflation has been running at 100 percent and is expected to continue doing so, workers will experience significant erosions of their real wage, even if α_1 is close to 1. The behavioral plausibility of imposing $\alpha_1 < 1$ in equation (8.5) becomes questionable, it would seem, at least when inflation rates are high.[9] This intuitive argument finds support in behavioral evidence on multiple representations and the dominance of those that are salient.

Rowthorn's anticipation of this argument could perhaps be seen as an indication that behavioral economics has added nothing new. I think such a conclusion would be incorrect. Rowthorn's paper has become influential primarily because of its focus on distributional conflict as the source of inflation; his suggestions about the influence of inflation on wage setting have received far less attention. Post-Keynesian inclinations have been to reject the presence of vertical segments of the Phillips curve (thereby diminishing the significance of Rowthorn's distinction between states of high and low inflation), while mainstream economists have insisted on the "rationality" of decision makers and the validity of the natural rate hypothesis. Both groups need strong arguments to give up these presumptions, and Rowthorn's brief, intuitive comments had little effect on subsequent post-Keynesian or orthodox expositions. Many hypotheses are hard to dismiss out of hand, and behavioral evidence is essential to decide which ones deserve to be taken seriously. The behavioral findings, it turns out, imply that the Rowthorn hypothesis does have support.[10]

Second, post-Keynesians posit the presence of a range of employment and utilization rates within which inflation remains constant. This conclusion may be attractive – if it holds, demand policy can be used to influence output and employment without having to worry about inflationary effects. But the behavioral plausibility of the assumption is not obvious. Had there been compelling econometric evidence for Phillips curves with a flat segment and positive slopes above and below this segment, one could reasonably use this as a benchmark assumption. This is not the case, however. Some empirical studies of the Phillips curve, including Eisner (2003), have suggested that the shape of the Phillips curve may be concave (rather than convex), and I know of one study that finds a flat segment in estimates of the Phillips curve for the US (Filardo 1998). Most studies, however, find convex wage Phillips curves and linear or convex price Phillips curves. The interwar evidence and the missing disinflation in the aftermath of the financial crisis in 2008 offer striking illustrations of the insensitivity of inflation to variations in unemployment in depressed economies, and examples of strong inflation effects of changes in employment within a normal range are legion.

As indicated above, finally, post-Keynesian discussions of inflation often make reference to conventions and norms of fairness, including suggestions that norms and conventions change endogenously. The above formalization of endogenous adjustments is simple and has intuitive appeal as well as evidence to support the basic mechanism. But it may be too simple, and other intuitive mechanisms can produce very different outcomes. As an example, Skott (2005, 2023, ch. 6) discusses the sensitivity to changes in functional forms, but one can also point to a more fundamental tension within a post-Keynesian conflicting-claims approach to inflation.

Kalecki (1971 [1943]) pointed to the way in which prolonged periods of near full employment can erode discipline in the factories. This cumulative effect of high employment is plausible but has effects that are completely opposite to those associated with the adjustment of norms towards outcomes. Kalecki's argument implies that distributional conflict will intensify gradually if employment is kept high; path-dependent norms and conventions suggest that the initial effect of a rise in employment is to raise the aspiration gap but that distributional conflict gradually subsides as norms adjust. It is easy to set up formal models that include both mechanisms – after all, many models imply that changes in a variable can have several, potentially offsetting effects. One mechanism could be deemed as invariably dominant or the mechanisms may operate with different adjustment speeds; or the question can be left open with a general suggestion that one mechanism may dominate in some historical contexts, the other when circumstances are different.

The point here is not to make claims about the relative weight and importance of the two mechanisms. We shall probably never achieve full and definite answers to that question. But it would be desirable to go beyond general statements about the dependence of the degree of conflict and the rate of inflation on historical, cultural and institutional features.

Howell et al. (2006) have provided an insightful analysis of the misleading claims about the employment-generating virtues of deregulating the labor market. But the absence in their study of clear and definite patterns in the relation between labor market institutions and economic performance does not suggest that institutions are unimportant or that we should not examine the effects of different institutional settings on wage and price setting. Likewise, perfect optimization and rational expectations can be rejected as a description of microeconomic behavior without dismissing the relevance of contemporary insights into microeconomic behavior and the way it deviates systematically from optimization. Behavioral evidence from psychology, sociology and behavioral economics can help identify and untangle macroeconomically relevant behavioral assumptions.

Theory has policy implications, and the issues are important. Post-Keynesians recognize the great damage that has been done by macroeconomic policies based on a belief in the natural rate hypothesis, austerity policy in Europe being a prime example. But, as noted by Rowthorn (1977, p. 229), it appears that many countries were "pushed over the expectations threshold" in the late 1960s and 1970s, "leading to an economic crisis characterised by a combination of high unemployment and fast inflation." Policy based on a belief that aggregate demand can always be expanded without inflationary consequences clearly can also have costly consequences.

OLD BEHAVIORAL THEORY AND POST-KEYNESIAN THEORY

While dismissive of new behavioral economics, post-Keynesians have expressed greater interest in, and affinity with, older strands of behavioral economics. Often, however, the lessons that post-Keynesians draw from this literature stay at a general level. As an example, consider the listing in Lavoie (2014, p. 91) of procedures suggested by Keynes and Simon for decision making under conditions of uncertainty.

The first procedure states that "when a satisfactory solution has been reached, stop searching." Elaborating on this procedure, Lavoie explains that the decision maker "sets aspiration levels that allow him to distinguish between what is acceptable and what is not," thereby avoiding the problem of ranking all possibilities. This is fine, but for the procedure to become operational we need to know what constitutes a satisfactory solution. Presumably, the range of satisfactory outcomes depends on circumstances – the range of satisfactory consumption decisions, for instance, may depend on past, present and expected future income. Without some detail on how the satisfactory range is determined, the procedure tells us very little. Depending on the determination of the range, it may even generate outcomes that are quite similar to those derived from constrained optimization.

The second procedure says "take the present and the recent past as guides for the future." This rule may seem more operational. But when decision makers take the present and recent past as guides, what do they look at? Do wage setters assume that future price levels will be like some average of current and recent price levels, or do they believe that current and recent inflation rates will persist? Or are they perhaps guided by some other simple economic model of the determination of inflation by present and recent variables? These different hypotheses are consistent with the procedure but have radically different implications for wage formation and the Phillips curve.

Similar questions can be asked with respect to all eight procedures on Lavoie's list. The procedures seem plausible but don't tell us much beyond the fact that decision makers do not operate as envisaged by models with perfect optimization and rational expectations. The lack of detail does not invalidate the procedures. In fact, they are presented by Lavoie as describing decision "on a general plane" with specific procedures pertaining to different areas like firms' payback periods for investment and households' routine consumption decisions.

Addressing consumption decisions, Lavoie devotes considerable space to "post-Keynesian theory of consumer choice." The discussion focuses mainly on lexicographic preferences and their implications for the substitutability between goods. Lexicographic preferences are well-defined, complete, reflexive and transitive, and therefore perfectly compatible with mainstream microeconomic theory.[11] More importantly, the specification of preferences over the composition consumption at a point in time says nothing about the macroeconomically important, intertemporal consumption and saving decisions, decisions that new behavioral economics have helped shed light on.

Satisficing, conventions and rules of thumb "reflect the rationality of reasonable agents" and have "microeconomic foundations that are more solid, from a realist point of view, than those of the standard mainstream models" (Lavoie 2014, p. 95). But without the study of decision making by individual agents, how will we ever be able to say anything more precise about the influence of conventions and the determination of the range of satisfactory outcomes? An emphasis on procedural rationality makes the detailed examination of actual behavior even more pressing for post-Keynesians than for economists who assume exogenously given preferences and perfect rationality. To be clear, the need for studies of individual behavior obviously does not deny the crucial importance of structural and institutional forces; studies of individual behavior are necessary but by no means sufficient.

CONCLUSION

Most "new behavioral economists" may see themselves as quite mainstream. But researchers sometimes interpret their own research findings in one way while their readers see them quite differently. A behavioral economist may view behavioral economics as merely providing minor refinements of traditional microeconomic theory, but why accept this assessment?

Evidence on the role of fairness norms, framing effects and loss aversion in wage setting undermines the natural rate hypothesis, while present bias and other behavioral findings pull the rug from under macroeconomic saving and consumption theories that are based on microeconomic assumptions of intertemporal optimization. Had the assessment been correct, furthermore, would that have made it sensible for economists who want to base their theories on realistic assumptions to dismiss the behavioral evidence? Whatever the methodology, vision or political leanings of the researchers, behavioral economics may produce information and research that can be extremely useful. Clearly, not all behavioral results are equally convincing, interesting or useful from the perspective of post-Keynesian macroeconomics. But dismissing the possibility of engaging with – and learning from – researchers who may come from a different school of thought can only, it seems to me, hurt the post-Keynesian tradition.

The questionable use of behavioral evidence to patch up models with untenable core assumptions does not justify a wholesale rejection of behavioral economics. We can and should be dismissive of the way in which mainstream macroeconomists have introduced behavioral modifications in dynamic stochastic general equilibrium models, but that should not make us overlook the importance of behavioral evidence.[12] Post-Keynesian models – like all macroeconomic models – contain behavioral relations that describe the aggregate outcomes of the behavior of individual decision makers. In the formulation of these relations, whether they are stated verbally or formalized mathematically, it should be recognized that individual behavior is shaped by a social context and subject to structural constraints. It would be a serious mistake, however, to ignore the insights and empirical evidence from behavioral economics, old and new, even if some contributors to this literature see their research as falling within the orthodox economic paradigm.

NOTES

1. Other prominent surveys by Hein (2014) and Blecker and Setterfield (2019) devote less attention to microeconomic behavior and make no reference to behavioral economics.

2. A dependence of firms' target on the utilization rate will be irrelevant for the stationary solution if stationarity is associated with an exogenous "normal rate of utilization."
3. The argument is outlined briefly in Hein (2014) and Lavoie (2014) and in greater detail in other contributions, e.g. Hein (2002) and Kriesler and Lavoie (2007).
4. Behavioral, experimental and econometric studies support workers' willingness to punish firms for unfair treatment, even if the punishment is costly to themselves (e.g. Fehr and Gächter 2000).
5. An extension of the model with heterogenous workers generated more interesting conclusions: if fairness is defined over relative wages, groups with low wages also tend to experience high rates of involuntary unemployment.
6. Loss aversion is also used as the key element in McDonald's (2021) analysis of Keynesian unemployment.
7. Seemingly unfamiliar with Rowthorn's paper, Akerlof et al. (2020) present a model with the same key assumption and implications. Behavioral evidence, they argue, suggests that "when inflation is low, a significant number of people may ignore inflation when setting wages and prices" (p. 3).
8. The Akerlof and Yellen model of fair wages missed this implication, but their contribution set the stage for extensions that incorporate the path dependence of social norms, including wage norms. In their model with heterogenous labor, path-dependent norms produce relative-wage hysteresis, an implication that becomes particularly interesting in light of the large increase in earnings inequality that occurred in many Organisation for Co-operation and Development countries from the late 1970s.
9. Blecker and Setterfield (2019, pp. 219–220) note that the rate of pass-through may depend on the speed of inflation. Their formulation avoids vertical Phillips curve by assuming the absence of any feedback effects from wage inflation to price inflation: firms adjust prices without taking into account expected wage increases, an assumption that seems behaviorally questionable.
10. Speaking for myself, I became familiar with Rowthorn's paper shortly after its publication but, while not finding the assumptions implausible, failed to be persuaded that the basic hypothesis behind the Phillips curve in Figure 8.1 had empirical support.
11. Lavoie's (2014) illustration on pp. 109–114 of the implications of lexicographic preferences for ecological economics points to limitations of marginal analysis: it may give misleading conclusions if the change that is being contemplated is not marginal. Lexicographic preferences represent an extreme case in which errors remain, even if the size of the change approaches 0.
12. As Fung (2010–2011, p. 247) observes, the findings and tools of behavioral economics are resources that can be put to either productive or unproductive use. Post-Keynesians may dislike the unproductive use to which neoclassical economists have put these resources, but they have only themselves to blame if they do not show in their own work how these resources can be put to productive use.

REFERENCES

Akerlof, G.A. and Yellen, J.L. (1990). "The fair wage-effort hypothesis and unemployment." *Quarterly Journal of Economics*, 255–283.

Akerlof, G.A., Dickens, W.T. and Perry, G.L. (1996). "The macroeconomics of low inflation." *Brookings Papers on Economic Activity*, 1, 1–75.

Akerlof, G.A., Dickens, W.T. and Perry, G.L. (2000). "Near-rational wage and price setting and the long-run Phillips curve." *Brookings Papers on Economic Activity*, 1, 1–60.

Bewley, T.F. (1998). "Why not cut pay?" *European Economic Review*, 42, 459–490.

Blanchard, O.J. (2021). *Macroeconomics*, 8th edition. Pearson.

Blecker, R.A. and Setterfield, M. (2019). *Heterodox macroeconomics: Models of demand, distribution and growth*. Cheltenham, UK and Northampton, MA, USA: Edward Elgar Publishing.

Eisner, R. (2003). "The NAIRU and fiscal and monetary policy for now and our future: Some comments." In Nell, E.J. and Forstater, M. (eds) *Reinventing functional finance: Transformational Growth and Full Employment*. Cheltenham, UK and Northampton, MA, USA: Edward Elgar Publishing.

Fehr, E. and Gächter, S. (2000). "Fairness and retaliation: The economics of reciprocity." *Journal of Economic Perspectives*, 14(3), 159–181.

Filardo, A.J. (1998). "New evidence on the output cost of fighting inflation." *Federal Reserve Bank of Kansas City Quarterly Review*, 83(3), 33–61.

Fung, M. (2010–2011). "Comments on 'can Post Keynesians make better use of behavioral economics?'" *Journal of Post Keynesian Economics*, 33(2), 235–248.

Hein, E. (2002). "Monetary policy and wage bargaining in the EMU: Restrictive ECB policies, high unemployment, nominal wage restraint and inflation above the target." *Banca del Lavoro Quarterly Review*, 222, 299–337.

Hein, E. (2014). *Distribution and growth after Keynes*. Cheltenham, UK and Northampton, MA, USA: Edward Elgar Publishing.

Hicks, J. (1975). *The crisis in Keynesian economics*. Oxford: Blackwell.

Howell, D.R., Baker, D., Glyn, A. and Schmitt, J. (2006). "Are protective labor market institutions at the root of unemployment? A critical review of the evidence." *Capitalism and Society*, 2(1), article 1.

Jefferson, and King, J. (2010–2011). "Can post Keynesians make better use of behavioral economics?" *Journal of Post Keynesian Economics*, 33(2), 211–234.

Kahneman, D., Knetsch, J.L. and Thaler, R. (1986). "Fairness as a constraint on profit seeking: Entitlements in the market." *American Economic Review*, 76, 728–741.

Kalecki, M (1971 [1943]). "Political aspects of full employment." *The Political Quarterly*, 322–330.

Kriesler, P. and Lavoie, M. (2007). "The new consensus on monetary policy and its post-Keynesian critique." *Review of Political Economy*, 19(3), 387–404.

Lavoie, M. (2014). *Post-Keynesian economics*. Cheltenham, UK and Northampton, MA, USA: Edward Elgar Publishing.

McDonald, I. (2021). "A Keynesian model of aggregate demand in the long-run." *Metroeconomica*, 72(3), 442–459.

Rowthorn, R. (1977). "Conflict, inflation and money." *Cambridge Journal of Economics*, 215–239.

Shafir, E., Diamond, P. and Tversky, A. (1997). "Money illusion." *Quarterly Journal of Economics*, 341–374.

Skott, P. (2005). "Fairness as a source of hysteresis in employment and relative wages." *Journal of Economic Behavior and Organization*, 57, 305–331.

Skott, P. (2023). *Structuralist and behavioral macroeconomics*. Cambridge: Cambridge University Press.

9. How not to do monetary policy

Louis-Philippe Rochon

INTRODUCTION

The 'art of central banking' (Hawtrey, 1932) has not changed much in the last four decades or so. Central banks always reacted to inflation in the same way: by increasing rates of interest in the hope that this would slow down economic activity sufficiently to bring down inflation, without engineering a recession. Abandoning money supply as the control variable of central banks, as in old monetarist incarnations, in favour of control over the rate of interest rates, as in New Consensus (NC) or New Keynesian models, has changed very little in terms of the overall design of mainstream monetary thinking. As Lavoie (2006, p. 167) has said, this rather minor change amounts simply to 'new wine in an old bottle'.

Best represented by the so-called New Consensus model, this approach today nevertheless appeared dormant in the last few decades, largely as a result of the fact that inflation was relatively low and stable. We must remember that since 2008, especially, we have been living in very strange and unusual times. In the specific case of central banks, interest rates were pushed to the lower bound and left there for a considerable period of time, during which inflation was dormant. In fact, in many countries, this period of low interest rates amounted to the longest stretch of time where interest rates were kept so low for so long (Borio and Hofmann, 2017).

In this sense, it certainly gave the impression that this model was, well, also dormant. But dormant is not the same as dead. As we see now, with inflation roaring back to life, in a post-pandemic world, in some places reaching double-digits, though it has been coming down more recently from those highs, all the old monetary reflexes are coming back, accompanied by all the old rhetoric about the use of interest rates to fight inflation. As expected, the more knee-jerk reaction of central banks also came roaring back, with eight increases in interest rates in Canada and nine in the United States in a matter of mere months, marking it certainly as one of the most aggressive monetary policy stances in history.

So, in this sense, yes, the model is still alive and well. This is consistent with an observation made by Hakes, Gamber and Shen (1998, p. 195), some 25 years ago: 'Thus, although the Fed may respond modestly (or not at all) to its policy objectives for extended periods of time, this pattern of behaviour may be interrupted by periods when the Fed responds more aggressively to a single objective.' This is what I think precisely describes monetary policy since the 2007–2008 financial crisis.

Moreover, as recently as 2022, Lavoie argued that this NC model was still the most relevant model to figure out the official arguments behind the present monetary policy, or 'the bread and butter of central bank researchers' (Lavoie, 2022, p. 10). So, the model is still a relevant point of referral for understanding current monetary policy, especially in the post-pandemic inflation era.[1]

In this short contribution, I will explore the relevant transmission mechanism of monetary policy as found in the NC model, but will conclude that the thinking behind the model is grossly inadequate to actually help bring down inflation, unless under the conditions of a hard landing. This is largely because of the weak statistical relationship embedded in the model's theoretical equations.

In the next section, I will explore the theoretical and policy assumptions embedded in the model. I will then criticize them and conclude they are inadequate to deal with current inflation, which is largely cost-plus or even conflict-driven, whereas the NC model largely assumes demand-pull inflation.[2] For instance, this was made clear by Jerome Powell, Chair of the Federal Reserve, when stating that: 'We are tightening the stance of policy in order to slow growth in aggregate demand. Slowing demand growth should allow supply to catch up with demand and restore the balance that will yield stable prices over time' (see Powell, 2022). The problem has thus been identified as one of excess demand, and meets the mainstream criteria of inflation resulting from 'too much money chasing too few goods'.

THE NEW CONSENSUS MODEL

NC models represent the standard mainstream explication of the relationship between monetary policy and inflation. Woodford (2003) was certainly one of its early exponents, and can be said to form a clear consensus among macroeconomists and policy makers today.

It encapsulates two essential and core components: first, it relies on a theoretical part, based around both a standard investment and savings (IS) curve and a Phillips curve. This part of the model is about the transmission mechanism of monetary policy, in theory, that is how changes in the rate of interest filter through the economy, in order to deliver on its ultimate goal of price stability or rather on how changes in interest rates bring inflation back to its target. Most commonly, this target is taken to be around 2 per cent or a corridor system from 1 to 3 per cent. First adopted by New Zealand in 1990 and Canada in 1991, inflation targeting is at the heart of this approach, and is now adopted by over 50 countries and the European Central Bank. Inflation targeting is claimed to be successful in reducing inflation largely by keeping inflationary expectations low and using fine tuning to adjust interest rates.

Second, it contains a policy component as well, usually referred to as the Taylor Rule, so named after John Taylor's 1993 article (see Taylor, 1993). Accordingly, this interest rate rule, or policy reaction function, suggests that central banks should change its policy rate, firmly under the control of independent central banks, whenever inflation deviates from its (natural) target (or outside the target corridor of unemployment).

There is much to criticize about this approach to monetary policy, in particular the belief in some natural rate of interest and the notion of central bank independence, both at the core of this approach. One could also criticize the notion of monetary policy dominance, that is the concept that only monetary policy is suited to fight inflation, or even the issue of fine tuning.[3] Indeed, there is very little room for fiscal policy to play any role, let alone when it comes to fighting inflation. If anything, fiscal policy is assumed to contribute to higher inflation and higher interest rates, and as such austerity or balanced budgets are considered the preferred policy stance.

We can also criticize the adoption of the 2 per cent target itself. Indeed, after extensively researching the research and policy documents from the Bank of New Zealand prior to 1990, I could not find any document that identified, explained or justified the decision to target around 2 per cent. This conclusion is confirmed as well by Benjamin Friedman (2018, p. 187), who argued that 'there is the arbitrariness surrounding the current 2 percent target. In retrospect, the paucity of serious empirical research underlying the identification of the 2 percent norm, now quite some time back, is a professional embarrassment.'

As a policy approach to inflation, the NC model suggests therefore that when inflation is above its chosen target, say 2 per cent, central banks should raise interest rates, which in turn should bring economic activity down (the IS relationship), which then should raise unemployment and bring inflation down (as established by the Phillips curve relationship). The notion of fine tuning assumes that this convergence to price stability should continue until the target is attained. Moreover, it is assumed that both of these curves are well behaved and stable, in the sense that the IS curve is elastic and downward sloping, the short-run Phillips curve has its standard downward-sloping curve and some sort of long-run non-accelerating inflation rate of unemployment exists. Both of these relationships are crucial for monetary policy to be successful and effective, from a mainstream perspective.[4]

The elasticity of the IS curve is of great importance as central banks must have degrees of freedom in setting monetary policy. After all, what good would the model be if changes in interest rates did not lead to significant changes in output? Indeed, as Hall (1977) stated some 45 years ago, the notion of monetary policy efficiency rests upon an interest-elastic IS curve: 'The more sensitive the response, the more potent is monetary policy.' So, a first question is how sensitive is it to changes in rates of interest.

Similarly, once output is impacted, it is imperative for changes in output to have an impact on unemployment, which in turn must impact inflation. In other words, inflation must respond to changes in output in a significant way for monetary policy to be effective. Yet, from a post-Keynesian perspective, there are a lot of 'ifs'. This is the essence of Arestis and Sawyer's (2003, p. 5) criticism that 'It is a long and uncertain chain of events from an adjustment in the interest rate controlled by the central bank to a desired change in the rate of inflation.' It also informs my own criticism of mainstream monetary policy, and the 'general ineffectiveness of monetary policy' (see Rochon, 2022a).

THE INTEREST AND SAVINGS RELATIONSHIP

Let us consider these relationships in turn. In general, the above description leaves much to be desired from a post-Keynesian or heterodox perspective. In particular, post-Keynesians generally reject the existence of an IS curve, or stipulate that its slope is rather steep. In other words, they specifically reject the notion that changes in interest rates have a significant impact on the demand for consumption goods, or that monetary policy has a significant impact on investment.[5]

Post-Keynesians have argued that investment in particular is not influenced much by monetary policy. Rather, investment is influenced by aggregate demand, or rather by expectations of growth of aggregate demand in the future, and whether this growth is thought to be sustained through time, that is over the life of the investment (see Rochon, 2022b). This was recognized early by Robinson (1943, p. 25) in a largely forgotten contribution: 'Firms producing consumption goods would make greater profits, and, if they had sufficient confidence that the higher demand would continue in the future, they would enlarge their capacity by building more plant.'[6]

A number of post-Keynesians have studied the statistical relationship embedded in the IS curve and found it lacking. For instance, Deleidi (2018, p. 186) has studied this relationship within the European context. According to the author, some heterodox economists would argue:

> investment is never influenced by interest rates but is positively affected by the level of the effective demand … firms' credit demand, as well as the investment

> demand, has to be represented as a vertical curve, which is perfectly inelastic with respect to the interest rate … loans provided by banks to firms and for the purchase of consumption goods are not influenced by the rate of interest … Such empirical findings allow us to maintain that interest rates do not have any effect on the volume of loans provided to enterprises and consequently cannot stimulate the demand for investments and for capital goods. (p. 203)

A number of other authors, both from the heterodox and the orthodox traditions, have reached this same conclusion. For instance, according to Cynamon et al. (2013, p. 13):

> The transmission mechanism from monetary policy to aggregate spending in new consensus models relies on the interest sensitivity of consumption. It is difficult, however, to find empirical evidence that households do indeed raise or lower consumption by a significant amount when interest rates change. Some authors have generalized the link to include business investments (see Fazzari, Ferri, and Greenberg, 2010 and the references provided therein) but a robust interest elasticity of investment has also been difficult to demonstrate empirically.

Moreover, Sharpe and Suarez (2015, p. 1) have made it clear that 'a large body of empirical research offers mixed evidence, at best, for substantial interest-rate effects on investment. [Our research] find[s] that most firms claim their investment plans to be quite insensitive to decreases in interest rates, and only somewhat more responsive to interest rate increases.'

Krugman (2018) calls the lack of empirical evidence supporting the traditional IS curve relationship a 'dirty little secret of monetary analysis … Any direct effect on business investment is so small that it's hard even to see it in the data. What drives such investment is, instead, perceptions about market demand.'

For their part, Kopp, Leigh, Mursula and Tambunlertchai (2019, p. 4) reach the same conclusion. According to the authors, there 'appears to be little unexplained component of business investment beyond the expected demand effect. Other factors, such as reductions in the cost of capital, thus appear to have played a relatively minor role.' Finally, Robert Hall (1977, p. 61) stated 'the evidence is disappointingly weak'.

THE PHILLIPS CURVE

Turning our attention now to the Phillips curve, it is the assumption that lies at the very heart of the mainstream approach to monetary policy. It is the holy grail of central banking: the pursuit of a soft landing, that is the Goldilocks of central bank policy. Central banks must slow down economic activity, not too little but not too much, to allow prices to come down to target with little social cost.

According to Bullard (2019): 'U.S. monetary policymakers and financial market participants have long relied on the Phillips curve – the correlation between labor market outcomes and inflation – to guide monetary policy.' In an NBER working paper, Hooper, Mishkin and Sufi (2019) stated the same opinion, and argued that the relationship between inflation and the unemployment rate is a key input to the design of monetary policy.

But it has become quite evident that the Phillips curve relationship has weakened considerably in the last four decades or so, revealing the vulnerability of monetary policy. Indeed, without the stable Phillips curve, the full mainstream monetary policy approach collapses, leading many to search for that elusive relationship. 'Without the PC, the whole complicated paraphernalia that underpins central bank policy suddenly looks very shaky. For this reason, the Phillips Curve will not be abandoned lightly by policy makers' (Davies, 2017).

Admissions of the collapse of the Phillips curve are numerous, spanning the spectrum of mainstream pundits. For instance, Janet Yellen (2019), former Chair of the Federal Reserve, has pointedly admitted that 'The slope of the Phillips curve – a measure of the responsiveness of inflation to a decline in labor market slack – has diminished very significantly since the 1960s. In other words, the Phillips curve appears to have become quite flat.' In an issue of the *Review of Keynesian Economics* that I edited, Bob Solow (2018) stated 'The slope of the Phillips curve itself has been getting flatter, ever since the1980s, and is now quite small … there is no well-defined natural rate of unemployment, either statistically or conceptually' (see Solow, 2018, p. 423). In that same issue, Gordon argues that 'the slope of the short-run inflation–unemployment relationship has flattened' (Gordon, 2018, p. 427).

Claudio Borio, Chief Economist of the Bank for International Settlement, has recently argued that 'the response of inflation to a measure of labour market slack has tended to decline and become statistically indistinguishable from zero. In other words, inflation no longer appears to be sufficiently responsive to tightness in labour markets' (see Borio, 2017, p. 2). Finally, Mary C. Daly, President of the Federal Reserve Board of San Francisco (see Daly, 2019), argues that 'as for the Phillips curve … most arguments today center around whether it's dead or just gravely ill. Either way, the relationship between unemployment and inflation has become very difficult to spot.'

For post-Keynesians, the Phillips curve is best represented with a long flat portion, reflecting precisely the breakdown in the relationship between output and inflation, and precisely emphasizing the lack of 'demand-pullness' in inflation.

But this flatter portion, as in Figure 9.1 for instance, poses considerable challenges for monetary policy and describes well the current situation. Indeed, this flat-curve means that in order to bring inflation down, central bank must push output (or capacity utilization) to considerable low levels, sufficient to deflate the economy. Hence, the possibility of soft landings becomes difficult to achieve, if not impossible.

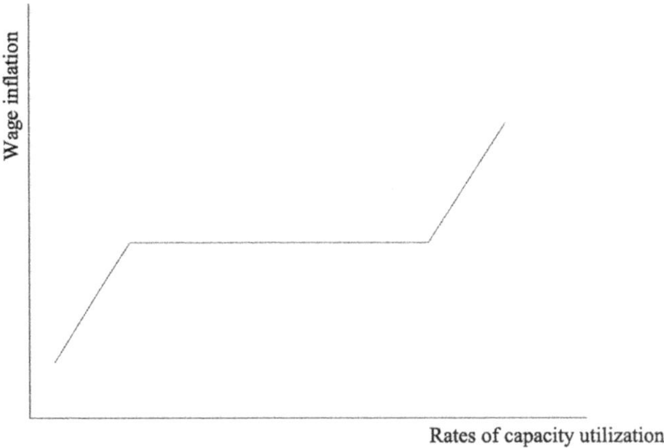

Figure 9.1 The post-Keynesian Phillips curve

Central bank policy is thus best described as a wait-and-see approach: rates increase incrementally and central bankers wait and consider the impact on output. Yet, what is happening is the economy is simply moving along the flat portion of the post-Keynesian Phillips curve. As Borio stated in the above quote, the response is 'statistically indistinguishable from zero'. So, central bankers keep raising rates and keep sliding along the curve. They continue until output has fallen sufficiently to bring inflation down. This has led some post-Keynesians to argue that monetary policy is a blunt instrument, akin to a sledgehammer used to kill the inflation fly on the economic table.

But in light of this discussion the question then becomes: why do central banks insist on pursuing a policy that is being discredited empirically? Surely, they must have access to the same data as we all do, and they must surely pay attention to our mainstream colleagues who advise them on the demise of the Phillips curve. This is not an easy question to answer. Fundamentally, I think, it is due to two things. First, it is the result of an ideological belief in the idea that inflation is demand-driven and the supreme belief in monetary policy dominance – both left-over concepts of the early days of monetarism. It is in this sense that the model is also referred to as the New Neoclassical Synthesis.

Second, I believe there is the question of credibility, where central banks must be seen to be credible in fighting inflation. Indeed, in the post-Covid-19 pandemic inflation era, central banks were accused of being slow to respond to the 'inflation threat' and were seen as non-credible. In many ways, I am prepared to argue, the current aggressive monetary austerity is the result of the desire to be seen as credible by financial interests. Credibility is defined with respect to inflation targeting and the appropriateness of policy in ensuring the goal of price stability is met. The many increases in interest rates, coming after central banks had claimed inflation was temporary, can be seen as an attempt to regain credibility.[7]

From this, we can conclude a few things: first, central bankers question the validity of the data, and all sorts of arguments are made to somehow claim the data are wrong or do not capture the true dynamics at play. Second, the concept of TINA (there is no alternative) applies to monetary austerity (as well as to fiscal austerity). Central bankers simply don't know much better and believe that monetary policy is the only game in town. Vacant from this discussion is the role fiscal policy can play, and as such, only central banks can bring inflation down. In order not to lose credibility, they must be seen to do something, and so they raise interest rates, perhaps knowing it may not entirely work.

This explains the persistence central bankers show in the face of inflation. This is precisely what Dennis Lockhart, former President of the Federal Reserve Bank of Atlanta, says: 'I think a policymaker has to act on the view that the basic relationship in the Phillips curve between inflation and [un] employment will assert itself in a reasonable period of time as the economy tightens up, as the resource picture in the economy tightens' (Hilsenrath, 2015).

Similarly:

> Even in the face of strong evidence for the flattening of the short-run Phillips curve (i.e., decreases in unemployment have a much smaller impact on inflation than in earlier periods), central banks are reluctant to omit it from their macroeconomic models ... All of the forgoing examples show that central bankers are not yet willing to discard the Phillips curve as a policy tool, even though the evidence for a downward sloping curve is meager. (Dorn, 2020, pp. 141, 143)

This then explains clearly Powell's insistence in adhering still to the Phillips curve in setting monetary policy: 'That connection has weakened over the past couple of decades, but it still persists, and I believe it continues to be meaningful for monetary policy' (see Powell, 2018, pp. 6–7).

CONCLUSION

The deconstruction of the NC model above poses enormous challenges for the conduct of monetary policy by central banks, and points to an urgent need to rethink how precisely do changes in interest rates affect economic activity.

Post-Keynesians have pointed to the income distributive nature of monetary policy (see Kappes, Rochon and Vallet, 2023). Rochon and Seccareccia (2023), in particular, have emphasized the revenue side of interest rate policy, thereby linking monetary policy to the functional distribution of income. They point to an income distributive channel of the transmission mechanism (see Kappes, 2023, for a discuss of the mainstream discussion of the relationship between monetary theory and the personal distribution of income) – an argument that goes back to earlier post-Keynesians like Niggle (1989), for instance.[8]

This rethinking is urgently needed, especially in light of current inflation. As argued above, central bankers see most inflation as being demand-driven, even in light of statements by so many economists now that point the finger to (mostly) supply-side reasons. But this insistence on seeing inflation as a demand-pull phenomenon justifies the continued use of monetary policy. Recognizing otherwise would in essence nullify the mainstream edifice of argumentation in favour of monetary policy.

Yet, a critical analysis shows there really is nothing left of mainstream macroeconomic and monetary theory. This has been a consistent refrain from post-Keynesians.

In the end, interest rates are not a good way of controlling inflation. We need a better approach, one that is inspired by the very specific sources of inflation. We must understand the sources of inflation as being specifically rooted in social conflict and temporary supply constraints. Once this is done, we can devise better policy to fight inflation with fewer social costs, one that relies more on the role of fiscal policy than monetary policy.

NOTES

1. Apparently, however, not everyone agrees. For instance, while giving a talk at Complutence University in Madrid, on 11 May 2022, a heterodox economist in attendance informed me that the New Consensus model was dead!
2. This is part of a greater research endeavour in the content of a book I am currently writing, simply titled *Monetary Policy*.
3. The Parking-It rules, which I developed in a series of articles with Mark Setterfield (see Rochon and Setterfield, 2007, 2008, 2012), stand most in contrast with this approach, in its rejection of monetary fine tuning.
4. Arestis and Sawyer (2008) give an exhaustive description of the model, in its more formal New Keynesian form, with intertemporal optimization and inflation expectations.
5. Many New Consensus models deal with intertemporal effect and utility maximization, such as TANK and other New Keynesian models. Yet, the basic assumptions of the IS curve remain.
6. I recognize that real estate is sensitive to interest rates. We often see real-estate markets collapsing after only a few increases in interest rates, as happened in Canada in 2022–2023. In fact, in the Krugman quote above, he argues ‘It’s a dirty

little secret of monetary analysis that changes in interest rates affect the economy mainly through their effect on the housing market.'

7. It can be asked whether the notion of credibility is consistent with the concept of central bank independence. As Epstein (2015, p. 106) argues, monetary policy decisions are made from '"finance coloured" glasses'.
8. As in Rochon and Seccareccia (2023), we also recognize the wealth effect of monetary policy, both directly on various asset values (including real estate) and through quantitative easing policies.

REFERENCES

Arestis, P. and M. Sawyer (2003), 'Reinstating Fiscal Policy', *Journal of Post Keynesian Economics*, 26 (1), pp. 3–25.

Arestis, P. and M. Sawyer (2008), 'New consensus macroeconomics and inflation targeting: Keynesian critique', *Economia e Sociedade*, 17, pp. 629–653.

Borio, C. (2017), 'Through the looking glass', Talk, Bank for International Settlement, 22 September.

Borio, C. and B. Hofmann (2017), 'Is monetary policy less effective when interest rates are persistently low?', in J. Hambur and J. Simon (eds), *Monetary Policy and Financial Stability in a World of Low Interest Rates*, Federal Reserve Bank of Australia.

Bullard, J. (2019), 'Three themes for monetary policy in 2019', Speech at 57th Winter Institute, St Cloud State University. www.stlouisfed.org/-/media/project/frbstl/stlouisfed/files/pdfs/bullard/remarks/2019/bullard_st_cloud_state_university_7_february_2019.pdf

Cynamon, B.Z., S. Fazzari and M. Setterfield (2013), *After the Great Recession: The Struggle for Economic Recovery and Growth*, Cambridge University Press.

Daly, M.C. (2019), 'A new balancing act: Monetary policy tradeoffs in a changing world', Speech, Reserve Bank of New Zealand, 29 August.

Davies, G. (2017), 'The (non) disappearing Phillips curve: Why it matters'. *Financial Times*, 22 October. www.ft.com/content/e1d27c20-b34d-339e-a15f-21f1b3d 87857

Deleidi, M. (2018), 'Post Keynesian endogenous money theory: A theoretical and empirical investigation of the credit demand schedule', *Journal of Post Keynesian Economics*, 41 (2), pp. 185–209.

Dorn, J.A. (2020), 'The Phillips curve: A poor guide for monetary policy', *Cato Journal*, 40 (1), pp. 133–151.

Epstein, J. (2015), 'Contested terrain', in L.-P. Rochon and S. Rossi (eds), *Encyclopedia of Central Banking*, Edward Elgar Publishing, pp. 105–107.

Fazzari, S., P. Ferri, and E. Greenberg (2010), 'Investment and the Taylor rule in a dynamic Keynesian model', *Journal of Economic Dynamics and Control*, 34 (10), pp. 2010–2022.

Friedman, B. (2018), 'The future of central banking', in European Central Bank (ed.), *The Future of Central Banking: Festschrift in Honour of Vítor Constâncio*, European Central Bank, pp. 187–190.

Gordon, R.J. (2018), 'Friedman and Phelps on the Phillips curve viewed from a half century's perspective', *Review of Keynesian Economics*, 6 (4), pp. 425–436.

Hakes, D.R., E.N. Gamber and C.-H. Shen (1998), 'Does the Federal Reserve lexicographically order its policy objectives?', *Eastern Economic Journal*, 24 (2), pp. 195–206.

Hall, R. (1977), 'Investment, interest rates, and the effects of stabilization policies', *Brookings Papers on Economic Activity*, 1, pp. 61–121.
Hawtrey, R.G. (1932), *The Art of Central Banking*, Longmans, Green and Company.
Hilsenrath, J. (2015), 'Excerpts from Atlanta Fed's Lockhart interview'. Wall Street Journal, 4 August.
Hooper, P., F. Mishkin, and A. Sufi (2019), 'Prospects for inflation in a high pressure economy: Is the Phillips curve dead or is it just hibernating?', NBER Working paper 25792.
Kappes, S. (2023), 'Monetary policy and personal income distribution: A survey of the empirical literature', *Review of Political Economy*, 35 (1), pp. 211–230.
Kappes, S., L.-P. Rochon and G. Vallet (2023), *Central Banking, Monetary Policy and Income Distribution*, Edward Elgar Publishing.
Kopp, E., D. Leigh, S. Mursula and S. Tambunlertchai (2019), 'U.S. investment since the tax cuts and Jobs Act of 2017', IMF Working Paper 120.
Krugman, P. (2018), 'Why was Trump's tax cut a fizzle', *New York Times*, 15 November. www.nytimes.com/2018/11/15/opinion/tax-cut-fail-trump.html
Lavoie, M. (2006), 'A post-Keynesian amendment to the New Consensus on monetary policy', *Metroeconomica*, 57 (2), pp. 165–192.
Lavoie, M. (2022), *Post-Keynesian Economics: New Foundation*, Edward Elgar Publishing.
Niggle, C. (1989), 'Monetary policy and changes in income distribution', *Journal of Economic Issues*, 23 (3), pp. 809–822.
Powell, J. (2018), 'The outlook for the U.S. economy', Speech, Economics Club of Chicago, 6 April.
Powell, J. (2022), 'Inflation and the labor market', Speech, Hutchins Center on Fiscal and Monetary Policy, Brookings Institution, 20 November. www.federalreserve.gov/newsevents/speech/powell20221130a.htm
Robinson, J. (1943), *The Problem of Full Employment*, Workers' Educational Association and Workers' Educational Trade Union Committee.
Rochon, L.-P. (2022a), 'The general ineffectiveness of monetary policy or the weaponization of inflation', in S. Kappes, L.-P. Rochon and G. Vallet (eds), *The Future of Central Banking*, Edward Elgar Publishing, pp. 20–37.
Rochon, L.-P. (2022b), 'The post-Keynesians', in H. Bougrine and L.-P. Rochon (eds), *A Brief History of Economic Thought*, Edward Elgar Publishing, pp. 246–272.
Rochon, L.-P. and M. Seccareccia (2023), 'A primer on monetary policy and its effect on income distribution: A heterodox perspective', in S. Kappes L.-P. Rochon and G. Vallet (eds), *Central Banking, Monetary Policy and Income Distribution*, Edward Elgar Publishing, pp. 20–34.
Rochon, L.-P. and M. Setterfield (2007), 'Interest rates, income distribution and monetary policy dominance: Post Keynesians and the "fair" rate of interest', *Journal of Post Keynesian Economics*, 30 (1), pp. 13–41.
Rochon, L.-P. and M. Setterfield (2008), 'The political economy of interest rate setting, inflation, and income distribution', *International Journal of Political Economy*, 37 (2), pp. 2–25.
Rochon, L.-P. and M. Setterfield (2012), 'A Kaleckian model of growth and distribution with conflict-inflation and post-Keynesian nominal interest rate rules', *Journal of Post Keynesian Economics*, 34 (3), pp. 497–519.
Sharpe, S. and G. Suarez (2015), *Why Isn't Investment More Sensitive to Interest Rates: Evidence from Surveys*, Federal Reserve Board.

Solow, R. (2018), 'A theory is a something thing', *Review of Keynesian Economics*, 6 (4), pp. 421–424.

Taylor, J. B. (1993), 'Discretion versus policy rules in practice', *Carnegie-Rochester Conference Series on Public Policy*, 39, pp. 195–214.

Woodford, M. (2003), *Interest and Prices: Foundations of a Theory of Monetary Policy*, Princeton University Press.

Yellen, J. (2019), 'Former Fed Chair Janet Yellen on why the answer to the inflation puzzle matters', Remarks delivered at 'What's (Not) Up with Inflation?', Hutchins Center on Fiscal and Monetary Policy at Brookings, 3 October.

10. Inflation, monetary policy and the hierarchy of consumer goods

Thibault Laurentjoye

INTRODUCTION

The recent years have seen the return of inflation in Western economies, to levels unseen since the 1970s. In the euro area, annual inflation in 2022 ranged from 5.9 per cent in France to nearly 20 per cent in the Baltic countries. Countries like Denmark, Germany and the United States have witnessed annual increases in prices in the vicinity of 8.5 per cent, while only Switzerland and Japan have managed to keep inflation relatively under control – albeit above their official monetary policy target – at respectively 2.5 and 4 per cent.

These price increases have occurred against the backdrop of global instability. Initially linked to the disorderly reopening of global supply chains in the aftermath of the COVID-19 pandemic, inflation has been prolonged and amplified by the Russian invasion of Ukraine in February 2022, which has led to significant disruption in the gas supply and pushed energy prices, notably in Europe, to unprecedented levels. This is reminiscent of the 1970s inflationary episode, which was driven by the increase in energy prices following the oil shocks.

In parallel, we have recently witnessed a new dissociation in the economic policy mix. Prior to the pandemic, monetary policy was relatively expansionary while restrictions were placed on fiscal policy, particularly in the European Union. During the pandemic, extraordinarily accommodating policies were led by both central banks and governments. We are now witnessing a tightening of monetary policy, while fiscal policy is remaining expansionary in many countries, mostly due to price energy subsidy and household disposable income support schemes. Although that policy mix divergence is not the topic of the chapter, it is a fascinating topic in itself.

Monetary tightening has been met with mixed reactions from politicians, ranging from neutral to negative. The Prime Minister of Finland, Sanna Marin, has openly criticised the current trend in monetary policy by quoting a piece from Ronkainen (2022). Beyond disagreements regarding the appropriate level of unemployment–inflation trade-off, monetary policy critiques have pointed to two aspects of the current inflationary process which supposedly render monetary tightening inappropriate.

A first aspect concerns the supply- versus demand-driven nature of the current inflation, which resonates with the theoretical opposition between mainstream and post-Keynesian economics. The disorderly reopening of the global supply chains in the aftermath of COVID-19, in 2020 and 2021, followed by the fallouts of the Russian invasion of Ukraine at the beginning of 2022, seem to weigh in favour of the supply-side explanation. On the other hand, the expansionary fiscal policies put in place in the wake of COVID-19 have been invoked to underpin a demand-based explanation.

Another debate, not unrelated to the previous one, concerns the internal versus external origin of the current inflationary process. Inflation can be considered internal in the case of an economy at full employment, where any additional demand or expenditure would lead to overheating and therefore higher prices – at least on flexible price markets. On the other hand, inflation has an external source when it is the result of extraneous events leading to higher import prices, either due to a lower exchange rate or higher prices of goods transacted on international markets, such as oil and other commodities. Again, the expansionary fiscal policies during COVID-19 can be used to underpin an internal approach to inflation, while the disorderly reopening of supply chains and the invasion of Ukraine can be used to put forward an external explanation.

While these aspects are certainly important to get an overall and nuanced understanding of inflation, I would like to argue that another and potentially more important aspect to consider pertains to the structure of final consumers' demand. In the real world, demand for goods is hierarchical: not all consumers buy the same basket of goods depending on their level of disposable income. Instead, they first satiate their demand for a good or a type of good, before moving to the next one and so on. As a result, policy-triggered changes in disposable income will not affect the demand for all goods uniformly.

To represent the basic intuition and consequences of hierarchical demand for goods, I will operate a distinction between two types of goods, called respectively 'basic goods' and 'comfort goods'. It therefore contrasts with explanations of inflation based on one-good models.[1] I will aim to demonstrate that when inflation is primarily driven by basic goods, monetary policy can be ineffective or even counter-productive.

The chapter is organised as follows. In the next section, I will discuss some of the literature on the drivers of inflation, focusing particularly on establishing the logical preconditions for the occurrence of inflation. In the third section, I will present a simple model based on the distinction between basic goods (high-priority goods in the consumption hierarchy) and comfort goods (low-priority goods). In the fourth section, shocks will be introduced to show how the efficacy of monetary policy is affected by the structure of inflation. In the fifth section, I will discuss how the supply-versus-demand and internal-versus-external debates can be enriched using insights derived from the model, before concluding.

THE LOGICAL DRIVERS OF INFLATION

Asked about what causes price changes, the average layman – as well as many economists – will reply 'supply and demand', or more precisely: the respective amounts, or *magnitudes*, of supply and demand. Supply greater than demand must lower prices, while excess demand will raise them. Falling prices are meant to stimulate demand and reduce supply, while increasing prices are supposed to attract supply and discourage demand.

The theory of supply and demand magnitudes (S&DM) as a driver of price changes is a perfect example of the vagueness that sometimes characterises economics. Although S&DM has been disproved by facts on plenty of occasions, it remains a cornerstone of the collective unconscious understanding of economics. Furthermore, its theoretical underpinnings were proved inconsistent almost a century ago by Sraffa (1925, 1926). Despite the acknowledgement by most economists of the existence of structural market imperfections, the theory of S&DM remains part of the mainstream narrative.

According to Lavoie (2014), in mainstream economics price inflation is essentially an excess demand phenomenon. This excess demand can either arise from an excess supply of money, from an excessive growth rate of the money supply or in a more Wicksellian perspective associated with the New Consensus, from a market rate of interest too low compared to the natural rate of interest. Indeed, a negative discrepancy between the market and the natural rate of interest creates an output gap that leads to an acceleration of the inflation rate, supported by growth in the money supply. Other variants include the vertical Phillips curve, based on the natural rate of unemployment or the non-accelerating inflation rate of unemployment: whenever the actual rate of unemployment is below this rate, wage and price inflation speeds up.

By contrast, still according to Lavoie (2014), in the post-Keynesian view inflation is a supply-side issue mostly driven by the cost-push channel. While price or wage inflation may accompany increased activity, excess demand is generally not the cause of continually rising prices. The growth of the money supply or the natural rate of unemployment do not play any role in the explanation of inflation, and the influence of demand is only an indirect one. In the post-Keynesian view, inflation arises from conflicting views about the proper distribution of income.

While I agree that the cost-based explanation of inflation is overall more plausible than the excessive demand narrative, I also find the post-Keynesian theory of inflation to be incomplete. In an article that triggered consternated reactions by prominent post-Keynesian authors, Lerner (1977) accused Keynesianism of having brought about an 'overconcentration on macroeconomics', which he saw as the symmetric extreme to the pre-Keynesian 'overconcentration on microeconomics'. For Lerner, stagflation in particular could only be understood – and fought – by combining both micro and macro elements.

While I do not dismiss the importance of repartition conflict as a consolidating factor of inflation, I feel that a theory of inflation only based on repartition conflict does indeed overconcentrate on macroeconomic factors, as per Lerner's words. (Interestingly, the explanation of inflation put forward by the mainstream falls under a similar criticism, as it relies on monetary policy variables and aggregate labour market factors.[2])

The main flaw of the S&DM approach is precisely that it focuses on absolute amounts, and at one point in time. As Kalecki (1954) put it, 'an increase in the number of paupers does not broaden the market': it is not the number of demanders that matter, but the price each of them is willing to put – and whether they can afford to do so – especially once price changes have taken place. This is why Bilger (1985) suggests moving away from S&DM-based explanations, to supply and demand *price elasticity* explanations, as they better capture the supply and demand dynamics.

The price elasticity of supply, or its deficiency, has long been a prominent feature of heterodox economics, which emphasises the importance of imperfect competition in the real world. A recent example is offered by Nersisyan and Wray (2022), who highlight the importance of supply-side factors in their account of the current episode of inflation:

> Mainstream economics treats prices as if they were determined by markets. In the real world, only a limited set of prices is determined this way (some commodity prices, for instance). Most prices are set by firms with the degree of pricing power dependent on the amount of competition that exists in the industry. Traditionally, firms with monopoly power are believed to restrict output and raise prices (above marginal cost) to maximize profit. There is an incentive to restrain capacity to keep prices up. At the same time, the threat of new entry by competitors can temper exercise of pricing power. (p. 25)
>
> The COVID-19 crisis clearly started as a supply-side crisis that spilled over into demand. It has continued to be a supply-side problem because of the pandemic, while policy has been able to temper the demand problem. One could of course argue that if we didn't provide pandemic relief, which prevented a downward spiral in the economy, we might have less measured inflation. (p. 34)

The very fact that supply decreased because of the pandemic or the measures taken to limit the propagation of the virus indicates that supply could not react to prices in any way. Furthermore, the ability for firms with market power to raise their prices constitutes another case of inelastic supply to prices.[3]

One element is missing from this narrative: how can firms afford to raise their prices, especially in the case when they decide to increase these more than their costs – which corresponds to an increase in their mark-up? The answer to this question can only be found in the behaviour of the other price elasticity, that of demand. After all, if firms used their market power to raise prices, but demand fell so much as to reduce profits, this would force even the best-established monopoly to restore the initial price.

It is usual to consider that a price elastic demand is the norm, while abnormal elasticities occur in specific instances only, the most famous being Giffen goods and Veblen goods:

- Giffen goods correspond to situations when the price of a basic good increases and leads to an increase in the demand for that good – note that this effect involves a simultaneous substitution effect.
- Veblen goods correspond to conspicuous consumption behaviour, in the context of which a higher price can be used as a social signal.

To put it somewhat caricaturally, Giffen goods are associated with poor people's inelastic or perverse demand, while Veblen goods are associated with rich people's. In between these two extreme situations, in the 'middle class' of demand patterns, the price elasticity of demand is assumed to be well behaved, i.e. algebraically around minus one.

Bilger (1985) highlights another situation when microeconomic demand can become inelastic, which occurs when using durable and complementary goods. Typically, when an investment has been made that requires the use of specific inputs, an increase in the price of these inputs will at best trigger only a marginal reduction in their use, since a signification reduction would require switching to another technology, which would necessitate making a new costly investment.

Furthermore, in parallel with microeconomic inelasticity, Bilger (1985) argues that from the firms' perspective, which is the level at which the reaction of demand is supposed to provide an incentive to limit price increases, the relevant elasticity is not only the product of microelasticity, but also the result of demographic change. In effect, if individual demand decreases as prices increase while the number of demanders increase due to demographics,[4] the net effect could still be an increase in demand despite higher prices, which provides no incentive to companies to limit price increases.

The field of economics which has arguably made the most operational use of the concept of demand price elasticity is international economics, where the theorem of critical elasticities explicates the conditions under which changes in the exchange rate can lead to an improvement or a degradation of the trade balance (see Lavoie 2014, p. 520 for a presentation of Marshall-Lerner-Robinson Theorem). Outside of international economics, Lerner (1934) associated the price elasticity of demand with the inverse of the monopoly power, while Harrod (1936) claimed the existence of a 'law of decreasing elasticity of demand' and Bilger (1985) argued that macroeconomic inelasticity of demand to prices is a fundamental, logical requirement for inflation.

In this chapter, I would like to come to similar considerations from a slightly different angle. Using the post-Keynesian theory of consumer choice from Lavoie (1994), which relies on several principles, including satiability, separability and subordination of needs, I will aim to show how the existence of a hierarchical demand for consumption goods effectively implies discontinuous patterns in demand price elasticities for the various goods. These discontinuous patterns, which to the best of my knowledge have never been highlighted in the literature, have important implications for the effectiveness of economic policies aiming to stabilise inflation through a compression in disposable income.

A SIMPLE MODEL OF HIERARCHICAL DEMAND

In this section, I will put forward a very simple formalisation to show how demand structure and demand reaction to changes in prices and economic policy are important aspects to consider when addressing inflation. I will argue that the existence of a hierarchical demand for goods makes the reaction of demand a function of the relative level of disposable income compared to the threshold between goods of varying priority.

Model Setup

The population is made up of a finite number of identical households, who take part in the production and consumption of two goods: basic goods and comfort goods. Basic goods are necessary to the survival and reproduction of households, while comfort goods are nice to have.[5] This follows Lavoie's (1994) principles of separability and subordination of needs.

The characteristics of the demand for basic goods[6] are as follows:

- High priority: households spend in priority on basic goods.
- Finite: the need for basic goods is satiable.

On the other hand, the demand for comfort goods is characterised by:

- Low priority: households spend on comfort goods only once they have satiated their need for basic goods.
- Infinite: the desire for comfort goods has no a priori limit. This is obviously a simplifying assumption, a more realistic alternative would be to add more goods to the model, all associated with finite demand.

In the model, disposable income (YD) is split between consumption of basic goods (C_B), consumption of comfort goods (C_C) and savings (S):

$$YD = C_B + C_C + S \tag{10.1}$$

Disposable income is initially entirely spent on basic goods, until the subsistence threshold is reached:

$$C_B = p_B q_B = \min(YD,\ p_B q_B^*) \tag{10.2}$$

where p_B is the price of basic goods, q_B the real production of basic goods and q_B^* the volume of basic goods that satiates the demand for them.

Once the subsistence threshold is reached, additional disposable income is allocated between consumption of comfort and saving, with a proportion α going to the former and $(1 - \alpha)$ going to the latter:

$$C_C = p_C q_C = \begin{cases} 0 \text{ } if \text{ } YD \in [0,\ p_B q_B^*] \\ \alpha(YD - p_B q_B^*) \text{ } if \text{ } YD > p_B q_B^* \end{cases} \tag{10.3}$$

$$S = \begin{cases} 0 \text{ } if \text{ } YD \in [0,\ p_B q_B^*] \\ (1-\alpha)(YD - p_B q_B^*) \text{ } if \text{ } YD > p_B q_B^* \end{cases} \tag{10.4}$$

where p_C is the price of comfort goods and q_C the real production of comfort goods.

The demand for basic goods admits a maximum at the individual household level – and for the economy as a whole, as long as the size of the household population remains constant. Considering the price of basic goods, the level of disposable income that enables households to satiate their demand for basic goods will be referred to as the ‘subsistence threshold’ – which resonates with the subsistence wage of classical economists (Figure 10.1). Past that threshold, the volume of basic goods demanded does not vary as disposable income increases.

Until the subsistence threshold is reached, agents spend all their disposable income on basic goods. For any amount of nominal demand inferior to the

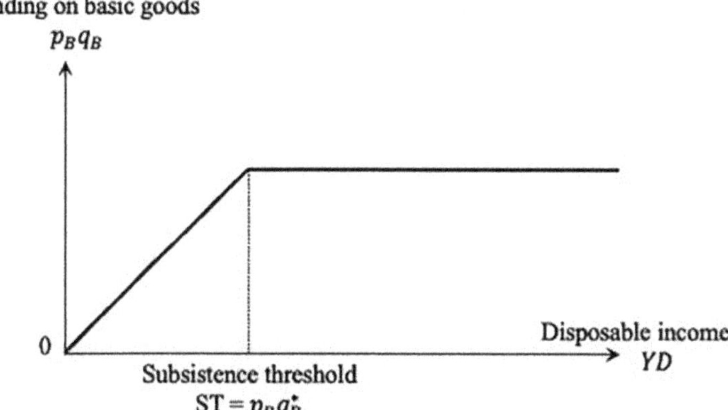

Figure 10.1 *Relationship between disposable income and spending on basic goods*

subsistence threshold, a change in the price of basic goods will therefore result in an inverse reduction in the volume of basic goods demanded (corresponding to an algebraic cross-elasticity value of −1). Past the subsistence threshold, the nominal demand for basic goods will follow exactly any change in prices (corresponding to an elasticity of 0).

Once households' disposable income exceeds the subsistence threshold, households will split the marginal amount they received between spending on comfort goods and savings in the form of various financial assets (whose precise allocation is beyond the scope of this chapter) (Figure 10.2).

Note that from equation (10.3) it can be derived that:

$$q_C = \frac{\alpha\,(YD - p_B q_B^*)}{p_C} \text{ when } YD > p_B q_B^* \tag{10.5}$$

The demand for comfort goods is defined so that it remains constant in nominal terms, for a given level of disposable income. An increase in the price of comfort goods will result in a symmetric decline in the quantity of comfort goods demanded by households, so that the quantity of labour employed in the production of comfort goods will remain unchanged.

To keep the model as simple as possible, I only consider one factor of production, homogenous labour, which can be used interchangeably in the production of both goods:

$$p_k = \frac{w}{\sigma_k}\,(1 + \theta_k) \tag{10.6}$$

where the subscript k stands for the sector, w is the wage rate, σ_k is the labour productivity in sector k and θ_k is the rate of mark-up over cost in sector k.

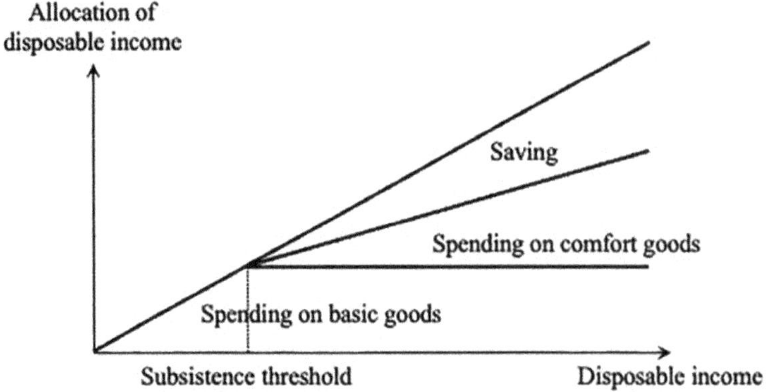

Figure 10.2 Allocation of disposable income

PRICE AND POLICY SHOCK REACTIONS

I now introduce five shocks to study how they influence the various variables of the model:

- An increase in the price of basic goods caused either by:
  - A decrease in the productivity of labour used to produce basic goods σ_B (shock 1A);
  - Or an increase in the mark-up coefficient on basic goods θ_B (shock 1B).
- An increase in the price of comfort goods caused either by:
  - A decrease in the productivity of labour used to produce comfort goods σ_C (shock 2A);
  - Or an increase in the mark-up coefficient on comfort goods θ_C (shock 2B).
- A reduction in households' disposable income (shock 3).

The first four shocks correspond to the various ways prices can increase in the model (apart from an autonomous wage increase). For each good, price increase can be the result of a decline in labour productivity or an increase in the mark-up. The last shock is there to highlight the effect restrictive monetary (or fiscal) policy could have on aggregate demand. The two shocks leading to a rise in the price of basic goods will be presented together, and so will the two shocks leading to a rise in the price of comfort goods.

Increase in the Price of Basic Goods

Both a decrease in σ_B and an increase in θ_B trigger an increase in the price of basic goods, which brings about an increase in the nominal subsistence threshold (Figure 10.3).

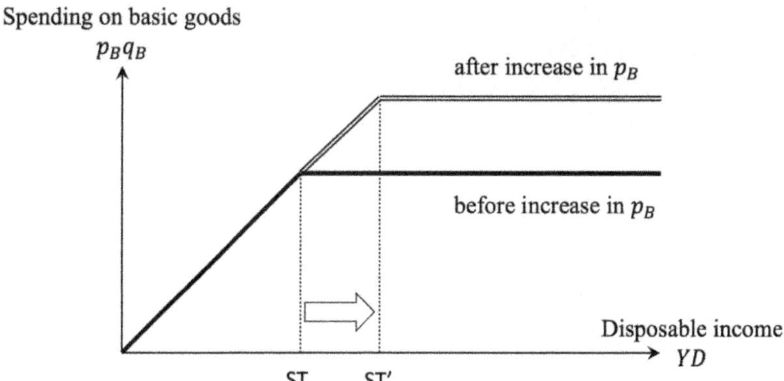

Figure 10.3 Subsistence threshold shift following an increase in the price of basic goods

This further reduces the amount of savings as well as spending on comfort goods. The main difference between the two sources of increase in p_B concerns the impact on the quantity of labour used to produce basic goods.

In the case of the decrease in σ_B, the quantity of labour needed to produce basic goods increases exactly in the same proportion as prices, since the volume of basic goods demanded is constant (whereas it stays constant in the case of a mark-up increase). But in both instances, for a given amount of disposable income, the increase in the price of basic goods reduces the amount of savings as well as the nominal (and real) demand for comfort goods.

The effect of the decrease in σ_B on overall employment depends on the value of α. When α is equal to 1, which means the disposable income exceeding the subsistence threshold is entirely spent on comfort goods, the decrease in σ_B has no effect on employment, because the additional labour needed to produce a constant volume of basic goods is compensated by the lower labour required to produce comfort goods whose demand has declined. When $\alpha \in [0, 1]$, which means the disposable income exceeding the subsistence threshold is partly or entirely saved, the decrease in σ_B provokes an increase in overall employment, because households reducing their savings doesn't affect the demand for labour.

Increase in the Price of Comfort Goods

A decrease in σ_C or an increase in θ_C trigger an increase in the price of comfort goods. Unlike what happened with the rise in the price of basic goods, the subsistence threshold is not affected, which means that neither the nominal demand for basic goods nor the amount of savings vary. However, the volume of comfort goods demanded still declines, as it is inversely related to the price, as the nominal demand for comfort goods remains constant – a property of the demand function when isoelasticity is equal to -1.

The only difference between the decrease in σ_C and the increase in θ_C concerns the quantity of labour employed in the production of comfort goods: it stays constant when the rise in comfort good prices comes from a decrease in productivity, but diminishes in the case of an increase in the mark-up.

Reduction in Disposable Income

The last shock consists in a reduction in households' disposable income. If the economy is developed, disposable income should initially be significantly greater than the subsistence threshold. In this case, unless the fall in disposable income is extremely large, the fall in disposable income should not affect the consumption of basic goods, but instead reduce the consumption of comfort goods, as well as saving.

Restrictive monetary policy, in the form of higher interest rates, aims to reduce the nominal spending on consumption goods and services – through a decline in the share of disposable income available for consumption purposes, or through a higher incentive to save. It is therefore useful to look at this shock in addition to one of the previous shocks, as the reduction in disposable income is the consequence of a policy reaction to higher prices (Table 10.1). The effects on the various variables are as follows:

- None of the shocks immediately affect the real demand for basic goods. Large enough increases in the price of basic goods or large enough falls in disposable income could have an impact (shown by the minus sign between brackets), but an increase in the price of comfort goods will not.
- The demand for labour in the basic goods sector increases in the case of a fall in the labour productivity of the sector and stagnates otherwise.

Table 10.1 *Summary of the effects of the various shocks*

Shocks →	**Shock 1: increase in p_B**		**Shock 2: increase in p_C**		**Shock 3: disposable income reduction**
Variables ↓	**1A: Decrease in σ_B**	**1B: Increase in θ_B**	**2A: Decrease in σ_C**	**2B: Increase in θ_C**	
q_B	0 (–)	0 (–)	0	0	0 (–)
N_B	+	0 (–)	0	0	0 (–)
C_B	+	+	0	0	0
q_C	–	–	–	–	–
N_C	–	–	0	–	–
C_C	–	–	0	0	–
S	–	–	0	0	–

- All the shocks reduce the real demand for comfort goods and reduce the demand for labour in that sector – with the exception of the shock on the productivity associated with comfort goods which leaves the latter magnitude unchanged.
- The nominal demand for comfort goods as well as saving decrease in the case of an increase in the price of basic goods and a decline in disposable income, but stagnate in the case of a fall in the price of comfort goods.
- It could be argued that the model should have included the possibility that a more restrictive monetary policy increases saving. This is worth reflecting upon with further improvement of the model – for the time being, it might suffice to note that this increase in saving would only reinforce the negative effect on the demand for comfort goods.

The main conclusion that can be drawn from the simple model presented here is that the efficacy of monetary policy varies greatly depending on whether inflation comes mainly from basic or comfort goods.

Two channels of efficacy should particularly be highlighted.

Firstly, does restrictive monetary policy affect the demand for the most inflationary subset of goods? Although I have not considered explicitly any channel through which the demand for a certain type of goods could affect their price, it is at the very least an official channel of transmission of monetary policy to inflation through aggregate demand, which underpins the whole working of current monetary policy.

Secondly, how does the change in demand composition influence the price index used to calculate inflation? This apparently technical effect is nevertheless important, insofar as the official inflation index is used as a basis for future remuneration negotiations and therefore determines the path of future inflation through repartition conflict.

If the increase in prices primarily concerns comfort goods, a reduction in households' disposable income will trigger a reduction in both savings and the nominal demand for comfort goods. Furthermore, assuming that both basic and comfort goods enter the price index used to calculate inflation, the reduction in the real demand for comfort goods (due to the constant nominal demand for these goods associated with a unitary price isoelasticity) means that their weight in the inflation basket is reduced. Both channels can therefore be considered as having a stabilising effect on inflation.

If the increase in prices primarily concerns basic goods, the reduction in households' disposable income will trigger a reduction in savings and the nominal demand for comfort goods, but *not* a reduction in the demand for basic goods. Furthermore, the increase in the share of basic goods in the consumption mix, arising from the decline in the real demand for comfort goods, translates into higher inflation measures. The first channel seems non-operational, while the second channel amplifies inflation.

It therefore appears that restrictive monetary policy – and more generally restrictive economic policies aimed at reducing consumption spending – is relatively more effective when inflation arises from comfort goods. On the other hand, restrictive policies appear ineffective, or even counter-productive, when inflation comes from basic goods.

In a recent paper, Weber et al. (2022) identify sectors with 'systemically significant prices' which 'present systemic vulnerabilities for monetary stability' (p. 1), among which they find energy and basic necessities. This indicates that basic goods as defined in this chapter tend to be stronger drivers of inflation than other goods. One possible explanation depends on the place of goods in the supply chain – such as 'basic goods' in the sense of Sraffa (1960), which enter directly or indirectly the production of every good in the economy. Another explanation, along the lines of this chapter, is that monetary policy is less effective in taming inflation when it is driven by necessary goods.

ON SOME IMPLICATIONS OF HIERARCHICAL DEMAND

Despite its simplicity, the model presented above can shed an interesting light on the aforementioned debates between supply-versus-demand and internal-versus-external inflation.

Supply versus Demand

In the model, additional demand would concern comfort, which means that demand-driven inflation would manifest in the form of higher prices for comfort goods, not basic goods. Looking at the data for the Eurozone in 2022, where headline inflation stood at 9.2 per cent, it can be seen that the main contributions came from 'housing, water, electricity, gas and other fuels' (2.90 per cent), 'food and non-alcoholic beverages' (2.66 per cent) and 'transport' (1.01 per cent), which together explained over 70 per cent of inflation.

Admittedly, not all use of food, energy and transport by households falls under 'basic' needs, but most of it does. For that reason, it seems fair to reject the idea that inflation is demand-driven.[7] In the context of the model, the current inflation would thus be described as supply-driven, but it would be interesting to enrich the model with market mechanisms to see if this observation still holds.

Internal versus External

It can be argued that the current inflation comes from world markets, especially commodity markets. Unfortunately, the model presented above does not include features of an open economy, although this is something that shall be added in the future. For instance, it would be interesting to add the possibility of inflation being imported, or of foreign demand leading to shortages in the domestic economy.

Nonetheless, it is possible to derive a few intuitions without going through the whole process of formalising a new model. One way the results of the above two-good model could be refined would be depending on the proportion of basic imported goods and comfort imported goods.[8] If the price of imported comfort goods increases, the demand for these goods will be reduced, and any subsequent restrictive economic policy will help reduce the trade imbalance by reducing the demand for these imports. On the other hand, if the price of imported basic goods increases, the nominal demand for these goods will increase, thereby deteriorating the trade balance – and if restrictive policies can have any chance to improve the trade balance, it will not be through reducing demand for these goods, but the demand of imported comfort goods.

Given that Europe relies on energy imports, which have been immensely disrupted by the recent geopolitical developments, the spectacular deterioration of the trade balance of a country like Germany makes sense in that respect.

CONCLUSION

Monetary policy aims to control inflation by affecting the amount of money spent on consumption. In this chapter I have argued that the composition of demand, in particular the existence of a hierarchy of needs, should be taken into account when assessing the effectiveness of monetary policy. Inflation is rarely evenly spread across all categories: instead, the price of certain goods tends to rise faster than others. It should not be expected that monetary policy has the same impact regardless of which category of goods drive the inflation process.

To substantiate this claim, I formalised a simple model distinguishing between basic goods and comfort goods. Households spend on comfort goods (and save) only once they have satiated their need for basic goods. I then introduced several shocks in the model, consisting of located price increases and reduction in disposable income – taken as a proxy for restrictive monetary policy as it reduces aggregate demand.

The results indicate the existence of an asymmetry between the case when inflation mostly comes from comfort goods, as opposed to when it comes from basic goods. When inflation is driven by comfort goods, restrictive monetary policy will reduce the demand for the most inflationary segment of the consumption, which can be considered effective – at least for argument's sake. On the other hand, when price increase is driven by basic goods, restrictive monetary policy will leave the most inflationary segment of the consumption basket untouched, while reducing the demand for relatively less inflationary goods, which appears as a clear failure of monetary policy. From what precedes, I conclude that the category composition of inflation, and the location of the most inflationary goods in the consumption hierarchy (Lavoie, 1994) are even more important concerns than the supply-versus-demand or internal-versus-external nature of inflation.

Although the above presentation is mostly theoretical, the conclusions of the model have potential implications for the real world. Indeed, the current inflation in Europe has been driven mostly by the price of goods which broadly fall into the category of necessary goods. Although adjustments in the demand for necessary goods are possible, such as buying budget food items and waiting for commercial offers, there is a consumption floor below which spending cannot go – unless extreme economic events take place, forcing people to turn to food banks or even go hungry. Relying on a reduction in the demand for necessary goods to keep inflation under control is therefore misguided.

NOTES

1. The fundamental idea behind this chapter comes from a remark by my colleague Sebastian Valdecantos, who I would like to thank and cannot be held responsible for any of the mistakes made.
2. Weber et al. (2022, p. 2) similarly write: 'In policy debates, most economists have until recently tended to see inflation as a purely macroeconomic phenomenon: Monetarists as the result of "too much money chasing too few goods" and New Keynesians as a matter of the relation between aggregate demand and capacity utilization. The key variables to control inflation from both perspectives are thus macroeconomic: the quantity of money and government spending.'
3. It can be argued that the concept of price elasticity of supply only applies to perfect competition, while in a context of imperfect competition the monopolist or the oligopolists decide the price, thus rendering the whole concept of price elasticity of supply a self-centered, circular, and rather irrelevant notion. It would then be more proper to talk about 'inelastic supply' instead of 'price inelastic supply'. This point was brought to my attention by Peter Skott.
4. This demographic effect can be seen as a particular form of income effect. This point was brought to my attention by Jesper Jespersen.
5. I have avoided using the term 'luxury goods' as I think luxury goods are only a subset of comfort goods. A sofa is a comfort good, in the sense that it is not needed for survival, but it would be excessive to consider all sofas, including the cheapest ones, as luxury goods.
6. Note that the meaning of 'basic goods' in this chapter differs from the meaning adopted by Sraffa (1960).
7. One nuance should be made: even the most basic goods can see their prices affected by demand conditions in the real world. This is due to the conjunction of a few reasons. Fixprice and flexprice markets cohabit and interact: goods transacted on markets where prices fluctuate according to supply and demand can be used in the production of goods whose prices are administered (by companies or the government), and conversely. Supply and demand determinants of inflation are often intertwined.
8. This will add trade balance considerations – in line with the Marshall-Lerner-Robinson theorem – to the ones raised in the above model.

REFERENCES

Bilger, François (1985) *L'expansion dans la stabilité*, Economica, Paris.

Harrod, Roy (1936) *The Trade Cycle*, Clarendon Press, Oxford.

Kalecki, Michał (1954) *Theory of Economic Dynamics*, Routledge, London.

Lavoie, Marc (1994) 'A post Keynesian theory of consumer choice', *Journal of Post Keynesian Economics*, 16 (4), pp. 539–562.

Lavoie, Marc (2014) *Post Keynesian Economics: New Foundations*, Edward Elgar Publishing, Cheltenham, UK and Northampton, MA, USA.

Lerner, Abba P. (1934) 'The concept of monopoly and the measurement of monopoly power', *Review of Economic Studies*, 1 (3), pp. 157–175.

Lerner, Abba P. (1977) 'From pre-Keynes to post-Keynes', *Social Research*, 44 (3), pp. 387–415.

Nersisyan, Yeva and Wray, L. Randall (2022) 'What's causing accelerating inflation: Pandemic or policy response?', Levy Economics Institute, Working Papers Series, No 1003.

Ronkainen, Antti (2022) 'Tunnen kuinka vauhti kiihtyy, mutta kuinka kauan kansa viihtyy?', *Suomen Kuvalehti*, https://suomenkuvalehti.fi/vallan-mahotonta/tunnen-kuinka-vauhti-kiihtyy-mutta-kuinka-kauan-kansa-viihtyy/

Sraffa, Piero (1925) 'Sulle relazioni tra costo e quantità prodotta', *Annali di economia*, 2, pp. 277–328.

Sraffa, Piero (1926) 'The laws of returns under competitive conditions', *Economic Journal*, 36 (144), pp. 535–550.

Sraffa, Piero (1960) *Production of Commodities by Means of Commodities*, Cambridge University Press, Cambridge.

Weber, Isabella M., Jauregui, Jesus Lara, Teixeira, Lucas and Nassif Pires, Luiza (2022) 'Inflation in times of overlapping emergencies: Systemically significant prices from an input–output perspective', Economics Department Working Paper Series, No 340.

PART III

Methodology and theory

11. On Keynes's uncertainty: a tragic rational dilemma

Anna Maria Carabelli

INTRODUCTION

Keynes's uncertainty is a legacy of Greek tragedy: uncertainty as tragic choice. In general, Keynes's uncertainty is characterised by three conditions: ignorance, low weight of argument (evidential weight) and incommensurability of probability. It is this third condition that I address in my chapter. The non-comparability and incommensurability of Keynes's logical probability is intrinsic, due to the nature of the material constituting his probability. In Keynes, the material of probability is – in general, apart from a few specific cases – non-homogeneous, since the reasons, grounds or evidence are heterogeneous and incommensurable. There is no possibility to reduce this heterogeneity characterising the material of Keynes's probability with the use of a common or homogeneous unit of measure, since no common unit of quantities of probability exists; nor is there any possibility of introducing tacit assumptions of atomicity and independence. I consider Keynes's uncertainty as an incommensurable magnitude; thus, I view uncertainty from a new perspective.

When reasons are heterogeneous and compelling, irreducible and irresolvable conflicts arise. In these situations, decision-making (human conduct in general and economic decision in particular) is not based on reasonableness: it poses a rational dilemma. In my view, Keynes's uncertainty characterises situations of rational dilemma. When uncertainty reigns, indecision, vacillation of judgement and cognitive instability result. In Carabelli (1998a, 1998b, 2021) I suggested that, for Keynes, the case of uncertainty as non-comparable and incommensurable probabilities is loosely connected with Greek tragedy and I showed that tragedy influenced Keynes from the outset of his intellectual career. In a few words, Keynes moves on from Greek tragedy to incommensurable probability, and then on to economics.

In the earliest period, in 1904–1906, Keynes is interested in moral dilemmas and irreducible conflicts, typical of ancient Greek tragedy and classical drama.

In my 1998 article I examined the evidence of the early influence of tragedy on Keynes, and the themes of tragedy in which he was interested – in particular, the theme of the noble hero and situations of moral and rational conflicts and dilemmas. I also examined his tragic view of ethics and aesthetics. Keynes's constant attention to the non-comparability and incommensurability of magnitudes (probability and economic magnitudes such as aggregate utility, the general level of prices, real capital and aggregate real income) derives from this early interest in dilemmas; in particular, his concept of uncertainty as incommensurability can be associated with tragic rational dilemmas and choices. Dilemmas characterise situations of indecision, of irreducible conflict where compelling moral claims or reasons (in Keynes, *some* claims or reasons) cannot be weighed one against the other on a common scale, using a common, homogeneous unit of measure. These situations are within the domain of radical uncertainty, a concept that is relevant to Keynes's thinking in general, but which came to dominate his mature economic writings, and in particular the 1936 *General Theory* (GT; Keynes, 1971–1989, VII) and his 1937 *Quarterly Journal of Economics* article.[1] Also behind Keynes's uncertainty as incommensurability is his notion of partial similarity or likeness (partial analogy arising from shared features of similarity) and partial dissimilarity (partial negative analogy arising from shared features of dissimilarity), which he uses in his approach to generalisation from instances by inductive arguments. There are cases in which it is impossible to draw comparisons between two (three or more) complex objects or situations. In *Treatise on Probability* (TP; Keynes, 1971–1989, VIII) Keynes refers to the difficulties of comparing complex objects. He takes the example of comparing three books (TP, p. 39), recalling, as we will see, the GT passage on comparison of the two queens, Queen Victoria and Queen Elizabeth (GT, p. 40).

WHAT IS KEYNES'S UNCERTAINTY?

Unfortunately, Keynes does not define his notion of uncertainty. However, it can be characterised by three situations:

1. *Ignorance*, when there are no – even partial – reasons. In this case, there is no probability and no reasonableness. It is a situation of total ignorance; if a probability exists, it is unknown due to our want of reasoning power or cognitive skill. O'Donnell (1989, 2021) reduces Keynes's uncertainty to this case alone.
2. *Low weight of argument*. In TP, Keynes distinguishes two attributes of probable judgement: probability and the weight of argument. Probability concerns the balance between the favourable and unfavourable evidence, while the weight of argument concerns the total amount of knowledge

available. When the total amount of available knowledge is very limited, there is very low weight in probable belief (low 'intensity of belief', low confidence, using Keynes's own words). This means that reasonable beliefs are not firm, they are unstable and prone to high volatility when new knowledge, evidence or reasons become available; they easily change if a new piece of relevant information or knowledge becomes available. If two probabilities (two probable judgements) are equal and one has a greater weight, in TP Keynes suggests that the probability with greater weight is more reliable. Obviously, in Keynes, when the weight changes, the probability changes too. In which direction? It depends on the relevant new piece of knowledge, whether it is favourable or unfavourable. In any case, the weight of argument always increases.

3. *Intrinsic incommensurability* holds when Keynes's probabilities exist but are non-comparable and intrinsically incommensurable. Intrinsic incommensurability of probabilities does not depend on our inability to measure or know them. Keynes then transfers his philosophy of measurement and his notion of incommensurability from probability to economic magnitudes. Keynes's 'complex or manifold' economic magnitudes are the following: utility, the general price level (Keynes, 1910), aggregate capital and aggregate real output (GT, ch. 4).

KEYNES'S UNCERTAINTY AS INTRINSIC INCOMMENSURABILITY

In this contribution, I will focus mainly on uncertainty as intrinsic incommensurability of probabilities. Thus, I will not deal with ignorance or the weight of argument. Intrinsic incommensurability is not due to a lack of our knowledge of logical or calculable probabilities or on our inability to measure them: it is not a problem of measurement or of statistics.[2]

Further, uncertainty is not ontologically based (it does not depend on Davidson's non-ergodicity of the world system, nor on statistical mechanics) and does not concern the structure of material reality (empiricism). Uncertainty regards the intrinsic nature of probability: the material of Keynes's probabilities consists of propositions.

In TP, Keynes stresses this idea:

> It is not the case here that the method of calculation, prescribed by theory, is beyond our powers or too laborious for actual application. No method of calculation, however impracticable, has been suggested. Nor have we any *prima facie* indications of the existence of a common unit to which the magnitudes of all probabilities are naturally referable. A degree of probability is not composed of some homogeneous material, and is not apparently divisible into parts of like character with one another … Probabilities do not all belong to a single set of magnitudes measurable

in terms of a common unit. (TP, pp. 32–33; on measurability in terms of a common unit see also pp. 35–36)

As we will see, Keynes's probability belongs to 'complex or manifold' magnitudes. To appreciate the reconstruction and interpretation of Keynes's uncertainty I advance here, the reader should bear in mind the chronology below, which is relevant to the developments of his notion of uncertainty as incommensurability:

- 1904: 'Ethics in relation to conduct';
- 1905–1906: Early papers on ethics and aesthetics;
- 1907 and 1908: Early versions of TP: *Principles of Probability*;
- 1909: 'Essay on index numbers' (1971–1989, IX);
- 1910: *Lecture notes on the Stock Exchange*, on risk and speculation;
- 1921: TP (1971–1989, VIII);
- 1930: *Treatise on Money* (1971–1989, V);
- 1936: GT (1971–1989, VII);
- 1937: *Quarterly Journal of Economics* article on uncertainty (1971–1989, XIV); and
- 1939: Exchange with Hugh Townshend (1971–1989, XXIX).

1910 LECTURE NOTES ON THE STOCK EXCHANGE AND THE NATURE OF SPECULATION AND CH. 12 OF *GENERAL THEORY*

In evidencing the dates in the above chronology relevant to the developments of Keynes's notion of uncertainty, I will briefly consider his 1910 *Lecture Notes on the Stock Exchange* (Keynes, 1910). These notes represent a strong link between Keynes's early 1907–1908 versions of TP and his more mature economic writings, and in particular chapter 12 of the 1936 GT.

In his 1910 manuscript *Notes* for the preparation of his lectures on the stock exchange, while examining the nature of speculation, Keynes distinguishes four main situations on the basis of the nature and calculability of risk (1910). He speaks of risk as calculable or incalculable but he never uses the term 'uncertainty', even though this term occurs in various passages by the authors he considers (e.g. Emery, 1896).

The four situations are the following:

1. When risk is not calculable. The example given by Keynes is insurance against political events with an insurance company ('some political insurances at Lloyd's').

2. When risk is more or less calculable. Keynes distinguishes it between two sub-cases:
   a. risk is 'not averaged'. The example is roulette at Monte Carlo; and
   b. risk is, instead, 'averaged'. The example is life or fire insurance.
3. Speculation.

Keynes sees situations (1) and (2a) as comparable to 'gambling'; in (1) the risk is not calculable, while in (2a) it is calculable but not averaged. (2b) is a situation assessed by insurance (averaged). Situation (3) is described only negatively, as not identical to 'taking risk'. It is also a situation differing from (1) and (2a), i.e. other than 'gambling'. As to speculation, Keynes points out:

> the essential characteristic of speculation is, it seems to me, the possession of superior knowledge. We do not mean by the risk of an investment its actual future yield – we mean the degree of probability of the yield we expect. The probability depends upon the degree of knowledge. In a sense, therefore it is subjective. What would be gambling for one man would be sound speculation for another (instance from betting). (1910, p. 93)

Thus, in 1910, speculation is dealt by Keynes in terms of his degrees of probability. The early distinction between speculation and gambling is fundamental to Keynes's analysis of financial markets and recurrent in all his thoughts (see Carabelli and Cedrini, 2013).

KEYNES'S PROBABILITY IN *TREATISE ON PROBABILITY*

Let us take a further step back and start from the beginning of the story. What is Keynes's probability? Keynes's probability is logical judgement; better, it is reasonable judgement: it is *having some reasons to believe*. 'Probability is concerned with *arguments*' (TP, p. 126, italics in original). It is not a frequency and Keynes is not an empiricist: 'Experience, as opposed to intuition, cannot possibly afford us a criterion by which to judge whether on given evidence the probabilities of two propositions are or are not equal' (TP, p. 94). And further: 'Under the aegis of an empirical philosophy they have sought in probability a quality belonging to the entities of phenomenal experience and have imagined that events have probabilities just as men belong to nations' (1907, p. 18). It deals with logically relevant and reasonable arguments. It is not a subjective degree of belief (à la Ramsey, De Finetti or Savage). It is not reducible to betting. In general, it is not numerical, not additive and linear; and it does not follow Bayes's theorem.

KEYNES'S DIFFERENT TYPES OF PROBABILITY IN *TREATISE ON PROBABILITY*: PHILOSOPHY OF MEASUREMENT

According to Keynes, there are, in general, many types of probability (precise; imprecise; orderable or comparable in terms of equal, more or less; indeterminate). Let us consider it in more in detail, using a classification based on three main cases and further sub-cases, broadly following TP's classification.

Case 1

a. *Precise (exact) probability*. Probability can be numerically measured, i.e. precisely measured: cardinal probabilities. This is the notion of calculable risk, to which the calculus of probability applies.
b. *Imprecise (inexact) probability*. Probability can be imprecisely measured with a numerical approximation or interval-valued probabilities. (TP, pp. 159–160)[3]

Case 2

Orderable and comparable probability in terms of equal, more or less. This case of orderable or comparable probability opens out the notion of probability to new situations other than those in which there are precise or approximate numerical probabilities: orderable probabilities. This case, for example, is highly relevant to Keynes's economics. It covers Keynes's analysis of speculation in monetary and financial markets, that is, for example, his liquidity preference in chapter 17 and also his view on long-term expectations in chapter 12 of GT (see Carabelli, 2021; Carabelli and Cedrini, 2013). As Keynes points out, the term 'probability' is commonly used in a broader sense than that implicit in its mathematical interpretation: 'mathematicians have employed the term [probability] in a narrower sense; for they have often confined it to the limited class of instances in which the relation is adapted to an algebraical treatment. But in common usage the word has never received this limitation' (TP, p. 6).

A requirement for comparison and ordering is *homogeneity* in kind, or in dimension, as we will see. In the 1907 version of *Principles of Probability* (p. 65) he writes of 'kinds of the same species of quantity'. In this case, we can properly speak of degrees of probability in conditions of limited knowledge and, because Keynes's logical probability is reasonableness, we can speak of degrees of reasonableness (TP, pp. 37–38).

Case 3

Indeterminate probabilities. These probabilities are non-comparable and even non-orderable. They are intrinsically incommensurable. There is *heterogeneity* in kind. This gives rise, as we will soon see, to rational dilemmas like Buridan's ass and the dilemma of the umbrella. It means indecision and uncertainty. In this case, we cannot speak of degrees of uncertainty.

Case 3 is the most relevant to Keynes's philosophy of measure, and indeed to my interpretation of his method, as it implies the intrinsic incommensurability ('indeterminateness') of probabilities. This idea of intrinsic incommensurability and indeterminateness is then transferred by Keynes from probability to economic 'complex or manifold magnitudes', through his 1909 'Essay on index numbers' (Keynes, 1971–1989, XI) and then to his economics. These probabilities can be non-comparable or even non-orderable.

Case 3 can be further split into two sub-situations (see Keynes's figure on p. 42 of TP):

a. when probabilities can be arranged in an order of magnitude; and
b. when probabilities cannot even be arranged in an order of magnitude.

In Case 3a, we cannot generally compare probabilities belonging to different orders. Quantitative comparison of the probabilities belonging to different orders is possible only if the different orders intersect with each other. The same degree of probability, therefore, may belong to more than one order. The two orderings intersect at a point. Anyway, Case 3a concerns situations in which different orders of probability exist:

> [I]t is possible … to find several sets, the members of which are measurable in terms of a unit common to all the members of that set; so that it would be in some degree arbitrary which we chose … Some probabilities are not comparable in respect of more and less, because there exists more than one path, so to speak, between proof and disproof, between certainty and impossibility; and neither of two probabilities, which lie on independent paths, bears to the other and to certainty the relation of 'between' which is necessary for quantitative comparison. (TP, pp. 36–38)

Keynes draws an analogy with the relations of orders of likeness between objects; we have the example of the three books mentioned above, and we will go on to see the comparison of the two queens in the GT:

> When we say of three objects A, B, and C that B is more like A than C, we mean, not that there is any respect in which B is in itself quantitatively greater than C, but that, if the three objects are placed in an order of similarity, B is nearer to A than C is. There are also … different orders of similarity. For instance, a book bound in blue morocco is more like a book bound in red morocco than if it were bound in blue calf;

> and a book bound in red calf is more like the book in red morocco than if it were in blue calf. But there may be no comparison between the degree of similarity which exists between books bound in red morocco and blue morocco and that which exists between books bound in red morocco and red calf. (TP, p. 39)

Case 3b is when there is not even ordering. This is due to the 'intrinsic' incommensurability of magnitudes. In his 1907 version of *Principles of Probability*, Keynes refers to the units of probability, which belong to 'different kinds' of magnitudes of probability:

> they are 'essentially' indeterminate ... I say 'essentially', because this indeterminacy is not simply relative to our knowledge or to a particular set of premises, but is absolute. We have to do with different kinds of the same species of quantity, whose units are essentially indeterminate in terms of one another, but which are sometimes comparable within certain limits. The case is not to be compared to that of a real number ... and a rational number ... In these probability scales a new conception of relative indeterminacy of units of magnitude must be introduced. For although we can always express one unit in terms of another to some degree of approximation, there are strict limits to this and we cannot increase at will the closeness of the approximation. (1907, p. 65)

In 1921, in TP, the same idea is stressed anew:

> It is not the case here that the method of calculation, prescribed by theory, is beyond our powers or too laborious for actual application. No method of calculation, however impracticable, has been suggested. Nor have we any *prima facie* indications of the existence of a common unit to which the magnitudes of all probabilities are naturally referable. A degree of probability is not composed of some homogeneous material, and is not apparently divisible into parts of like character with one another ... Probabilities do not all belong to a single set of magnitudes measurable in terms of a common unit. (TP, pp. 32–33; on measurability in terms of a common unit see also pp. 35–36)

Case 3b and Rational Dilemmas

In Case 3b, as seen, quantitative comparison of probabilities is not possible because the degrees of probability cannot be arranged even in an order of magnitude. In TP, Keynes asks 'But in another class of instances is it even possible to arrange the probabilities in an *order* of magnitude, or to say that one is the greater and the other less?' (TP, p. 31, italics in original). He offers two examples where probabilities cannot be arranged in any order at all. The first is relative to inductive arguments. He refers to a difference in *kinds*, in quality, 'if the grounds in the two cases are different'. There is clearly a problem of heterogeneity and variety of reasons and grounds:

> Consider three sets of experiments, each directed towards establishing a generalisation. The first set is more numerous; in the second set the irrelevant conditions have been more carefully varied; in the third case the generalisation in view is wider in scope than in the others. Which of these generalisations is on such evidence the most probable? There is, surely, no answer; there is neither equality nor inequality between them. We cannot always weigh the analogy against the induction, or the scope of the generalisation against the bulk of evidence in support of it. If we have *more* grounds than before, comparison is possible; but, if the grounds in the two cases are quite different, even a comparison of more and less, let alone numerical measurement, may be impossible. (TP, pp. 31–32, italics in original)

Keynes's second example – let me call it the 'umbrella dilemma' – is as follows:

> Is our expectation of rain, when we start out for a walk, always more likely than not, or less likely than not, or as likely as not? I am prepared to argue that on some occasions none of these alternatives hold, and that it will be an arbitrary matter to decide for or against the umbrella. If the barometer is high, but the clouds are black, it is not always rational that one should prevail over the other in our minds, or even that we should balance them, – though it will be rational to allow caprice to determine us and to waste no time on the debate. (TP, p. 32)

In reading the first example, the reader should take note of Keynes's italics. If we have 'more grounds than before', the ordering of probabilities in terms of equal, more or less is possible; if, on the contrary, the 'grounds are quite different', it is impossible. Thus, the impossibility of ordering probabilities is due to the heterogeneity of reasons, grounds or evidence.

We can now fully grasp why the quantitative characteristics of probability can be considered only when we are in situations represented by *more or less reasons* (grounds or evidence), and why this is impossible in situations represented by *different* and *opposite* reasons. In fact, the arranging of reasons in terms of more or less requires, as a preliminary condition, that these reasons be *homogeneous*. In situations of heterogeneity of reasons, we cannot say that we have more or less reason for one conclusion than another. The ordering of probabilities is impossible.

In Keynes's second example, it is clear that the impossibility of ordering is due to heterogeneity of reasons. 'High barometer' and 'black clouds' are clearly heterogeneous and opposite reasons. It is this heterogeneity of reasons, therefore, that is at the basis of the impossibility of ordering and consequently quantitatively comparing probabilities.

In his letters to Townshend, dated 27 July 1938 and 7 December 1938, Keynes explicitly refers to his early position in TP. He deals with joint judgements of probability and goodness in a manner similar to Case 3b, where probabilities cannot be arranged in any order at all due to the heterogeneity of reasons underlying them. In the 1907 PP version and in 1921 TP, he cites the example that I call his 'umbrella dilemma'. In his letter to Townshend, he refers to the dilemma of Buridan's ass (but he also makes a reference to Buridan's dilemma in his 1907 version of PP, p. 75):

> But that still leaves millions of cases over where one cannot even arrange an order of preference. When all is said and done, there is an arbitrary element in the situation … [I]n making a decision we have before us a large number of alternatives, none of which is demonstrably more 'rational' than the others, in the sense that we can arrange in order of merit the sum aggregate of the benefits obtainable from the complete consequences of each. To avoid being in the position of Buridan's ass, we fall back, therefore, and necessarily do so, on motives of another kind, which are not 'rational' in the sense of being concerned with the evaluation of consequences, but are decided by habit, instinct, preference, desire, will, etc. (1971–1989, XXIX, pp. 289, 294)

The umbrella dilemma and the Buridan's ass dilemma are obviously situations in which it is impossible to decide on Keynes's degrees of probability, i.e. on degrees of reasonableness. Thus, Keynes's uncertainty is characterised by rational dilemmas. We have finally answered our initial question: what is uncertainty for Keynes? The answer is the following: uncertainty is a rational dilemma.

UNCERTAINTY, RATIONAL DILEMMAS AND TRAGEDY

Keynes actually starts from ethics, and in particular tragedy (on his ethics, see Keynes, 1904a, 1905a, 1905b) to move on to probability (1904a, 1907) and economics (Keynes 1909, 1910, 1930, 1936, 1937). In ethics, Keynes distinguishes between 'speculative ethics' and 'practical ethics' (or 'morals'). Speculative ethics deals with values, ends, desires, claims, tragedy and dilemmas. It concerns ultimate ends and values that are intrinsically good – what in his 1938 paper *My Early Beliefs* Keynes calls his 'religion', a religion that he got from Moore (Keynes, 1971–1989, X, pp. 433–450). Practical ethics (or morals) concerns itself with conduct: '[Practical Ethics] would concern itself with conduct; it would investigate the difficult questions of the probable grounds of actions, and the curious connection between "probable" and "ought"; and it would endeavour to formulate or rather to investigate existing general maxims, bearing in mind their strict relativity to particular circumstances' (Keynes, 1905b).

Practical ethics deals with probability, uncertainty, action, politics and economics. Keynes's TP published in 1921 (the earlier versions were written in 1907 and 1908) is actually devoted to practical ethics and human conduct. TP focuses on logical probability and uncertainty, of fundamental relevance to his economics.

GREEK TRAGEDY AND MORAL DILEMMAS

Human life involves difficult choices and dilemmas, for the circumstances of life do not always help us towards the harmonious realisation of all our distinct ends. In his speculative ethics, Keynes believes in the existence of a plurality of ends and values. This is also true of his views on aesthetics. These ends and values are heterogeneous. He sees 'many different kinds of beauty as of virtue' (Keynes, n.d.). There is irreducibility in the case of heterogeneous plural ends and values: Keynes's pleasure, goodness and happiness. On pluralism, Keynes follows Aristotle rather than Plato. Aristotle stresses the plurality and variety of goodness and the fact that good is not reducible to a univocal scale. On the contrary, the Platonic tradition – like utilitarianism – embraces the idea of the unicity of ends and values: it reduces goodness to one dimension alone. But heterogeneous values and desires cannot be ordered on a univocal scale and no common unit exists: this is the starting point of Keynes's philosophy of measure.

In *Virtue and Happiness* (1905a): values and desires, being multiple and heterogeneous, may clash. Both are ultimate, so they cannot be ordered on a univocal scale. Keynes sees the desire for pleasure and the desire for goodness as irreconcilable. Why are they irreconcilable? Because the two units of measure are incommensurable: 'In the attempt to reconcile these two incommensurable units. In *Egoism* (1906), he writes: 'claims which I cannot easily reduce to common terms and weigh against one another upon a common balance'. It means that there is no common unit of measure, no common balance on which to weigh the two heterogeneous desires. The two units of measure are heterogeneous; pleasure and goodness are qualitatively and dimensionally different.

On moral conflicts or dilemmas, Keynes refers to the conflicts of duties, moral claims, values, interests and desires:

- the conflict between rational egoism and rational benevolence (1905c, 1906);
- the conflict between 'being good' and 'doing good' (1906);
- the conflict between public and private life (1905c);

- the conflict between moral duties: between particular and general good; between the interest of the individual and the interest of the community (1904b, in which Keynes refers to Agamemnon's dilemma); and
- the conflicts of desires: in particular, the conflict between the desire for pleasure and for goodness.

In *Virtue and Happiness* (1905a), Keynes criticises all the methods of reconciling moral conflicts adopted in history in both religion and philosophy. He identifies four main methods:

1. affirming that the good is only the pleasurable – the solution adopted by utilitarians;
2. affirming that the good is always associated with the pleasurable;
3. denying the authenticity either of goodness or of pleasure (the second is Moore's method); and
4. accepting that it is a mystery.

The theme of rational conflict in rationality is strictly connected with that of moral conflict in ethics. In moral dilemmas the conflict is between moral claims, while in rational dilemmas the conflict is between reasons, grounds, arguments or evidence (the umbrella dilemma; the Buridan's ass dilemma). The good and virtuous life is often associated with tragedy, disasters and dilemmas. In these situations, whatever we do will cause pain to somebody else. It will cause something we will regret. This leads to indecision and vacillation in human judgement, decision and action, i.e. uncertainty.

MANIFOLD OR COMPLEX MAGNITUDES

Keynes deals with complex magnitudes first with considerations on goodness, beauty and probability, and then transfers his philosophy of measure of probability to economic magnitudes: utility, price level, aggregate product, aggregate capital and time.[4] In *Treatise on Money* (Keynes, 1971–1989, V), where we find his best-known reference to 'complex or manifold' magnitudes, Keynes refers to 'incommensurable directions':

> This difficulty in making precise quantitative comparisons is the same as arises in the case of many other famous concepts, namely of all those which are complex or manifold in the sense that they are capable of variations of degree in more than one mutually incommensurable direction at the same time. The concept of purchasing power, averaged over populations which are not homogeneous in respect of their real incomes, is complex in this sense. The same difficulty arises whenever we ask whether one thing is superior in degree to another *on the whole*, the superiority depending on the resultant of several attributes which are each variable in degree

> but in ways non commensurable with one another. (*Treatise on Money*, p. 88, italics in original)

In chapter 4 of GT on the choice of the units of measure, Keynes similarly takes the example of comparing two queens, Queen Victoria and Queen Elizabeth:

> To say that net output today is greater, but the price level lower, than ten years ago or one year ago, is a proposition of similar character to the statement that Queen Victoria was a better queen but not a happier woman than Queen Elizabeth – a proposition not without meaning and not without interest, but unsuitable as material for differential calculus. (GT, p. 40)

The central concepts in macroeconomics are complex and the magnitudes considered by macroeconomics are also complex. These concepts are the volume of real output/income, the stock of real capital and the general price level (GT, p. 37). Keynes defines them as 'incommensurable collections of miscellaneous objects' (GT, p. 39). In particular, 'the community's output of goods and services [is] a non-homogeneous complex which cannot be measured' (GT, p. 38). In GT, there is another complex and heterogeneous magnitude, namely probability. Keynes considers it separately in chapters 5 and 12. There is also another complex magnitude in GT: time and the units of time (Carabelli and Cedrini, 2016, 2018).

VAGUENESS: KEYNES'S ARGUMENTATIVE SUBSTANTIAL LOGIC VERSUS FORMAL RUSSELLIAN LOGIC – ARTIFICIAL INTELLIGENCE AND DEFEASIBLE REASONING

How are we to deal with vagueness? In TP, Keynes writes: 'The object of a logical system of probability is to enable us to know the relations, which can easily be perceived, by means of other relations which we can recognise more distinctly – to convert … vague knowledge into more distinct knowledge' (TP, p. 57). Complex or manifold magnitudes are theoretically vague concepts. Incommensurable and indeterminate probabilities (uncertainty), goodness, beauty and economic magnitudes such as utility, the general price level, aggregate capital and aggregate output raise theoretical difficulties. Keynes refers to the well-known 'element of vagueness which … attends the concept of the general price level' (1971–1989, VII, p. 39). Theoretical vagueness does not mean that these concepts are vague and ambiguous from an ordinary language point of view or in business practice. In ordinary language, their meaning is easily grasped and they can be used for practical purposes. Theoretically, however, they remain 'conundrums' with 'no solution' (1971–1989, VII, p. 39). They raise difficulties that are purely theoretical 'in the sense that they never perplex, or indeed enter in any way into business decisions and have no relevance to the causal sequence of economic events, which are clear cut and determinate in spite of the quantitative indeterminacy of these concepts' (1971–1989, VII, p. 39).

NOTES

1. I thank the Provost and Scholars of King's College, Cambridge, for kind permission to quote from Keynes's manuscripts, held in King's College Library, Cambridge. Parts of this chapter have already been published in Carabelli (2021). I thank Palgrave Macmillan for permission to publish them.
2. For O'Donnell (1989, 2021), Keynes's uncertainty reduces itself to unknown probabilities, i.e. ignorance: an interpretation of Keynes's uncertainty that is untenable and too restrictive.
3. On interval-valued probabilities in Keynes, see Brady and Arthmar (2012) and Zappia (2016). According to Brady, imprecise or inexact probabilities and interval-valued probabilities constitute the main and indeed only relevant contribution by Keynes in TP. Brady repeatedly shows scorn for all the other interpreters of Keynes's probability for – as he has it – not having read part II of TP and in particular chapter XV.
4. For a detailed investigation of how Keynes makes this transfer, see Carabelli (1992, 2021).

REFERENCES

Brady, M.E. and Arthmar, R. 2012, Keynes, Boole and the interval approach to probability, *History of Economic Ideas*, 20, 3, 65–84.

Carabelli, A.M. 1992, Organic interdependence and Keynes's choice of units in the *General Theory*, in Gerrard, B. and Hillard, J., eds, *The Philosophy and Economics of J.M. Keynes*, Cheltenham, UK and Northampton, MA, USA, Edward Elgar Publishing, 3–31.

Carabelli, A.M. 1998a, Alcune osservazioni sulle Note di Keynes del 1910 sulla speculazione, in Vercelli, S., ed., *Incertezza, razionalità e decisioni economiche*, Bologna, Il Mulino, 207–222.

Carabelli, A.M. 1998b, Keynes on probability, uncertainty and tragic choices, *Cahiers d'Economie Politique*, 30–31, 187–222.

Carabelli, A.M. 2021, *Keynes on Uncertainty and Tragic Happiness: Complexity and Expectations*, London, Palgrave Macmillan.

Carabelli, A.M. and Cedrini, M.A. 2013, Further issues on the Keynes–Hume connection relating to the theory of financial markets in the *General Theory*, *European Journal of the History of Economic Thought*, 20(6), 1071–1100.

Carabelli, A.M. and Cedrini, M.A. 2016, This time is … complex: Keynes on time. Mimeo.

Carabelli, A.M. and Cedrini, M.A. 2018, Expectations, equilibrium and time in the *General Theory*, in Dow, S., Jespersen, J. and Tily, G., eds, *The General Theory and Keynes for the 21st Century*, Cheltenham UK and Northampton, MA, USA, Edward Elgar Publishing, 70–82.

Emery, H.C. 1896, *Speculation on the Stock and Produce Exchange of the United States*, New York, Columbia University Press.
Keynes, J.M., King's College Archive Centre, Cambridge, *The Papers of John Maynard Keynes*:
—1904a, *Ethics in Relation to Conduct* (UA/19).
—1904b, *The Political Doctrines of Edmund Burke* (November, UA/20).
—1905a, *Virtue and Happiness* (after the Easter vacation, MM/24.2).
—1905b, *Miscellanea Ethica* (July–September UA/21).
—1905c, *Modern Civilisation* (28 October UA/22).
—1906, *Egoism* (24 February UA/26).
—1907, *The Principles of Probability* (TP/A).
—1910, *Notebook, 8 Lectures on Company Finance and Stock Exchange* (Lent term, UA/6/3).
—n.d., *On Beauty and Art* (UA/23).
Keynes, J.M. (1971–1989), *The Collected Writings of John Maynard Keynes*, Vols I–XXX, E. Johnson and D.E. Moggridge eds, London, Macmillan.
O'Donnell, R. 1989, *Keynes: Philosophy, Economics and Politics: The Philosophical Foundations of Keynes's Thought and Their Influence on His Economics and Politics*, London, Macmillan.
O'Donnell, R. 2021, Keynes's *A Treatise on Probability*: The first century, *Review of Political Economy*, 33, 585–610.
Zappia, C. 2016, Whither Keynesian probability? Impolite techniques for decision-making, *European Journal of the History of Economic Thought*, 23 (5), 835–862.

12. The *Principle of Effective Demand* – reconsidered: 'Anything we can actually *do*, we can afford'

Jesper Jespersen

INTRODUCTION

> As I now think, the volume of employment is fixed by the entrepreneur under the motive of seeking to maximise his present and prospective profits; whilst the volume of employment which will maximise his profit depends on the aggregate demand function given by his expectations of the sum of the proceeds. (Keynes, 1936, p. 77)

This chapter intends to draw together a number of points related to the dynamics of the private sector. However, *effective demand*,[1] as I will interpret the concept below, can best be understood by drawing on several methodological elements.

Effective demand is an epistemological concept developed by Keynes (1936, ch. 3) in order to better understand the dynamic structures within the macroeconomic landscape (see Jespersen, 2009, ch. 2). It draws on the theory of microeconomic behaviour under conditions of uncertainty with the aim of developing *macro*economic behavioural relationships (causal relationship). The *Principle of Effective Demand* is presented by Keynes as a series of analytical semi-closures of the market system including both supply and demand of goods and labour based on the Open System Ceteris Paribus method (Chick, 2003). The analysis produces a geometric presentation of the *Principle of Effective Demand* where supply and demand meet in the market system. The real microeconomic novelty is that Keynes introduces explicitly the real-world condition that expectations related to future events are notoriously uncertain and cannot, therefore, be calculated by standard Probability Theory.[2] Hence, the standard analytical assumptions of full knowledge within neoclassical macroeconomics (based on general equilibrium and hence relevant *ceteris paribus* preconditions) have to be cancelled, which by necessity will make the theory more complex, but also more realistic.

The *Principle of Effective Demand* was presented by Keynes as an epistemological strategy of how to establish macroeconomic behavioural relations and hence a macroeconomic analytical model with a microeconomic foundation.[3]

The chapter is organized as follows. The next two sections deal with aspects of Keynes's original theory of '*effective* demand' in *The General Theory* and are followed by a section on dynamic implications for short- and longer-run analyses. The chapter then sketches some policy implications and, finally, the chapter is concluded.

KEYNES CALLED HIS NEW MACROECONOMIC THEORY THE *PRINCIPLE OF EFFECTIVE DEMAND*

As mentioned, the intention of this chapter is to give an example of how a macroeconomic causal relationship can be modelled based on consistent microeconomic arguments related to supply and demand conditions with the inclusion of specific institutional conditions such as market power/competition and lack of certain knowledge (about the future). The choice of method plays a determining role for how macroeconomic 'behaviour' can be deduced on the basis of microeconomic theory and empirical data. Therefore, Keynes's micro foundation of macroeconomics went far beyond methodological individualism and stylized utility and profit-maximizing agents.

This was not an easy task to go beyond the simplistic neoclassical theory (re-erected 100 years later as the New Classical Economics by Robert Lucas et al.). The more heterogeneous and interrelated the underlying microeconomic structures are assumed to be, the more difficult it is to deduct a simple 1:1 macroeconomic causal relationship that is relevant for the analysis of the macroeconomic landscape.

Anyhow, I will use chapter 3 of Keynes's *General Theory*: *The Principle of Effective Demand* as an example of how important analytical results can be achieved by using an 'open-system method with semi-closures' (see Chick, 2003). When employing the *open system method*, there is no *a priori* requirement that the microeconomic behaviour and the institutional anchoring should be pre-designed, let alone reach a (general) equilibrium. On the contrary, it is an epistemological strength to employ an analytical procedure, where uncertainty causing future indetermination is a part of the outcome. In this case Keynes's macroeconomics is to be considered as more *general* than models where uncertainty is excluded by design, i.e. by *a priori* assumptions.

This methodological interpretation of the *Principle of Effective Demand* demonstrates that Keynes presented a (more) general theory of the economy as a whole based on an analysis of the supply side (production decisions) as well as the demand side (expected sales/proceeds) derived on companies' rational behaviour and expectations under uncertainty.

On the other hand, it should immediately be conceded that Keynes did not make it any easier for the reader to get this point by calling the theory the *Principle of Effective Demand.* It should be noted that Keynes used the term 'principle'. It is no coincidence that Keynes specifically wrote: *the principle* in the heading of the chapter. A 'principle' is more fundamental than just a theory. The unfortunate thing is that Keynes employed the expression 'equilibrium' as the outcome of his analytical model, where 'unemployment equilibrium' could prevail. He predicted in the Preface to the *General Theory* that his colleagues would waiver between thinking either 'totally wrong' (unemployment is a sign of disequilibrium in the labour market) or 'nothing new' (due to 'sticky wages') (Keynes, 1936, p. vii). Accordingly, Keynes's methodological practice of calling a short-run analytical standstill an 'equilibrium' has caused an endless row of misunderstandings.

It is a misreading of the *General Theory* to claim that the supply side is neglected. It is the interaction between the sum of the individual companies' sales expectations (aggregate demand) and their production costs (aggregate supply) that together determine the development in production and employment 'as a whole'[4] (see Box 12.1). Furthermore, it is my intention also to contribute to the eradication of the often presented point of view that Keynes's macroeconomic theory does not have a microeconomic foundation.[5]

BOX 12.1 AN OUTLINE OF THE *PRINCIPLE OF EFFECTIVE DEMAND*

The aggregate (and interrelated) supply function of the business sector dependent on costs, production conditions and market structure (competition)

\+

The companies' aggregate, but uncertain, sales expectations

\+

Institutional and competitive conditions

\+

Keynes's empirical statement: 'about the future we cannot know [with certainty]'

(Allow me to add, the longer into the future we look, the less we can know with any degree of certainty)

=

Principle of Effective demand

THE BUSINESS SECTOR'S FOCUS IS ON SUPPLY *AND* EXPECTED DEMAND

Aggregate Supply: Cost of Production

The supply side of the goods market is determined by the individual companies' cost functions. Keynes's *aggregate supply* function appears almost to be 'copied' from Marshall's *Principles of Economics*. It shows a connection between what Keynes calls 'supply price', the sales income/turnover that, given the cost structure, is necessary to ensure a 'normal profit'. Under the precondition of perfect competition, normal profit is what can be achieved in a branch that consists of profit-maximising companies. If a more than normal profit is earned in a branch it will attract new companies, which on the macro level will leave, *ceteris paribus*, the level of employment unchanged. This precondition entails that the *aggregate supply function that arises from 'horizontal addition' of companies' cost process*, which also represents the revenue that is necessary to cover the expected costs, mostly wage costs. Hence, the *supply function* looks like it has been taken directly from a standard, neoclassical textbook where *decreasing marginal productivity* is assumed, which explains the upward-sloping AS-curve in Figure 12.1 (Keynes calls it the Z-curve).

Aggregate Demand: Uncertain Expectations of Sales

> You will not find it [aggregate demand] mentioned even once in the whole works of Marshall, Edgeworth and Professor Pigou, from whose hands the classical theory has received its most mature embodiment. (Keynes, 1936, p. 32)

Today it is trivial to ascertain that the new analytical contribution, in relation to the *macro*economic standard literature in the 1930s, was Keynes's introduction of *aggregate demand for goods and services* at the *macro* level. Keynes mentioned in the quote above that it is peculiar that not even Alfred Marshall, who if anyone is the father of the supply *and* demand diagram at the micro/market level, leaves out the demand side at the macro level. The neoclassical view on macroeconomics was based on general market equilibrium theory, where 'supply creates its own demand'. Hence, the supply side is the determinant part of macroeconomic development – especially in the longer run ('when the ocean is flat again'). Keynes's *macro* theory differs from the neoclassical macro theory by introducing the term *aggregate demand*, i.e. the total *expected* sales at the macro level that forms the 'the other half' of the production plans decided by entrepreneurs at the micro level. The individual company is assumed by Keynes to plan its (optimal) production (and employment) on the basis of costs and the *expected* future receipts. If entrepreneurs are correct in their expectations, 'supply may be matched by expected demand'; but there is no adjustment mechanism in the macroeconomic system, which secures that 'equilibrium' corresponds with full employment. Individual firms care about their individual 'equilibrium'. The sum of the individual firms' rational behaviour does not necessarily add up to full employment. The macroeconomics system could be left in a persistent state of unemployment, where firms have no incentive to change the size of production or employment, as illustrated in Figure 12.1. However, in rare cases aggregate demand could add up to more than full employment, then the crossing of the Z- and D-curves would be to the right of full employment.

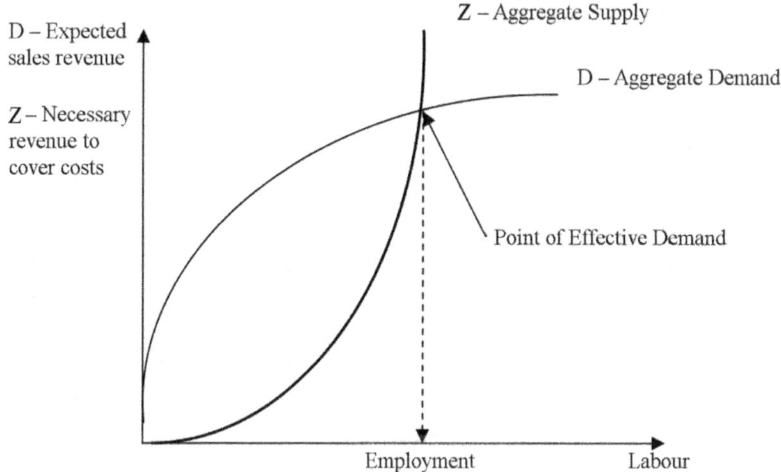

Figure 12.1 *A macroeconomic equilibrium: effective demand*

'Effective demand' is the intersection of these individual entrepreneurs' rational behaviour related to supply and demand towards a (partly) uncertain future. In this way, Keynes broke, as mentioned, with the neoclassical precondition of a self-adjusting market economic system securing full employment (Keynes, 1934). But he does not really explain how the business sector's macro expectations are formed. There seems to be a missing link from microeconomic behaviour by heterogenous agents acting under uncertain condition to the aggregate macro level. In some way Keynes jumps directly from the individual actor to the 'community level' of aggregate demand, where this D-curve is explained by *the psychological characteristics of the community, which we shall call the propensity to consume* (p. 28). Then, he concludes in the following paragraph: 'D is what we have called above effective demand' (p. 29). It would have been much clearer and more stringent if he had written: 'D is what we have called aggregate demand and the intersection of the Z- and D-curves is *effective demand* derived from the *Principle of Effective Demand.*

THE DYNAMIC CONTENT OF THE *PRINCIPLE OF EFFECTIVE DEMAND*

In the Short Run

Keynes's macroeconomic dynamics in the short run is summarized in *General Theory*, chapter 18, where capital equipment, labour force and productivity are assumed to be unchanged. Furthermore, to make the new theory as clear-cut as possible, he makes the assumption of entrepreneurs' expected sales proceeds being correct. No divergence between what is produced on a daily basis and what is sold, as the general case, as long as aggregate demand is unchanged.

Hence, Keynes concentrated in books 3 and 4 on aggregate demand consisting of private consumption (C) and private real investments (I) (being dependent on marginal efficiency of capital and the rate of interest). His new and revolutionary argument was that C + I do not by any self-adjusting market mechanism add up to full employment production of the private sector. When the propensity to save (depending mainly on consumers' uncertainty towards the future and less on the rate of interest) makes the amount of savings larger than real investments at full employment, the intersection of aggregate supply and aggregate demand, what Keynes called *effective demand* (see Figure 12.2) settles in a state of unemployment equilibrium. By calling this position an equilibrium outcome he already in the Preface of *General Theory* predicted that the neoclassical economists would accuse him of being either 'totally (analytical) wrong' or 'saying nothing new' (other than that inflexible/too-high wage level causes unemployment) (1936, p. vii).

Keynes called this situation with persistent unemployment, which if anything characterized Great Britain in the 1930s, deliberately an equilibrium; because a falling real or money wage level would not reduce unemployment (1936, ch. 19). In fact, Keynes argued that a falling wage would increase uncertainty and hence make wage earners (and households) even more parsimonious.

In this situation of aggregate demand being too small for full employment, demand management policy is the obvious answer. As Keynes expressed very clearly just before the inauguration of President Roosevelt in 1933: 'Look after Unemployment, and the Budget will look after itself' (Jespersen, 2018).

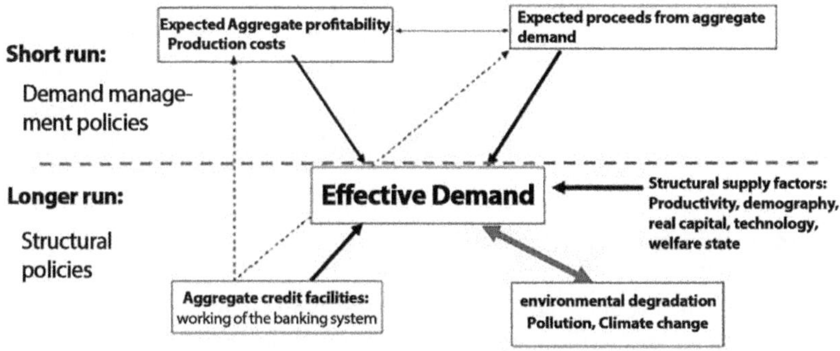

Figure 12.2 *Effective demand in the short and longer run*

In the Longer Run

Keynes mentions explicitly in the *General Theory* that he would consider a number of structural factors as frozen. In the lower part of Figure 12.2 I have listed a number of structural factors which would have an impact at either aggregate demand or aggregate supply and therefore on effective demand in the twenty-first century. Accordingly, only the first three arguments for changing structure listed below were explicitly mentioned by Keynes back in 1936:

1. Labour force: size, skills, age and preference for leisure time.
2. Growing real capital stock + improved technique = increased labour productivity.
3. Degree of competition (national and international).
4. Financial system.
5. Welfare state.
6. Environmental degradation, pollution and climate change.

Within this section I will make a few attempts to unfreeze some of these factors and look at the impact in a longer-run perspective. The task is rather speculative, because these frozen structural factors may or may not change and if they do it is often in an unpredictable way.

In many ways it would have been more respectful to Keynes and his theoretical contribution not to speculate on these longer-run perspectives. Because, as Keynes wrote in 1937, 'About the future we simply do not know' (and let me add 'cannot know'). On the other hand, in the early 1930s Keynes did make a similar long-run speculation, when he wrote the essay 'The economic possibilities for our Grandchildren'. In this essay he took an unconventional long-term view: '[T]ake wings into the future. What can we reasonably expect

… hundred years hence?'.[6] So, we may, like Keynes did, speculate on what impact changes in the frozen factors might have in the longer run. Of course, many post-Keynesian scholars have already made such exercises within Post-Keynesian Growth Theory (see for instance Chick and Freeman, 2018).

Within this chapter I must limit myself. There will not be space for a thorough analysis of the possible longer-term consequences of all these possible structural changes.

The Impact of Increased Macro Productivity

I will primarily look at changes in productivity, which has a permanent impact on the supply capacity of the business sector. Keynes, in his 1930 essay mentioned above, played with the idea that the overall productivity could continue to grow by 2 per cent per annum in the future, as it (according to his rough calculation) had done for the last centuries. The outcome of this rather simple assumption is somewhat astonishing, because it implies the potential gross domestic product (GDP) would double every 35 years, hence a quadrupling in 70 years. So, looking at the time of his grandchildren GDP could end up four times larger than in the 1930s. But, Keynes became doubtful, because this enormous potential growth capacity requires to be realized that aggregate demand grows in tandem with supply. In that case, effective demand would also quadruple. But, Keynes in the next paragraph asks the reader, would this development also mean a parallel rise in welfare? His answer was a clear-cut 'no': workers, he presumed, would much prefer a somewhat reduced working time/load than the unpresidential rise in material living standards. In this essay he suggested that his 'grandchildren' had the possibility to reduce the workload by a half and still experience a doubling in living standards compared to Keynes's generation. To many people in the middle of the misery of the 1930s this prospect must have sounded like Paradise on Earth.

In the year 2022, more than 20 years beyond Keynes's calculation, what do we see? A GDP in the Western countries which, in fact, has more than quadrupled compared to the 1930s and as a consequence a number of working hours for the ordinary family, which has hardly changed. One reason for this surprising development is the establishment of the welfare state, which today employs approximately one third of the labour force. Seemingly, increased material living standards together with this manifest welfare state have been preferred in the Western world by the population.

If we – like Keynes did 80 years ago – once again 'take wings into the future', what do we then see? If we turn our attention to the official economic institutions, for instance the Organisation for Economic Co-operation and Development (OECD) and its projections of GDP for the middle of this century, we see a calculation showing the doubling of GDP one more time.

Does that make sense? Keynes would immediately have responded: absolutely not. But, to modern politicians, the answer is an absolutely 'yes'.[7] The different answers seem to rely on different views of the role of government. To Keynes government was responsible for full employment and a reasonably fair distribution (see 1936, ch. 24). Modern economists see the rising tax revenue from an ever growing GDP as the ultimate financial source, making it possible to meet the ever expanding popular call for increased welfare and sustainable development. Growth in GDP is seen as the key to generating the income for the government, which is needed to overcome the negative side effects on distribution and environment caused by the growing economy. This is an argument which might in the end lead to a vicious cycle of degradation.

POLICY IMPLICATION: 'ANYTHING WE CAN *DO*, WE CAN AFFORD'

Once again there could be good reason to listen to Keynes.[8] We are approaching a climate crisis unfolding with increasing speed around us. A situation which makes me recall what Keynes argued in the middle of the Second World War, where the experiences and potential damages were even more scarring than today. He was looking around a bombed London and at a military budget taking up half of GDP and concluded: 'Anything we can *do*, we can afford'. So, when the war was over, nearly anything could be done by the government, if the population accepted high tax rates, this would secure the increased GDP necessary for growing productivity to be (partly) directed into the welfare sectors. In this way it became possible during the 1950s and 1960s to develop a welfare state contemporarily with expanding private consumption.

Today, there is still an increasing demand for welfare goods and for real investment in sustainable development to secure the future for our grandchildren. Can we afford these investments? Taking into consideration that productivity is projected, for instance by the OECD, to increase by 2 per cent each year and hereby to double the potential GDP within 35 years, it does not seem to be a relevant question. But investments in green economics require, like military expenses during the war, that a larger proportion of GDP goes to the public sector by rising tax rates. Fortunately, the green transition is much less expensive than fighting a war – and labour is not engaged in the army, but is available for green investments. To make this transformation happen public revenue as a percentage of (the growing) GDP has to be expanded. Hence, tax rates have to be higher in this transitory period. It would be obvious to increase CO2 taxes or raise the price of CO2 permits. This tax has the triple useful effects of: (1) supporting the change from black energy to green energy; (2) making energy in general more costly, which would change the behaviour of production and consumption; (3) using part of the revenue to support low-income families (in general) and the other part as subsidies to energy savings (for instance, insolation of public buildings and private homes) and green investments. By the way, when CO2 neutrality has been achieved, the CO2 tax will disappear by itself!

Probably the only thing Keynes would really have objected to, when giving advice on how to support our grandchildren, would have been the idea of zero growth, not to speak about negative growth as a cure for the upcoming climate crisis. When the transition to sustainability has been fulfilled in 30 years, then it might be time to think about a substantial reduction in average working time and to enjoy 'love, beauty and truth'.[9]

CONCLUSION

What have we learned by reconsidering the *Principle of Effective Demand*? First of all that 'effective demand' is the outcome of a dynamic macroeconomic market-based analysis involving, of course, aggregate demand, but equally important also aggregate supply. In the short-run analysis one could use a (semi-)closed model, where a number of structural factors are frozen – among other productivity. But, when we take 'wings into the future. What can we reasonably expect?'. Keynes gives two answers to this question – one is 'we don't know', because the future is fundamentally uncertain and the second is to point at the risk that an unregulated capitalist market economy undermines social morality, and thereby prevents us from pursuing a 'good society'. Both answers point at the necessity of government intervention and an active fiscal policy.

Accordingly, we (in fact, the elected politicians) should take the uncertain future in our hands by setting up social and physical safeguards to reduce the possible consequences of likely political, economic and environmental upheaval,[10] which is as relevant today as it was in the 1930s. So, what we collectively decide to do, i.e. plan with regard to private consumption and real investment and public expenditures, we can also afford, if real resources are available. Once again, I leave the word to Keynes, when he in his 1945 speech to the Economic Society gave a toast to his fellow economists. 'We, the economists, are the trustees, not of civilization, but of the *possibilities* of civilization' (Harrod, 1951, pp. 193–194, emphasis added). Keynes had at an earlier stage pointed at the seemingly ever growing productivity due to technical innovations and more industrial capital as opening the door to the future, 'where nearly everything is possible'.

Increased supply capacity together with aggregate demand, what Keynes called *effective demand*, both directed by market forces and by governments, are, if fulfilled, 'the possibilities for our grandchildren' to live a life, where 'love, beauty and truth' go hand in hand with sustainable development and a much shorter working load. But you have to be patient for another 30–40 years.

ACKNOWLEDGEMENTS

Finalizing this chapter in January 2023 gives me an opportunity to express my respect for the unlimited inspiration and intellectual support which I have through more than 30 years received from the late Victoria Chick. She as early as in her seminal book *Macroeconomics after Keynes* in 1983 pointed at chapter 3 of *The General Theory* as the key to Keynes's macroeconomics, which could be used as a platform for the development of post-Keynesian economics. In addition, I wish to thank Finn Olesen for many constructive comments and encouragement.

NOTES

1. A recommended textbook presentation of effective demand can be found at www .economicsdiscussion .net/ keynesian -economics/ keynes -theory/ the -principles -of -effective -demand -and -employment -determination -keynes -general -theory/ 14375.
2. If anything, this conclusion was the outcome of his fellow dissertation for King's College, Cambridge, published in a slightly revised form as *Treatise on Probability* in 1921 (Johnson and Moggridge, 1972–1989, vol. VIII).
3. Keynes's monetary theory summed up under the name of 'liquidity preference' is another example of such a macroeconomic causal relationship that is drawn up on the basis of microeconomic supply and demand behaviour on the financial markets under consideration of institutional conditions.
4. One can always discuss what the most effective strategy is when new theories are to be presented. For Keynes it was critical to include demand on an equal footing with the supply conditions, also in the macroeconomic analysis. This is probably part of the explanation for the choice of this terminology. This choice was so effective that nobody subsequently doubted the fact that Keynes placed special emphasis on demand, so effective that ever since, Keynes and Keynesian economy, in a more superficial reading, is often presented as exclusively a demand theory, which is an exaggeration of at least the same dimension. The 'inheritance from Marshall' had naturally to include the fact that *macro*economic development was also analysed as a result of the interaction between supply and demand decisions at the actor level.
5. Allow me to pay tribute to two important sources of inspiration for this reinterpretation of the *Principle of Effective Demand* – Chick (1983, ch. 4) and Hartwig (2007).
6. In fact, there has been published a collection of essays written by mainly Keynesian scholars celebrating the 75th anniversary of 'The economic possibilities'. These essays are remarkable by not mentioning environmental degradation nor sustainable development at all, see Pecchi and Piga (2008).

7. In Denmark, the new center government has put forward a law to cancel one of the traditional public holidays. The argument is to make it possible to finance tax reduction and increased military expenses, sic!
8. The quote in the chapter title and the above heading is Keynes's conclusion in 1942, when he on the radio was asked 'What to do?'. His answer was based on his still rather new macroeconomic insight in a condensed form: it is the availability of real resources, which is the determinant of *what is possible to do – not finance!*
9. See Keynes's paper 'My early beliefs' read to the Memoire Club at Charleston in 1937. The paper was on his request not published until after he had died. Later it was included in Johnson and Moggridge (1972–1989, pp. 433–450). This aspect of how to live in a society where the material capacity is abundant has, of course, been the concern of a number of post-Keynesian economists, for instance, Skidelsky and Skidelsky (2012).
10. In 1930, the revolution in Russia, the Wall Street financial collapse and San Francisco earthquake were still very present.

REFERENCES

Chick, V. (1983), *Macroeconomics after Keynes: A reconsideration of* The General Theory, Oxford: Philip Allan.

Chick, V. (2003), On open systems, *Brazilian Journal of Political Economy*, 24(1), pp. 3–16.

Chick, V. and A. Freeman (2018), The economics of enough: A future for capitalism or a new way of living?, in S. Dow, J. Jespersen and G. Tily (eds), *Money, Method and Contemporary Post-Keynesian Economics*, Cheltenham, UK and Northampton, MA, USA: Edward Elgar Publishing, pp. 148–159.

Harrod, R. F. (1951), *The Life of John Maynard Keynes*, London: Macmillan.

Hartwig, J. (2007), Keynes vs. the post Keynesians on the Principle of Effective Demand. *European Journal of the History of Economic Thought*, 14(4), pp. 725–739.

Jespersen, J. (2009), *Macroeconomic Methodology: A Post-Keynesian Perspective*, Cheltenham, UK and Northampton, MA, USA: Edward Elgar Publishing.

Jespersen, J. (2018), Look after employment, and the budget will look after itself, in T. Veggeland (ed.), *Keynesian Policies: A New Deal in the European Narrative: Employment, Equality and Sustainability*, New York: Nova Science Publishers, pp. 151–169.

Johnson, E. and D. Moggridge (eds) (1972–1989), *The Collected Writings of John Maynard Keynes*, 30 vols, London: Macmillan and Cambridge: Cambridge University Press.

Keynes, J. M. (1934), *Is the Economic System Self-Adjusting?*, London: The Listener, 21 November 1934, reprinted in Johnson and Moggridge (1972–1989), vol. XIII, pp. 485–492.

Keynes, J. M. (1936), *The General Theory of Employment, Interest and Money*, London: Macmillan.

Keynes, J. M. (1942), 'How much does finance matter?, in D. Moggridge (ed.), *Keynes on the Wireless*, London: Palgrave Macmillan, pp. 215–224, reprinted in Johnson and Moggridge (1972–1989), vol. XXVII, pp. 264–270.

Keynes, J. M. (1973 [1930]), *The Economic Possibilities for Our Grandchildren*, reprinted in Johnson and Moggridge (1972–1989), vol. IX, pp. 321–332.

Marshall, A. (2013 [1890]), *Principles of Economics*. Basingstoke: Palgrave Macmillan.
Pecchi, L. and G. Piga (eds) (2008), *Revisiting Keynes: Economic Possibilities for Our Grandchildren*, Cambridge, MA: MIT Press.
Skidelsky, R. and E. Skidelsky (2012), *How Much Is Enough*?, London: Allen Lane.

13. Lucas, modern macroeconomics and the post Keynesians

Finn Olesen

INTRODUCTION

Being one of the founding fathers of New Classical economics, Robert E. Lucas had a tremendous role to play in the development of modern mainstream macroeconomics.[1] As such, there are many seminal contributions in the writings of Lucas. In the present chapter, the focus is on the well-known Lucas critique.[2] Lucas (1976) presented not only a critique of the econometric practices of the Keynesian era, he also sketched a new way of how to perform better econometric policy evaluations. More so, he enhanced the search for an explicit microfoundation for macroeconomic theory. Basically, a Lucasian would argue, economics is about the study of individual decisions.[3]

The progressive power of Lucas' new research programme was so strong that consensus concerning methodological matters between the New Classicals and the New Keynesians later emerged.

Not only should macroeconomics rest upon explicit and antiquated, although accepted, microeconomic axioms; macroeconomic theory also had to be formulated exclusively by use of mathematical modelling.[4] Likewise, the focus of the macroeconomic analysis was primarily narrowed down to supply-side effects only. Demand-side effects, in fact only including shocks of an exogenous nature, were in general not able to affect the macroeconomic outcome.

Finally, after years of debate between the two schools of macroeconomic thought concerning theoretical aspects, but agreeing on methodological matters, a new synthesis gradually arose: the New Neoclassical Synthesis (NNS) with its dynamic stochastic general equilibrium modelling (DSGE) models took over and became synonymous with modern macroeconomics. As such, one could argue that the Lucas critique initiated a transformation of macroeconomics – it came to have a tremendous impact on macroeconomic theory and policy analysis.

The present chapter is organised as follows. The next section aims to give a review of Lucas (1976), pointing to some of the major consequences that the

Lucas critique had on the development of macroeconomics. Next, the focus is on Lucas and the post-Keynesians. In general, it is argued that Keynes himself, to some degree in his *General Theory* and elsewhere, addressed problems of a similar nature to those discussed in Lucas (1976). As such, post-Keynesians should be familiar with and accept much of what is included in the Lucas critique. Finally, the chapter is closed by some concluding remarks.

A REVIEW OF LUCAS (1976) AND SOME FUNDAMENTAL MACROECONOMIC CONSEQUENCES

Perhaps the name of Robert E. Lucas is primarily associated with the introduction of rational expectations in economics; however, he has contributed more to theory than just that. In 1976, he published what later became known as one of the most influential articles in macroeconomics of the 1970s: 'Econometric policy evaluation: A critique', as Lucas (2001: 291) himself seems to acknowledge: 'This "Lucas critique" ... is probably the most influential paper I have written'.

A core concern of Lucas was to state that there are limits to the use of short-term forecasting. A key point was that with the macroeconometric models of the 1970s you should not, in general, have expected to be able to make quantitative policy evaluations, as he noted, 'simulations using these models can, in principle, provide *no* useful information as to the actual consequences of alternative economic policies [due to] the deviations between the prior "true" structure and the "true" structure prevailing afterwards'; Lucas (1976: 20). That is, the 'true' structure of the economy in question is, at least to some degree, a function of the economic policy conducted, since policy actions might somehow change the behaviour of households as well as firms. Therefore, 'the kinds of policy simulations called for by the theory of economic policy are meaningless' Lucas (1976: 25), as you should expect the likelihood of systematic changes in parameters to be rather high.[5] That is, the parameters are policy regime dependent.

As emphasised by LeRoy (1995), Lucas (1976) should not only be seen as a critique particularly concerning Keynesian macroeconometric model building. More so, he criticised how policy analysis, in general, conflicted with general equilibrium theory. Therefore, the question of how economic policies should be evaluated changed from considerations concerning different changes in given policy instruments to considerations of alternative policy rules 'which allowed individual agents to formulate forward-looking dynamic optimization problems' Rudebusch (2005: 246) within a general equilibrium framework.[6] Because of this, the macroeconomic analysis had to undergo a fundamental change. From then on, 'it was necessary to put macroeconomics on a general equilibrium basis that incorporated rational expectations' (Lucas, 1995: 255). Such a change, of course, has consequences, not only theoretically and methodologically but also policy wise: 'the design of economic policy consists of three parts: a model to predict how people will behave under alternative policies, a welfare criterion to rank the outcomes of alternative policies, and a description of how policies will be set in the future' (Chari & Kehoe, 2006: 5).

In principle, without question, Lucas is quite right in his critique concerning the lack of stability for policy evaluation. However, you could argue that in general changes in economic policy are almost never of a significant magnitude. Rather, implemented changes in policy are more or less always of an incremental nature; making the Lucas critique right but not as important as it would be if changes in policy were of a more radical nature.

Likewise, politicians in the 1970s might perhaps traditionally have been more concerned with the short-run consequences of their policy actions rather than the longer ones. Later, it had to be admitted that due to the influence of the modern macroeconomic understanding of our time, politicians might nowadays have a keener eye on the longer-run consequences of changes in economic policy and other kinds of shocks to the economy. In some instances, the long-run perspective seems even more important than short-run considerations; take for instance the discussion about fiscal sustainability and how it restricts the manoeuvrability of short-run fiscal policy changes. However, due to the lessons learnt from the years of the Great Recession, e.g., the economic policy strategy of austerity, and the current Covid-19 pandemic, one could probably argue that concerns for the short run for some politicians have been put higher on the agenda than was hitherto the case in the years before these events took place (see, e.g., Byrialsen et al., 2021).

Finally, as changes in economic behaviour of households and firms and, more generally, changes in economic structure take time to unfold, Lucas' critique again is quite right but not that restrictive considering only the short-run effects of incremental policy changes.

Be that as it may, the conclusion made by Lucas is crystal clear: 'given that the structure of an econometric model consists of optimal decision rules of economic agents, and that optimal decision rules vary systematically with changes in the structure of series relevant to the decision maker, it follows that any change in policy will systematically alter the structure of econometric models'. Furthermore, such a fact is fundamental for 'issues involving policy evaluation', as it 'implies that comparisons of the effects of alternative policy rules using current macroeconometric models are invalid regardless of the performance of these models over the sample period or in ex ante short-term forecasting' (Lucas, 1976: 41).

Trying to overcome the fallacies of the macroeconometric policy evaluations of the 1970s, Lucas suggested that certain changes in the performance of macroeconomics were needed. Models should be explicit and complete, as all-important variables should be determined endogenously within the model rather than being postulated exogenously. As such, fluctuations in macroeconomic outcomes could be explained because of households and firms' decisions in an equilibrium-like process of adjustment. Likewise, you must do policy analyses that explicitly 'include a clear specification of how a current choice of policy will shape expectations of future policies' (Chari & Kehoe, 2006: 4, 5).

In sum, Lucas stated that (1) economic behaviour, in general, is governed by certain explicit rules, as behaviour is goal oriented, (2) the economic behaviour of both households and firms has, in some regards, an intertemporal character and (3) both households and firms act economically to some degree on expectations; (4) these expectations may change, for instance as a result of changes in economic policy, and thereby cause both households and firms to reconsider what to do in the future. (5) As such, reduced-form equations might be affected, in general, by (3) and (4), and might become unstable over time and, (6) economic models have to be based on an explicit microeconomic principles of optimisation.

That is, macroeconomics must be applied based on an intertemporal general equilibrium understanding with optimising agents using rational expectations. Using such expectations, 'agents learn from their mistakes, use their intellectual capacity to understand the way the economy works and exploit available information in an efficient way' (Svensson, 1996: 2). In trying to achieve this, macroeconomics is essentially transformed to become microeconomic as macroeconomic behaviour becomes similar to microeconomic behaviour – the representative agent seeking optimality and the policymaker seeking to minimise a social loss function.[7] As such, the efficient application of monetary and fiscal policy must be based on neoclassical welfare-economic principles. You must have 'a disciplined way of establishing the connection between particular policy actions and their consequences for resource allocation and individual welfare' (Lucas, 1986: 122); that is, you must use a welfare criterion when you have to choose between different policy proposals.

Furthermore, if economic fluctuations – business cycles – are to be explained by equilibrium-like reactions of agents to unanticipated changes in relevant variables, that must, in general, 'imply severe limitations on the ability of government policy to offset these initiating changes' (Lucas & Sargent, 1979: 10). The need to do economic policy to stabilise the macroeconomic outcome over time is hardly ever present seen from a Lucasian perspective. As such, to achieve optimal outcomes, the task of fiscal policy is restricted to minimise intertemporal distortions (due to various kinds of taxation). Likewise, as is the case with monetary policy, fiscal policy should be based on rules that are credible and transparent.

Today, modern macroeconomics is characterised by the NNS and their DSGE models. As mainstreamers would argue (see e.g., Woodford, 2009), they comply to the essence of the Lucas critique.

First, modern mainstreamers argue that macroeconomic analysis has to do with intertemporal optimisation within a general equilibrium framework. Having agreed on that, in general, you must acknowledge that 'microeconomic and macroeconomic analyses are no longer considered to involve fundamentally different principles' (Woodford, 2009: 269). Second, mainstreamers argue that you should base quantitative policy analysis on econometrically validated structural models. Third, a relevant macroeconomic analysis must incorporate expectations that have been endogenously formed. Furthermore, such policy analyses have 'to take into account the way in which expectations should be different in the case that an alternative policy was to be adopted' (Woodford, 2009: 271–272). Fourth, modern mainstreamers accept, in general, that real disturbances or shocks – that is, changes in technology, preferences and economic policy – are an important source behind economic fluctuations in real life. Fifth, and finally, economic policy wise, an optimal monetary policy defined by a Taylor Rule regime is seen as very effective, especially concerning inflation control.

The Lucas critique together with other Lucas theoretical contributions has had an important and lasting impact on macroeconomic theory and how macroeconomists evaluate economic policies, as, for instance argued by Snowdon (2007), Fischer (1996) and Hall (1996). Based on the victorious Lucasian impact on the creation of the NNS, Chari and Kehoe (2006: 3) argue that the advances in macroeconomic theory have not only 'been restricted to the ivory tower', but they have also influenced to a huge degree how economic policy is conducted.

KEYNES AND THE *GENERAL THEORY*: DID KEYNES FORESEE THE CRITIQUE?

As stated above, Lucas (1976) presented several core statements that had a tremendous influence on the development of modern macroeconomics. However, in general, most of the Lucas critique should not come as a total surprise to post-Keynesians, albeit that they are non-mainstreamers as Keynes in his *General Theory* and elsewhere touched on some of these statements.

According to Lucas, it is essential to have a microeconomic foundation of macroeconomics. As macroeconomics is the outcome of what happens on every market in the economy where households and firms act accordingly to their goal-oriented behaviour – basically, they try to do the best they can economically in given situations – Lucas is right in his quest for a microfoundation.[8] However, such a foundation need not be one of optimality. As we know empirically, neither households nor firms act precisely as intertemporal optimising agents with rational expectations making first-best solutions. With certainty, we know that both households and firms use 'rules of thumb' when they act economically. That is, they seek the best of the second-best solutions possible. In an economic environment of uncertainty – epistemologically as well as ontologically – they act on expectations determined by knowledge that, to some degree, is imperfect and sometimes even false. Therefore, their behaviour is not characterised by rational expectations in the traditional meaning of the concept. Rather, as Keynes expressed it, they act on rational beliefs.

As argued by McCombie and Negru (2014: 59), Keynes accepted the need of giving 'some sort of intuitive explanation of macroeconomic phenomena in terms of an individual's behaviour'. As such, in his *General Theory*, Keynes always started out by focusing on microeconomic behaviour. This can clearly be observed in his arguments concerning how firms invest, how households consume and how and why people demand liquidity. Furthermore, in his macroeconomic model in chapter 3 of the *General Theory* – the principle of effective demand – the focus is on how the individual firm tries to get an economic outcome where expected profit is maximised. Thereafter, Keynes tries, in detail, to explain why positions of maximised levels of expected profits – kinds of microeconomic optimal outcomes – in general, do not lead to a macroeconomic outcome of optimality (an example of atomistic fallacy).[9] At the beginning of the 1930s, the macroeconomic outcome in the real world was, of course, one of involuntary unemployment, as described by Keynes.

Akerlof (2007) explains that the Lucasian strategy for doing macroeconomics overturned the Keynesian understanding. That is, modern macroeconomics created a macroeconomic universe that in principle, as least in the longer run, is one of harmony. When the representative agent finds his optimal outcome so does automatically the macroeconomy. Therefore, as Lucas has stated on many occasions, with the rational expectations revolution, there is no longer any need to distinguish between micro and macroeconomic. We only need to talk about economics.

Furthermore, the introduction of an intertemporal planning representative agent – identifying equilibrium points on the productive frontier – gave way to another kind of neutrality: that of money and financial aspects in general. This approach allowed the concerns of money and pre-finance of production to be excluded from causal macroeconomic structures. To a post-Keynesian, of course, such a reduction completely distorts the structure of economic existence. It has no relevance.

More so, as any post-Keynesian would argue, such a representation of macroeconomics does not have much to do with reality. Macroeconomics must deal with the problems of the real world – historically, macroeconomics as a discipline was born due to the huge mismatch problems of the 1920s and early 1930s. To Keynes and other economists, economics is not for the ivory tower of academics alone. As argued in Mankiw (2006), economists also have a very important role as engineers. As noted by Mankiw (2006: 29): 'God put macroeconomists on earth not to propose and test elegant theories but to solve practical problems'. That was the case in the 1930s, and that is still the case in the 2020s. One has to be more than ordinarily tone deaf not to acknowledge this when considering what happened to most economies after the financial crisis of 2007–2009 and what happened in the recent years of the Covid-19 pandemic.

Such a view on economics is in good accordance with Baddeley (2014: 99), who stated that DSGE modelling is 'based on a number of unrealistic assumptions about rational, self-interested, atomistic behaviour'. From the school of behavioural economics, we know that individuals in their behaviour are influenced by many factors. As such, individuals act, at least to some degree, on conventions, social norms and social preferences. Likewise, in a less perfectly functioning world than that of the modern macroeconomic mainstream understanding, individuals also rely on herding behaviour and learn about economics in a social context. Such an understanding of economics comes as no surprise to post-Keynesians; they would argue exactly in the same manner. Actually, one could argue that Keynes in many ways should be considered as an early behavioural-like economist.

However important such considerations might be it is no simple task to implement the above-mentioned aspects in macroeconomics.[10] Although admittedly difficult, macroeconomists should not upfront reject to try to do so. Efforts to incorporate some of these aspects in macroeconomics might be a promising way to introduce relevant (and most needed) dimensions of heterogeneity in the theory.

Finally, as explained by Chick (2003), the mode of thought[11] to be found in the *General Theory* – and generally accepted by many post-Keynesians – is quite different from that of a more traditional mainstream mode of thought. And different modes of thought affect which methods that are defined as acceptable to use, how to build theoretical models and how to pose policy proposals and make policy conclusions within a given paradigm of economics. To Keynes, according to Chick (2003: 307), the *General Theory* 'is founded on a concern with time, uncertainty and organicism'. That is, the macroeconomic system presented in the *General Theory* is an open kind of system. To a Lucasian, the macroeconomic system should rather be seen as a closed system. Such a system is of course in nature more deterministic than the system of Keynes and the post-Keynesians.[12] That is, the two paradigms are incommensurable in the Kuhnian sense of the concept.

CONCLUSION

With the benefit of hindsight, Lucas (1976), together with other theoretical contributions, launched a revolution in macroeconomic theory. Based on his critique, the quest for an explicit microeconomic foundation for macroeconomics began. As we all know, the outcome of such a quest was the making of the representative agent who optimises intertemporal choices using rational expectations in a general equilibrium setup. In doing this, Lucas somehow unified the New Classical economists with the New Keynesians as both schools of thought accepted and advocated the same kind of methodology.[13] As such, Lucas laid down the bricks to the road for the DSGE understanding, which has become the baseline model of modern mainstream macroeconomics based on the NNS framework.

However, to a non-mainstream macroeconomist the road that macroeconomics has taken historically since the publication of Lucas (1976) is not a happy one. As Skott (2010, 342, 2014: 513) points out:

> The result has been a long and wasteful detour with enormous costs, both in terms of the loss of knowledge in the profession and, more importantly, mistaken policy ... [as such] ... the straitjacket of full intertemporal optimization misrepresents real-world decision making. It also reduces the ability of the theory to incorporate important aspects of reality in a tractable manner, and therefore encourages the theorist to ignore them.

That is, of course, not the same as to state that the Lucas critique in general is irrelevant. Nonetheless, the recommendations by Lucas, which made the modern mainstream macroeconomic understanding of the NNS and the DSGE models possible, must be rejected.

However, there is more than just one way to build a microeconomic foundation for macroeconomic theory. The solution need not be one of an intertemporal quest for optimality called forward by agents with perfect foresight or rational expectations or by aggregating the group of agents into a representative agent.[14] Instead, macroeconomic theory could be built on less perfect assumptions than those presented by the mainstreamers. As such, a case of bounded rationality concerning the economic behaviour of households and firms is not only a theoretical possibility; it is in fact also a case of empirical evidence (see e.g., Olesen, 2010).

Likewise, there is no one model for 'all seasons' regarding macroeconomics. And there is more than just *one* way to gain relevant knowledge about macroeconomic phenomena and macroeconomic processes of adjustment.[15]

Seen from the perspective of many post-Keynesians, the economic system is one of non-ergodicity rather than of ergodicity (or to use other concepts:

non-repetitiveness and repetitiveness). Therefore, ontology matters. As such, the macroeconomic landscape is expected to change over time. Naturally, the behaviour of households as well as firms and the way economic policy is conducted, just to mention two important aspects, are, at least to some degree, context determined and might change as the macroeconomic landscape itself undergoes changes through dynamic processes of path dependency.

Therefore, to a post-Keynesian, a modern economy is a monetary economy. That is, the real and the financial sectors of the economy depict deep patterns of interdependences. Seen from a post-Keynesian perspective – rather contrary to a Lucasian one – the influence of money (and financial aspects in general) is truly pervasive in nature economically as is the existence of uncertainty and the role of expectations.

NOTES

1. See, e.g., Olesen (2022), who gives a brief history of the development of modern macroeconomics. For a personal statement on the influence of Lucas in general, see e.g., Sargent (2022).
2. A more thorough presentation and discussion of the Lucas critique and its consequences is given in Olesen (2016). As such, the present chapter draws on Olesen (2016).
3. As Uhlig (2022: 49–50) points out: 'Macroeconomics had to be built on the foundations of general equilibrium theory and generates clear quantitative implications. Policy discussions should be done on the foundation of a fully specified model. Deep and stable parameters describing preferences and technologies were key to make them compelling. One should assume that agents have rational expectations and solve optimization problems. Everything had to have proper micro-foundations ... Lucas clearly put forward the idea that economic facts are to be understood in terms of individual decisions.'
4. This is in good accordance with Lucas (2001: 279, 294): 'I came to the position that mathematical analysis is not one of many ways of doing economic theory: It is the only way. Economic theory *is* mathematical analysis. Everything else is just pictures and talk ... It is a method to help us get to new levels of understanding of the ways things work.' Therefore, to Lucas, there is only one way to gain scientific progress in economics; it has to do with technical matters: 'better mathematics, better mathematical formulations, better data, better data-processing methods, better statistical methods, better computational methods' (Lucas, 2004: 22).
5. To strengthen his points, Lucas goes on to give some theoretical considerations concerning consumption, changes in the investment demand due to changes in taxation and a Phillips Curve example. In all three cases, he can illustrate that shocks affect crucial parameters making a policy evaluation of long-run consequences impossible. Only if the 'parameters describing the new policy ... are known by agents' (Lucas, 1976: 39) can we correctly forecast the consequences of a change in economic policy.
6. As pointed out in the press release from the Royal Swedish Academy of Sciences, Lucas was awarded the Nobel Memorial Prize in Economics 'for having devel-

oped and applied the hypothesis of rational expectations, and thereby having transformed macroeconomic analysis and deepened our understanding of economic policy' (Fischer, 1996: 11).

7. Actually, rather ironically, accepting the use of a representative agent in macroeconomic modelling is in conflict with the Lucas critique, as argued by Kirman (1992: 123). When an economic policy change is implemented, 'the change involved will frequently affect individuals differently. Indeed, many policy changes have this as their objective. As soon as this is the case, the representative constructed *before* the change may no longer represent the economy *after* the change.' Furthermore, as pointed out by McCombie and Negru (2014: 62), to accept the birth of the representative agent in macroeconomics is to accept that 'the single individual, devoid of social context and institutions, excludes the interactions of individuals with each other and the way this shapes, and is shaped by, social institutions'.
8. Somehow you may wonder why there is not a similar need of giving microeconomics a macroeconomic kind of institutional framework within which both the behaviour of the individual household and firm is conducted and the forces of the market mechanism on every single market unfolds itself. Neither households nor firms behave as free atoms in the universe. They are both somehow restricted by a given – although over time changeable – institutional setup.
9. As pointed out by Davidson (2015: 374): 'Keynes's general theory – using Marshallian microfoundations – could show that, as a matter of logic, less than full employment equilibrium could exist in a purely competitive economy with freely flexible wages and prices'.
10. 'The macroeconomy is a complex system, and any approach that does not properly address the behavioural and socio-psychological factors driving the individual actors that constitute the macroeconomy is unlikely to capture the instability effectively' (Baddeley, 2014: 109). The important question is just *how* this should be done in practice.
11. Mode of thought is defined by Dow (1996: 10) as 'the way in which arguments (or theories) are constructed and presented, how we attempt to convince others of the validity of truth or our arguments. It is concerned as much with the rhetoric used as means of communication as with the logical structure of the argument. It is a broader concept than "methodology", and indeed influences our judgement as to what constitutes an acceptable methodological position.'
12. A critical discussion of modern macroeconomic mainstream is given by Frydman and Goldberg (2013). Especially, they criticise the high degree of knowability that the mainstream requires of the individual agents in respect to their knowledge about market processes and market outcomes. As such, the mainstream model 'determines *exactly* all potential changes in participants' forecasts and the precise probabilities of their occurrence – in the past, present and future, all at once' (p. 119). That is, to a mainstreamer you can discover the one true model representing the macroeconomy. However, such claims have nothing to do with the facts of real life.
13. Although not all economists were that keen on accepting the hypothesis of rational expectations. As Blinder (1987: 131) pointed out: 'I think the weight of evidence – both from directly observed expectations and from indirect statistical tests of rationality … is overwhelmingly against the RE hypothesis … RE is theoretical coherent only in the context of a single-agreed-upon model.' In general, Blinder (1987: 135) concluded, 'The important thing is to make sure our models

are congruent with the facts. Lucasians, it seems to me, reverse the sequence. They want to begin with fully articulated, tractable models and worry later about realism and descriptive accuracy.'

14. As pointed out by Kirman (1992: 132, 134): 'the representative agent approach is fatally flawed because it attempts to impose order on the economy through the concepts of an omniscient individual. In reality, individuals operate in very small subsets of the economy and interact with those with whom they have dealings … it is clear that the representative agent should have no future.'
15. Or as Skott (2014: 503) states: 'There can be no single, correct theory or model of "the economy". The economy is not a well-defined object and, even if it were, a theory does not aim to provide a complete picture of reality … Equally self-evident … is the claim that there can be no single, correct method for gaining insights into the operation of the economy.'

REFERENCES

Akerlof, George A. (2007), 'The missing motivation in macroeconomics', *American Economic Review*, 97(1), pp. 5–36.

Baddeley, Michelle (2014), 'Rethinking the micro-foundations of macroeconomics: Insights from behavioural economics', *European Journal of Economics and Economic Policies: Intervention*, 11(1), pp. 99–112.

Blinder, Alan S. (1987), 'Keynes, Lucas, and scientific progress', *American Economic Review*, 77(2), pp. 130–136.

Byrialsen, Mikael Randrup, Olesen, Finn & Madsen, Mogens O. (2021), 'The macroeconomic effects of Covid-19: The imperative need for a Keynesian solution', *Revue de la regulation – Capitalisme, institutions, pouviors*, 29, pp. 1–20.

Chari, V.V. & Kehoe, Patrick J. (2006), 'Modern macroeconomics in practice: How theory is shaping policy', *Journal of Economic Perspectives*, 20(4), pp. 3–28.

Chick, Victoria (2003), 'Theory, method and mode of thought in Keynes's *General Theory*', *Journal of Economic Methodology*, 10(3), pp. 307–327.

Davidson, Paul (2015), 'What was the primary factor encouraging mainstream economists to marginalize post Keynesian theory?', *Journal of Post Keynesian Economics*, 37(3), pp. 369–383.

Dow, Sheila (1996), *The Methodology of Macroeconomic Thought: A Conceptual Analysis of Schools of Thought in Economics*, Edward Elgar Publishing.

Fischer, Stanley (1996), 'Robert Lucas's Nobel Memorial Prize', *Scandinavian Journal of Economics*, 98(1), pp. 11–31.

Frydman, Roman & Goldberg, Michael (2013), 'Change and expectations in macroeconomic models: Recognizing the limits to knowability', *Journal of Economic Methodology*, 20(2), pp. 118–138.

Hall, Robert E. (1996), 'Robert Lucas, recipient of the 1995 Nobel Memorial Prize in Economics', *Scandinavian Journal of Economics*, 98(1), pp. 33–48.

Keynes, John Maynard (1936), *The General Theory of Employment, Interest and Money*, in The Collected Writings of John Maynard Keynes, Vol. VII, Macmillan.

Kirman, Alan P. (1992), 'Whom or what does the representative individual represent?', *Journal of Economic Perspectives*, 6(2), pp. 117–136.

LeRoy, Stephen (1995), 'On policy regimes', in Kevin Hoover (ed.), *Macroeconometrics: Developments, Tensions, and Prospects*, Kluwer Academic Publishers, pp. 235–251.

Lucas, Robert E. (1976), 'Econometric policy evaluation: A critique', in Karl Brunner & Allan H. Meltzer (eds), *The Phillips Curve and Labor Markets*, North-Holland Publishing Company, pp. 19–46.

Lucas, Robert E. (1986), 'Principles of fiscal and monetary policy', *Journal of Monetary Economics*, 17(1), pp. 117–134.

Lucas, Robert E. (1995), 'Monetary neutrality', in Torsten Persson (ed.), *Nobel Lectures, Economics 1991–95*, World Scientific Publishing, Singapore, pp. 246–265.

Lucas, Robert E. (2001), 'Professional memoir', in William Breit and Barry T. Hirsh (eds), *Lives of the Laureates*, Fourth edition, pp. 273–297.

Lucas, Robert E. (2004), 'Keynote address to the 2003 *HOPE* Conference: My Keynesian education', *History of Political Economy*, Annual Supplements, pp. 12–24.

Lucas, Robert E. & Sargent, Thomas J. (1979), 'After Keynesian macroeconomics', *Federal Reserve Bank of Minneapolis Quarterly Review*, Spring, pp. 1–16.

Mankiw, Gregory (2006), 'The macroeconomist as scientist and engineer', *Journal of Economic Perspectives*, 20(4), pp. 29–46.

McCombie, John & Negru, Ioana (2014), 'On economic paradigms, rhetoric and the micro-foundations of macroeconomics', *European Journal of Economics and Economic Policies: Intervention*, 11(1), pp. 53–66.

Olesen, Finn (2010), 'Uncertainty, bounded rationality and post-Keynesian Macroeconomics', *European Journal of Economics and Economic Policies – Intervention*, 7(1), pp. 109–124.

Olesen, Finn (2016), 'The Lucas critique – is it really relevant?', *Working Papers - Macroeconomic Methodology, Theory and Economic Policy*, Aalborg University, WP 2016-7.

Olesen, Finn (2022), 'Macroeconomics: Developments and modern trends', *Journal of Behavioural Economics and Social Systems*, 4(1), pp. 64–80.

Rudebusch, Glenn D. (2005), 'Assessing the Lucas critique in monetary policy models', *Journal of Money, Credit and Banking*, 37(2), pp. 245–272.

Sargent, Thomas (2022), 'Learning from Lucas', *Journal of Economic Methodology*, 29(1), pp. 17–29.

Skott, Peter (2010), 'The great detour', *Homo Oeconomicus*, 27(3), pp. 338–343.

Skott, Peter (2014), 'Pluralism, the Lucas critique, and the integration of macroeconomics and microeconomics', *Review of Political Economy*, 26(4), pp. 503–515.

Snowdon, Brian (2007), 'The New Classical counter-revolution: False path or illuminating complement?', *Eastern Economic Journal*, 33(4), pp. 541–562.

Svensson, Lars E.O. (1996), 'The scientific contributions of Robert E. Lucas, Jr.', *Scandinavian Journal of Economics*, 98(1), pp. 1–10.

Uhlig, Harald (2022), 'The lasting influence of Roberts E. Lucas on Chicago economics', *Journal of Economic Methodology*, 29(1), pp. 48–65.

Woodford, Michael (2009), 'Convergence in macroeconomics: Elements of the New Synthesis', *American Economic Journal: Macroeconomics*, 1(1), pp. 267–279.

14. The *General Theory* as a macroeconomics of power

Geoff Tily

INTRODUCTION

In Tily (2010 [2006]) I argued Keynes's most important conclusions concerned monetary policies for the prevention of crisis, rather than fiscal policies for cure. While contemporaneous policy initiatives across left and progressive governments were reported, the political implications in their own rights were not adequately addressed. This chapter makes the case that politics are inherent to the *General Theory*, and fundamental context to the possibility of the change that Keynes had in mind.

As I argued of the economics, the politics of the *General Theory* are greatly different to those of 'Keynesianism'. Furthermore Keynes's own assessment of these politics falls far short, contributing to confusion. Above all, the majority of discussion, even his 'Concluding notes on the social philosophy towards which the *General Theory* might lead', is confined to technical economics and technocratic politics, when the most important implications concerned and still concern social, class and power relations.

At the most fundamental level, the *General Theory* shows – perhaps proves – that class rule by wealth is wholly and dangerously at odds with the interests of society as a whole. This conclusion was global in implication. As he touched on in the penultimate section of the book, setting power relations right meant resetting on positive grounds the economic relations between nations: 'if nations can learn to provide themselves with full employment by their domestic policy ... there need be no important economic forces calculated to set the interest of one country against that of its neighbours' (*CW* VII: 381). Such changes would be to the immense advantage and relief of the world. Indicating the relation between politics and theory, Hugh Gaitskell (Clement

Attlee's successor as leader of the British Labour Party) reasserted Keynes's approach in a commentary on the Bretton Woods agreement:

> It is recognised, at last, that the expansion of international trade depends on the maintenance of Full Employment – and not the other way round ... From this follows the idea of an undertaking by each nation ... *that it will not seek 'to maintain employment through measures which are likely to create unemployment in other countries'* ... i.e. a solid foundation on which we could build a *positive international full employment policy*. This, in my view, transcends in importance all else... (*Daily Herald*, 13 December 1945, cited in Williams 1979: 217, original emphasis)

The monetary policies that I emphasised in *Keynes Betrayed* – debt management techniques to set permanently low interest across the spectrum and a new global monetary architecture – should be understood as critical elements of this broader imperative. In 1977 lectures (published in 1984), Richard Kahn justly remarked of Keynes's statement: 'The world still has to accept this simple lesson taught by Keynes' (Kahn 1984: 158). With today the prolonged dysfunction of the global system and the re-emergence of nationalist politics, this argument – in effect for a labour internationalism – remains of uppermost relevance and importance.

Ahead of Bretton Woods certain left intellectuals seized the political implications of Keynes's book as soon as it was published. G. D. H. Cole recognised the *General Theory* as 'the supreme challenge to the practice of capitalism' (Cole 1999 [1936]: 102). The (Oxford University) historian and one-time Labour activist A. L. Rowse argued 'the book is ... at every point, without a single exception ... in full agreement with Labour policy in this country, and, what is even more significant, expresses in proper economic form what has been implicit in the Labour Movement's attitude all along' (Rowse 1999 [1936]: 110–111).

These reviews rightly situated Keynes's contribution in the wider context of the underconsumption analysis of J. A. Hobson, though the approach can be traced back at least a century earlier to Robert Owen (1771–1858). Beyond the analytical context, Rowse is vital to the present assessment because of his emphasis on the relation between power and ideas. He charged Keynes with a 'rationalist fallacy', for failing to see of ideas 'for the most part being effective in so far as there are interests behind them which make them effective' (Rowse 1936: 57). So not only did Keynes vindicate left analysis but, as Rowse urged in his (brilliant and short) book *Mr Keynes and the Labour Movement* (1936), it was vital for Keynes to make common cause with the left.

Rowse also sought to clear the landscape in terms of left opinion. He commended 'the plain common sense of the Labour Movement for a better international order and a progressive economic system, with its sober estimate of the means of reaching them' (Rowes 1936, p. 67). In contrast were 'The transports of Communism, the intellectual delights of a Marxism more or less divorced from the realities of politics' (p. 67). Several decades later, however, he was minded to contrast Marx's 'deeper insights into the process of history and the forces at work in society than Keynes ever had, with his superficial rationalism and his Bloomsbury superciliousness' (Rowse 1985: 18). A more constructive interpretation is that Keynes vindicated Marx's analysis of power relations, but instead offered an alternative means to their resolution. This resolution, as Cole conceded, did not mean 'destroy[ing] the system of private enterprise, but only that we should drastically re-fashion it' (Cole 1999 [1936]: 105).

Debate around the relation of Keynes to left politics is a live issue, as Nina Eichacker (2020) emphasises. Mann (2017) lambasts 'Keynesian' policies as serving only to protect capitalism; his Keynes is no Keynesian, but seemingly still falls short against Marx. Crotty (2019) has Keynes advocating and using the specific term 'liberal socialism'. This may yet be appropriate, but Keynes did so long before he had conceived of the *General Theory*. Contemporary assessments tend also to overlook the contemporaneous left literature, and moreover fail to address (as arguably did Keynes himself) the possibility that his new theory altered fundamentally the position.

This chapter is therefore concerned with showing how Keynes's theory leads to the claimed practical and political conclusions:

- the second section applies Keynes's analysis to show the dysfunction of the wealth setting and the great advantage of operating in the social interest;
- the third section sets Keynes in the context of Hobson's underconsumption thinking, and draws out connections to progressive and left initiative;
- the fourth section shows how Keynes's analysis affirms the operation of power relations, and challenges as greatly problematic his preference to operate only on technocratic grounds;
- the fifth section shows how power relations are resolved on the international domain; and
- the sixth section sets the orthodox account of economic history against an account according to the macroeconomics of power.

Mindful of the rationalist fallacy, the chapter nonetheless concludes by suggesting the *General Theory* is still vital to resolving the present global disarray.

KEYNES'S SCHEME

Keynes's reasoning points to two critical conclusions: negatively, the severity of the dysfunction of the wealth setting; and positively, the great advantage of resetting the economy in the social interest.

Keynes's deconstruction of the classical theory of interest – shown in greatly simplified form in Figure 14.1 – is both the appropriate point of departure to the *General Theory* and constitutes the substance of his scheme in practice. The same scheme is critical to the power and political perspective.

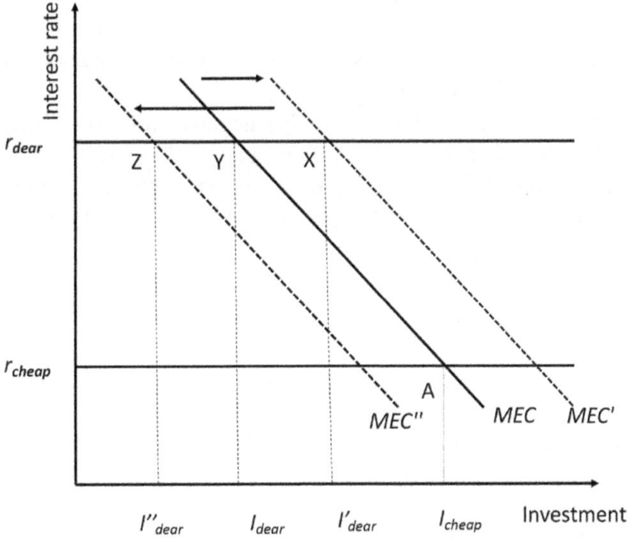

Figure 14.1 *Keynes's scheme, greatly simplified*

Taken as given here is the ability of policymakers to bring the long-term rate of interest under control (Tily 2010 [2006]). So Figure 14.1 focuses only on consequent investment outcomes – via the marginal efficiency of capital (MEC) that captures the 'animal spirits' of the business community – and is simplified according to two interest scenarios.

Warning that dear money should be avoided 'as we would hell-fire' (*CW* XXI: 389), Keynes argued dysfunction was a consequence of the authorities allowing high interest rates to prevail. Specifically, the scheme illustrates why capitalism operates both to restrict activity and to make conditions dangerously volatile.

At the most basic level, higher interest r_{dear} means lower investment I_{dear} on a given marginal efficiency of capital (*MEC*). Activity and then employment follow according to the multiplier and so marginal propensity to consume (MPC; inflation is briefly touched on in the penultimate section).

Moreover the system is prone to more optimistic animal spirits: the MEC shifts right to *MEC′* and means higher investment I'_{dear}. But it is likely that these conditions can only be temporary. Dear money may not prevent excess borrowing, but it reduces the likelihood of repayment. Keynes saw conditions reversing through a sharp leftwards shift in the MEC from *MEC'* to *MEC''*, leading to collapsed investment I''_{dear} and so recession.

Drawing on Fisher (1933) and Minsky (1985), I argued in *Keynes Betrayed* that the collapse in the MEC might be better understood as the consequence of associated inflations in private debt. Crotty (2019: 142) judges likewise: 'For Keynes, *balance sheets matter*!', and justly puzzles why he did not 'adequately stress' these mechanisms in the *General Theory*.

In contrast to this (potentially severely) negative trajectory, the positive conclusion follows the consequences of instead setting cheap money. In his chapter on his theory of the trade cycle, Keynes wrote of 'enable[ing] the so-called boom to last' (*CW* VII: 322). But this was too throwaway – his reading of contemporaneous conditions was that the United States boom of the 1920s still fell short of potential (e.g. *CW* XIII: 349). So Figure 14.1 suggests that setting cheap money will permit greater outcomes even than at the peak of the so-called 'boom'. This would be consistent with outcomes across the golden age, but that is to get ahead of the argument.

KEYNES AND THEORIES OF UNDERCONSUMPTION

Convention has Keynes's call for fiscal policy to *resolve* crisis as disrupting an orthodox economics concerned only with protecting market forces. Understood as a diagnosis of the *cause* of crisis, the better context for his analysis is the critique – outside academic economics – from left or progressive politics. Immediately, as the left understood at the time, this meant the underconsumption analysis of J. A. Hobson. G. D. H. Cole and A. L. Rowse respectively wrote of the *General Theory* as Keynes 'discovering ... Hobson [had] hold of the right end of the stick' (Cole 1999 [1936]: 104) and 'a tremendous vindication for Mr. J. A. Hobson' (Rowse 1936: 41).

Tracing precedent is beyond the scope of the present chapter, but it is vital to recognise the left-related thinking compelling since at least the contributions of the industrialist, social reformer and trade union leader Robert Owen. Maw (2011: 158) finds his motivating the start of a 'working-class anti-capitalist political economy'. In the same volume, Gregory Claeys (the editor of Owen's collected writings) cites Hobson himself looking back to 'the Owenite and early Socialistic analyses and proposals present[ing] a powerful and various challenge to the theory and accepted practice of the capitalist control of industry for private profit' (Claeys 2011: 36). Likewise, Klein and Pettis (2020: 7) look back to Hobson, and (too mildly) regret 'unfortunately his insights were ignored and forgotten'.

In chapter 23 of the *General Theory*, Keynes situated his own theory in this trajectory.[1] Previously culpable for a savagely critical approach ('sophistry, misunderstanding, and perverse thought' with only 'temporary concessions to reason' (*CW* XI: 388, 394)), Keynes came to see that orthodox economics had no answer to Hobson's challenge. While conceding his own serious error, Keynes still charged Hobson with a 'fail[ure] of completeness, essentially on account of ... having no independent theory of the rate of interest' (*CW* VII: 370).

Putting his own theory of the cycle in second place, Keynes emphasised the simple situation when a too high rate of interest meant too low investment (Figure 14.1, point X). He therefore emphasised underinvestment rather than underconsumption; Keynes's text continues:

> with the result that Mr. Hobson laid too much emphasis (especially in his later books) on under-consumption leading to over-investment, in the sense of unprofitable investment, instead of explaining that a relatively weak propensity to consume helps to cause unemployment by requiring and not receiving the accompaniment of a compensating volume of new investment. (*CW* VII: 370)

Only on the way to his conclusion is the cycle process mentioned: 'which, even if it may sometimes occur temporarily through errors of optimism, is in general prevented from happening at all by the prospective profit falling below the standard set by the rate of interest' (*CW* VII: 370).

With Hobson – and his predecessors – above all concerned with distributional considerations and in particular the pitiful recompense to labour, Keynes shifted the emphasis of the argument. Rowse (1936: 41–42) challenged Keynes on precisely this territory, emphasising the Labour Movement's 'resistance to wage-cuts, the demand for higher wages, better social services and all such measures which will increase consumption'. And he reckoned 'it may well be that the Labour Movement ... will attach more importance to keeping up the level of consumption than to increasing capital to the point of the euthanasia of the rentier'. Better to attach importance to both.

KEYNES AND POWER

The differing emphasis on investment and consumption is symptomatic of Keynes's problematic approach to power relations in a much broader sense. The same asymmetry recurs in his differing treatment of interest and wages. And throughout his work discussion keeps to technocratic territory, rather than the political grounds that Rowse urged him towards.

Underconsumption analysis both confronts power and does so in a more symmetrical way. In their contemporary account, Klein and Pettis (2020: 221) find a 'conflict mainly between bankers and owners of financial wealth on one side and ordinary households on the other – between the very rich and everyone else'. Ultimately, the *General Theory* affirms this conflict of interest between the holders of financial wealth and labour.[2] The immediate bridge to power relations is the liquidity preference theory of the rate of interest, with the latter viewed in broadest terms as the *return to wealth*.

Rather than identifying class forces, Keynes emphasised conventional opinion: 'It might be more accurate, perhaps, to say that the rate of interest is a highly conventional, rather than a highly psychological, phenomenon' (*CW* VII: 203). Responsibility for the 'objective of greatly reducing the long-term rate of interest' was allocated to the 'monetary authority'. And the mechanism was put succinctly: 'a complex offer by the central bank to buy and sell at stated prices gilt-edged bonds of all maturities' (*CW* VII: 206). The objective would fail if it was not pursued with 'sufficient conviction'.

The return to labour was also addressed in a technocratic, even abstract, way. In chapter 19, 'Changes in money-wages', Keynes assesses the viability of the classical prescription for (downward) wage adjustment within the framework of the *General Theory*. The question is resolved by comparing 'flexible wage' and 'flexible money' policies (with the latter defined as 'an open-market monetary policy'; *CW* VII: 267). He concludes only 'inexperienced', 'unjust' or 'foolish' persons would advocate flexible wages over flexible money (*CW* VII: 268–269). And, most categorically: 'To suppose that a flexible wage policy is a right and proper adjunct of a system which on the whole is one of *laissez-faire*, is the opposite of the truth' (*CW* VII: 269). Nonetheless his practical conclusion of a 'rigid wage policy' (*CW* VII: 271) is of a different order to his call for cheap money.

Likewise, in analytical terms, he links aggregate consumption to aggregate income and the MPC, rather than wages in their own right. In general, real wages are treated as a result rather than a cause of expansion (*CW* VII: 247–249). And to the extent that they are assessed in a causal role, as above, Keynes examines the consequences of a cut rather than an increase in money wages. There is no role here for trade unions operating directly to increase pay, and for what is today labelled 'wage-led growth'.

With the rate of interest understood simply as the return to wealth, a symmetrical approach would mean wages then follow as the return to labour. With any notions of natural rates rightly dismissed, the implication is that *both* are set according to power relations. For good social outcomes the return to wealth must go down and the return to labour must go up. Rather than technology, the industrial revolution may have followed more as a consequence of the Bank of England reducing the return to wealth (Tily 2010 [2006]: ch. 2), coupled, a century later, with strengthening trade unions and progressive political advance forcing an increased return to labour.

Keynes touches on power only in the final chapter. The first section dismisses the orthodox objection to a significant redistribution of income and wealth through taxation. The second addresses the implications of 'a much lower rate of interest than has ruled hitherto', arriving eventually at the 'euthanasia of the rentier' (*CW* VII: 375–376).

The following (quite contorted) remark from the third section exemplifies his consequent confusions on both political economy and politics:

> no obvious case is made out for a system of State Socialism which would embrace most of the economic life of the community. It is not the ownership of the instruments of production which it is important for the State to assume. If the State is able to determine the aggregate amount of resources devoted to augmenting the instruments and the basic rate of reward to those who own them, it will have accomplished all that is necessary. (*CW* VII: 378)

On *political economy*, Keynes's acknowledgement of class forces is only implied and limited to the return to capital. But the practical implications concern less a technocratic adjustment of the monetary system (and the government's fiscal policies), and more a wider reorientation of the economic system with the needs of labour rather than wealth paramount. Here the idea of a trajectory to the 'euthanasia of the rentier' may be problematic, better to see the change in binary terms according to power. As elaborated in his fourth section (and the next section here), with class forces operating on a global basis, this changed orientation must operate on a global basis.

On *politics*, Keynes's confusions are two-sided: neglecting power and misinterpreting the left challenge. The *General Theory* affirmed the critical fault line in capitalism, and the need to reorientate towards Labour. But Keynes regarded this as a technocratic adjustment, with (in his fifth and final section) the power of his ideas defeating the power of vested interest. In terms of politics, in effect he stood down (his perception of) socialism, with the collective ownership of the means of production not necessary to repair the dysfunction of capitalism.

Rowse challenged Keynes on both fronts. As noted in the introduction, he charged Keynes with the 'rationalist fallacy': ideas served power and therefore power would refuse his ideas. 'To imagine that you can persuade him [the capitalist] to another course than his interest dictates, in other words, to suppose that you can change capitalist behaviour without changing the system is merely silly – another example of the rationalist fallacy' (Rowse 1999 [1936]: 119). Only the Labour Movement was incentivised to embrace and effect Keynes's initiative: 'It remains for *us* to carry these tremendous gains in intellectual strength and self-confidence forward into practical effect' (Rowse 1936: 68, my emphasis).

Second, Rowse (1936: 34–35) stressed that – given a significant role for public ownership – Labour saw 'ample room for private enterprise' and the party was 'completely at one with [Keynes] on the question of individual initiative and its advantages'. Later, the British Labour Party affirmed this position: their 1945 manifesto proposed (and in large part delivered) an 'industrial programme', including public ownership of fuel and power, inland transport and iron and steel, but also emphasised: 'There are many smaller businesses rendering good service which can be left to go on with their useful work' (Labour Party 1945). The most important fault line in capitalism was not the orthodox economic account of market rivalling state, but that between labour and wealth.

THE INTERNATIONALISM OF LABOUR

The means to reset power relations is to reset the economic relations between countries. As cited in the introduction, both Keynes and Gaitskell addressed this practical conclusion; the latter continued: 'These risks [of non-discrimination] will be enormously diminished if at the forthcoming international conference we can really get agreement on an International Full Employment Policy. To this great task the skill and energies of our representatives should now be primarily directed' (Williams 1979: 217). Set on power terrain: permitting countries full employment policies means a high return to labour, rather than the present system of liberal finance permitting a high return to wealth.[3]

On this view, internationalism can be done on the terms of labour or on the terms of capital. Labour internationalism is at first sight paradoxical, with policies focused internally rather than externally. But Gaitskell wanted the policy to apply to all countries, and moreover maintained that labour internationalism would be the greater internationalism, for one on the grounds of better trade. Above all, labour internationalism rivals nationalism, with the latter understood as the degenerate form of internationalism on the terms of wealth.

In the *General Theory*, Keynes was returning to ideas he first outlined in July 1933 as 'National Self-Sufficiency' (*CW* XXI: 233–246), championing what is usefully labelled the 'domestication' of economic activity and finance (not, I stress, of labour). Yet, in spite of his contributions to contemporaneous practical initiatives, Keynes did not in the *General Theory* discuss how to change the external environment to enable this repositioning. Space permits only the briefest overview, and this must begin with international monetary and financial arrangements usefully separated on current and capital accounts.

On the *current account* Keynes sought an exchange regime that would ensure an elastic supply of currencies under normal conditions. His clearing union scheme was in effect a banking system for national currencies, with a world central bank supplying a notional world money (i.e. money of account). The system might have intermediate levels according for example (and most obviously) to continent. Surplus countries would lend automatically to deficit countries at fixed but adjustable rates of exchange, with various restraints according to the rules of the system (e.g. on country imbalances and the amount of money created). The system is very misleadingly – but far too commonly – described as forcing adjustment on surplus as well as deficit countries. Notably Keynes did not set out a theory of exchange in his main works, but he deferred, in his celebrated biography essay (*CW* X: 161–231), to Marshall's theory of purchasing power parity, and adopted that approach in practice.[4]

Paramount on the *capital account* was domestic autonomy, put succinctly in correspondence with R. F. Harrod: 'In my view the whole management of the domestic economy depends upon being free to have the appropriate rate of interest without reference to the rates prevailing elsewhere in the world. Capital control is a corollary to this' (*CW* XXV: 149). In the context of domestic policy, Keynes emphasises that there are 'no intrinsic reasons for the scarcity of capital' (*CW* VII: 376). The point is no less fundamental to the financial relations between nations: no country should be short of financial capital for investment or reliant on any other for trade finance.

International development is a different matter. The purpose of an international development fund was to address shortfalls in the quality and quantity of fixed capital stock for lower-income countries. After the Bretton Woods Conference the United States confused arrangements by switching roles, so the World *Bank* was concerned with *funding* development, and the International Monetary *Fund* with *banking*. In keeping with the broader asymmetry of his approach, Keynes has little to say about the International Labour Organization. The Labour Party document 'The international post-war settlement' is clear sighted and better balanced (though the language at the end jars today):

> The I.L.O. was one of the best creations of the Peace Treaties. It must be greatly developed and strengthened in the future. It must become a powerful and vital instrument, not only for international understanding among the workers of all lands, but for raising standard of life throughout the world, and especially in backward countries. (National Executive Committee of the Labour Party 1944)

TWO VIEWS OF THE PAST

In Tily (2010 [2006]) I argued that Keynesianism was 'a different theory opposed, and indeed rival, to Keynes's work' (back cover). On political and power grounds, the implications go much further. Harvard historian Charles S. Maier observed what he called the 'politics of productivity': 'American blueprints for international monetary order, policy towards trade unions, and the intervention of occupation authorities in West Germany and Japan sought to transform political issues into problems of output, to adjourn class conflict for a consensus on growth' (Maier 1977: 607). Keynesianism should be understood in the context of shifting to this broader technocratic framework, helpfully labelled a 'GDP [gross domestic product] standard' – to imply a degree of continuity with the gold standard. The framework has underpinned for 80 years both the orthodox assessment of economic outcomes in the past as well as monetary and fiscal policy in the present.

Outcomes are understood as an interplay between structural change, affecting productivity/aggregate supply, and the impact of policy on aggregate demand. Diane Coyle's (2014) *GDP: A Brief but Affectionate History* offers in effect a textbook account of this history. So, for example, the post-war golden age resulted from 'Keynesian policy' coupled with the Marshall Plan permitting demand to keep up with strong supply-side growth caused by a continuously improving level of education, new technologies and the steadily improving availability of consumer goods. But then the inflation of the 1970s came as the result of expanding demand (including wage bargaining) to sustain post-war growth, when the growth of potential output had contracted (or rather reverted to older norms).

After 80 years the approach has surely failed even in its own terms. In spite of relentless focus, since the 1980s supply-side policies have not prevented progressively worse productivity outcomes. Moreover, on a monetary view, the outcomes refute the classical theory of interest, as a (now *ex*) Bank of England official concedes: 'Global growth was much higher in the 1950s to 1970s than in the 1980s, yet real interest rates were significantly lower on average' (Kindberg-Hanlon 2017).

On the view of the macroeconomics of power, the critical factors in outcomes are those that affect the relative position of capital and labour in global terms. These depend on the interplay of political change and established authority in central banks, finance ministries and global institutions.

A brief overview is necessary to rival the orthodox account, which above all downplays the importance of political change for both good and ill. Moreover, viewed over a century, there is a sense of events turning full circle back to the 1930s – understanding the past is therefore critical to the future.

After the First World War, financial interests were dominant. The world was held hostage by high interest and colossal international debts, as a result of reparations and inter-allied war debts. The gold standard did not prevent excess but imposed restraint when excess turned to violent debt deflation and global depression (Tily 2014).

The way forward was only secured following political change. Socialist and social democrat parties in a number of advanced economies had reached a critical political mass; the Great Depression exposed elites as failed, and electorates were ready to risk change.

The exception initially was Britain, as the first country to come off gold, operate a managed exchange and to take interest rate policy out of the hands of central banks in order (imperfectly) to set cheap money. While the actions marked the beginning of a significant rebalancing in power relations, the change only came *after* a minority labour government was forced from office by global finance.[5]

Decisive change for the world came in 1933 when Franklin Delano Roosevelt took office, and momentarily over 1936–1937 under Leon Blum's popular front coalition in France. Both brought national central banks under public control, and legislated to strengthen workers and trade unions (under the Wagner Acts and Matignon Accords). There was also change in smaller countries. Clement Attlee (1937: 18–20) found the best examples in Sweden and New Zealand – the former under Per Albin Hansson from 1932 to 1946 and the latter under Michael Joseph Savage over 1933–1940. In fact, the change in Scandinavia was more widespread – see the Appendix for a fuller picture.

In parallel, there was a sequence of more formal and substantial global initiatives, as follows:

- the establishment of the Bank for International Settlements (1930);
- the Tripartite Agreement between the United States, United Kingdom and France (1936);
- the emergence of the Sterling Area in the Second World War;
- Keynes's (and likewise the British government's) plan for an International Clearing Union;
- the Bretton Woods conference and agreement (1943–1944);
- the Marshall Plan (1947);
- the European Payments Union (1951–1958); and
- the European Monetary Agreement (from 1959).

While the necessary forensic analysis is beyond the scope of this chapter, the vital point across this landscape is the tension between progressive forces and established financial authority. The leadership of the new global institutions under Camille Gutt at the International Monetary Fund ('the ultra-orthodox Belgian ex-Minister of Finance' (Williams 1979: 218)) and Eugene Meyer at the World Bank (whose role as Chairman of the Federal Reserve ended shortly after Roosevelt taking office) is indicative of the latter quickly having the upper hand.

Nonetheless, for a fleeting moment, the Attlee government attempted an unprecedented and deliberate reset towards labour and away from wealth. The domestic arrangements are reasonably well understood: nationalisation of the Bank of England, an explicit cheap money policy, repeal of anti-trade union legislation, a wider nationalisation programme (as above) and greatly increased expenditure on social infrastructure (Tily 2010 [2006], 2021). Under Ernest Bevin (formerly the founder and first head of the Transport and General Workers Union, at one point the largest trade union in the world) at the Foreign Office and Gaitskell at the Treasury, the Labour Government pursued the goal of an International Full Employment Policy across the Western European Union and beyond. Having been on the receiving end of harsh financial medicine from the United States, they turned the table and channelled Marshall Aid as the foundation for the clearing mechanism of the European Payments Union (Tily 2021). One of Bevin's final initiatives as Foreign Secretary was to support and arrange funding for a development agenda for South and South-East Asia – known as the Columbo Plan (Bullock 1983: ch. 20).

But orthodox forces soon had the upper hand. In summer 1950, at the Economic and Social Council of the United Nations, Gutt blocked Gaitskell's proposals for an international commitment to full employment (Williams 1979: 218). After the 1951 Federal Reserve–Treasury Accord central banks began again to influence monetary policy across the world. Likewise, they were instrumental in the ending of the European Payments Union and the signing in 1955 of the more orthodox European Monetary Agreement (Fford 1992; Faudot 2022).

At this point, at the end of the 1950s, the agenda indicated by Maier (1977) began decisively to operate. In practice, 'Keynesianism' amounted to the use of fiscal policy to aim aggregate demand at GDP growth targets set by the Organisation for Economic Co-operation and Development.[6] Under near full employment in many European economies, the inevitable inflation provided the ideal opportunity for political parties of the right. The critical moment for the decisive shift back to wealth was less Thatcher and Reagan on behalf of the market and more Paul Volcker on behalf of finance. The monetary policy 'shock' known by his name switched abruptly and decisively higher the lower real interest rates of the so-called golden age (Tily 2010 [2006]).

These changes in power relations and the corresponding switch of goal from full employment to the growth of real GDP provide an alternative interpretation of economic outcomes since the Second World War.

Of potentially vital importance, economic and financial conditions today resonate strongly with those at the end of the 1920s and the start of the 1930s: the ongoing disarray in global financial markets and emerging market economies; the immense levels of global private and public debt; and the relentless imposition of austerity policies. On this view, nationalist politics should come as no surprise. The International Monetary Fund in October 2022 warned of 'waves' of deleveraging and risks in particular to the non-bank financial system, concluding: 'the level of risk we are flagging at the moment is the highest outside acute crisis'.[7] While there is a sense of events turning full circle, the difference today is an inability even to identify – let alone dislodge – established authority. But the class struggle cannot be over: people will not endure indefinitely oppression by the plutocracy.

CONCLUSION

Keynes observed 'The great puzzle of effective demand … vanish[ing] from economic literature', only to 'live on furtively, below the surface, in the underworlds of Karl Marx, Silvio Gesell or Major Douglas' (*CW* VII: 32). Implicit to Rowse's critique is the restraining influence on academic doctrine of vested interest. Hobson was more direct, charging academia with 'setting up new earthworks against the attack the disinterested masses upon the vested interests of the plutocracy' (Hobson 1965 [1902]: 218). Maybe these 'earthworks' required the assimilation of the *General Theory* into a framework wholly at odds with the substance its conclusions. This framework sets economic outcomes as largely predetermined by natural forces, and so neutralises any role for power.

Instead, the *General Theory* offers the possibility that economic outcomes are dictated by social forces. In today's context the perceived constraints on activity are wholly artificial, and bind only for as long as the system is aimed at the interest of the wealthy. Likewise, the unfolding environmental catastrophe follows from the consequences of the GDP standard that is inherent *only* to the wealth orientation.

With the nature of these constraints properly understood, as Keynes had argued – and the Attlee government demonstrated – 'Anything we can actually *do* we can afford' (*CW* XXVII: 270, original emphasis).[8]

NOTES

1. Keynes himself has nothing to say about Owen, beyond in his biographical essay (*CW* X: 279) commending Herbert Somerton Foxwell's extensive commentary on the 'influence of Owen'.
2. This fault line is inevitably blurred, and its relation with previous interpretations (e.g. capital and labour, unearned and earned income) merits further exploration.
3. Symmetry would suggest the (pejorative) notion of financial repression that is applied to the post-war decades should be set against labour repression since then.
4. On practical considerations, his 16 November 1931 'Notes on the currency question' (*CW* XIII: 16–28) prepared after Britain left the gold standard for the Treasury looked at a 'somewhat crude index number of the main raw commodities of international trade' and used the production index of the League of Nations for 'a general indication of what is in view'. Wider remarks show his

making a distinction between 'internal' and 'external' values of currencies (e.g. *CW* XXV: 16), again originating in purchasing power parity theory.

5. Coined by the City editor of the *Daily Herald* as a 'Bankers' ramp' (Williams 1970: 101). Notably and disappointingly Keynes's decisive intervention on the gold standard came after Labour was out of office.
6. Schmeltzer (2016) traces the underlying thinking to the newly established Council of Economic Advisers in the United States, and sees the sequence of Organisation for European Economic Co-operation/Organisation of Economic Co-operation and Development growth targets as the vehicle for promoting the same discourse in European countries. In Tily (2023), I argue the GDP standard (though I don't use this label there) was the price for Marshall Aid.
7. Press conference for the *Global Financial Stability Review*, 12 October 2022.
8. This statement is regularly cited, but, vitally, is contingent on – not alternative to – system change in the wider social interest.

REFERENCES

Attlee, Clement (1937) *The Labour Party in Perspective*, London: Victor Gollancz.

Bullock, Alan (1983) *Ernest Bevin: Foreign Secretary*, London: Heinemann.

Claeys, Gregory (2011) 'Robert Owen and some later socialists', in Noel Thompson and Chris Williams (Eds), *Robert Owen and His Legacy*, Cardiff: University of Wales Press.

Cole, G. D. H. (1999 [1936]) 'Mr Keynes beats the band', in Roger E. Backhouse (Ed.), *Keynes: Contemporary Responses to the* General Theory, South Bend, IN: St Augustine's Press.

Coyle, D. (2014) *GDP: A Brief but Affectionate History*, Princeton, NJ: Princeton University Press.

Crotty, James (2019) *Keynes against Capitalism: His Economic Case for Liberal Socialism*, London: Routledge.

CW: Keynes, J. M. (1971–1989) *The Collected Writings of John Maynard Keynes*, 30 Volumes, Donald E. Moggridge and Elizabeth S. Johnson (Eds), London: Macmillan and New York: Cambridge University Press for the Royal Economic Society.

Eichacker, Nina (2020) 'Can America truly turn socialist?', *Challenge*, 63:1, 40–51.

Faudot, Adrien (2022) 'The dual context of Keynes' International Clearing Union: Theoretical advances meet history', *European Journal of the History of Economic Thought*, 29:2, 349–368.

Fforde, John (1992) *The Bank of England and Public Policy, 1941–1958*, Cambridge: Cambridge University Press.

Fisher, Irving (1933) 'The debt deflation theory of great depressions', *Econometrica*, 1:4, 337–357.

Hobson, J. A. (1965 [1902]) *Imperialism: A Study*, Ann Arbor MI: University of Michigan Press.

Kahn, Richard F. (1984) *The Making of Keynes's* General Theory, Cambridge: Cambridge University Press.

Kindberg-Hanlon, Gene (2017) 'Low real interest rates: Depression economics, not secular trends', Bank Underground blog, 16 February. https://bankunderground.co.uk/2017/02/16/low-real-interest-rates-depression-economics-not-secular-trends/

Klein, Matthew C. and Michael Pettis (2020) *Trade Wars Are Class Wars: How Rising Inequality Distorts the Global Economy and Threatens International Peace*, New Haven, CT: Yale University Press.

Labour Party (1945) 'Let us face the future: A declaration of Labour policy for the consideration of the nation'.

Maier, Charles S. (1977) 'The politics of productivity: Foundations of American international economic policy after World War II', *International Organisation*, 31:4, 607–633.

Mann, Geoff (2017) *In the Long Run We Are All Dead: Keynesianism, Political Economy, and Revolution*, London: Verso.

Maw, Ben (2011) 'Robert Owen's unintended legacy: Class conflict', in Noel Thompson and Chris Williams (Eds), *Robert Owen and His Legacy*, Cardiff: University of Wales Press.

Minsky, Hyman P. (1985) 'The financial instability hypothesis, a restatement', in Philip Arestis (Ed.), *Essays in Post Keynesian Economics*, Cheltenham, UK and Northampton, MA, USA: Edward Elgar Publishing.

National Executive Committee of the Labour Party (1944) 'The International Post-War Settlement', Prepared for the Annual Conference, London, 29 May–2 June.

Rowse, A. L. (1936) *Mr. Keynes and the Labour Movement*, London: Macmillan and Co.

Rowse, A. L. (1985) *Glimpses of the Great*, London: Metheun.

Rowse, A. L. (1999 [1936]) 'Mr Keynes and the Labour Movement', in Roger E. Backhouse (Ed.), *Keynes: Contemporary Responses to the* General Theory, South Bend, IN: St Augustine's Press.

Schmelzer, Matthias (2016) *The Hegemony of Growth: The OECD and the Making of the Economic Growth Paradigm*, Cambridge: Cambridge University Press.

Tily, Geoff (2010 [2006]) *Keynes Betrayed*, Basingstoke: Palgrave Macmillan.

Tily, Geoff [writing as Douglas Coe] (2014) 'Reparations, orthodoxy and fascism', in Jens Hölscher and Matthias Klaes (Eds), *Keynes's Economic Consequences of the Peace: A Reappraisal*, London: Routledge.

Tily, Geoff (2021) 'A second internationalism of labour', in Patrick Allen, Suzanne J. Konzelmann and Jan Toporowski (Eds), *The Return of the State*, Newcastle upon Tyne: Agenda Publishing.

Tily, Geoff (2023) 'National Accounts and macroeconomic methodology', in Victoria Chick, Jesper Jesperson and Bert Tieben (Eds), *Handbook of Macroeconomic Methodology*, London: Routledge.

Williams, Francis (1970) *Nothing So Strange: An Autobiography*, London: Camelot Press.

Williams, Philip M. (1979) *Hugh Gaitskell: A Political Biography*, London: Jonathan Cape.

APPENDIX

Table 14A.1 Left governments in Scandinavia

Country	Prime minister	Party	Date(s)	Other points of interest
Denmark	Thorvald Stauning (1873–1942)	SDP	1924–1926 1929–1942	Leader of cigar sorters union (1896–1908)
Finland	Väinö Tanner (1881–1966)	SDP	1926–1927	Trained as lawyer; managed Turun Vähäväkisten Osuusliike, then the largest cooperative retail society in Finland; socialists banned from cabinet over 1929–1937
	Mauno Pekkala (1890–1952)	Finnish People's Democratic League	1946–1948	Initially SDP; Minister of Finance in wartime Cabinet from 1939 to 1942; left SDP after 1941–1944 Continuation War
	Karl August Fagerholm (1901–1984)	SDP	1948–1950 1956–1957 1958–1959	Chairman (1920–1923) of the Barbers' Union
Norway	Christopher Hornsrud (1859–1960)	Labour	January–February 1928	Shopkeeper and farmer, sympathetic to Liberals; undone by financial intrigue?
	Johan Nygaarsvold (1879–1952)	Labour	1935–1945	Lumber mill worker, involved (from Canada) in international workers of the world; led exiled government from London in Second World War; resigned 25 June 1945 when the King appointed an interim government of all political parties

Country	Prime minister	Party	Date(s)	Other points of interest
Sweden	Hjalmar Branting	SDP	1920 1921–1923 1924–1925	Astronomer, journalist and founder member of SDP; first socialist prime minister in the world?
	Rickard Sandler (1884–1964)	SDP	1925–1926	
	Per Albin Hansson (1885–1946)	SDP	1932–1946	Minister of Finance (1932–1949): 'We refuse to admit that [10 per cent unemployment] is necessary and natural despite how much people come armed with theories stating that this must be so'
	Tage Erlander (1901–1985)	SDP	1946–1969	

15. Economics for the future: inspiration from the writings of Karl Polanyi

Mogens Ove Madsen

INTRODUCTION

After the global financial crisis of 2007, there has been widespread dissatisfaction with conventional economic theories, which provided no warning signs.

This gave rise to restrained optimism among post-Keynesians. Marc Lavoie (2010) asked if this gave rise to a second Keynesian revolution. He gives the answer himself: government employers have become disillusioned with economics as the financial crisis has shown the futility of standard economic advice and theories. This may give rise to heterodox dissenters (including post-Keynesians) to improve their standing in the social sciences in general, as they will be more likely to look for alternative views. However, there will also be forces within the economics profession and the population that are resistant to a new Keynesian revolution.

Later, Lavoie (2019) gave a lecture in Berlin with the title "History and fundamentals of post Keynesian macroeconomics," where he called for engaging more with other heterodox schools to improve or complete some aspects of post-Keynesian economics. These can be themes such as ecology, feminism, behavioral economics, or development of clear sets of policy recommendations.

With his unconventional writing, Karl Polanyi (1886–1964) is a clear candidate that Lavoie must be looking for. Not least Polanyi's book *The Great Transformation* from 1944 has a surprisingly great relevance in these years. Today's crises can rightly be regarded as another movement through a major transformation, where the current neoliberal era has triggered similar crises as Polanyi described for the nineteenth century.

In Polanyi's historiography of the failure of liberal capitalism in the nineteenth century, he mentions four elements that helped liberal capitalism thrive and at the same time hastened its collapse – these are the self-regulating market, the gold standard, international peace, and liberal constitutionalism.

There are, of course, notable differences between the liberal capitalism of the nineteenth century and the variety of capitalism that has emerged especially since the 1970s in the era known as globalization. Thus, it can also be stated that the social structures which are Polanyi's four elements do not completely determine the actual situation (Goldmann 2017).

The unique and thought-provoking *The Great Transformation* is Polanyi's absolutely alternative approach to the classics' assumptions about factors of production – the three fictitious goods: labor is thus another name for a human activity that accompanies life itself, which in turn is not produced for sale but for completely different reasons, neither can that activity be separated from the rest of life, stored or mobilized; land is another name for nature which is not produced by man; and money is merely a sign of purchasing power, which is usually not produced at all but is created through the banking or government financing mechanism (Polanyi 1944: 75–76).

However, it is not just a matter of a new breakthrough in economic thinking and thus a showdown with the classics' thinking about land, labor, and capital. Polanyi also takes a methodological stand against the mainstream view of economics. There is a fundamental need for a different set of concepts to understand sweeping transformations that balance economy, society, and environment. Polanyi sets out to distance himself from a formal definition of economy and develops instead a substantive alternative which is based on the relationship between basic needs, nature, and institutions (Alenda-Demoutiez 2022).

In the following, it is the intention, based on Polanyi's methodological and theoretical approach, to assess what consequences these insights may have for the subject of post-Keynesian economics in the future.

First, we begin by defining Polanyi's methodological approach. This is decisive for the analytic results he reaches. Next, the purpose is to give a brief characterization of his theoretical framework, including especially the phenomenon of the self-regulating market, as well as the notions of the embeddedness of the economy in society as a whole and the so-called double movement. Polanyi gave a characterization of the collapse of the self-regulating market in the nineteenth century. This realization is reassessed in a contemporary setting by taking a closer look at three examples of the fictitious goods in a European Union (EU) context – especially after the establishment of the internal market and the common currency. In the last section, some more general consequences of Polanyi's approach are described in relation to how this can be envisaged in post-Keynesian economics for the future.

POLANYI'S METHODOLOGICAL APPROACH

Polanyi (1977: 3) sets out two perspectives from which to approach economic analysis: the two basic meanings of "economic," the material and the formal, have nothing in common. The latter derives from logic and the former from facts.

A formalist approach is based on a deductive and logical way of thinking, where the material or substantivist meaning is descriptive and based on experience. In other words, a formalist orientation is based on the idea of economic rationality with the maximization of individuals. A substantivist argues that economics is embedded in a sociocultural context (Machado 2011).

Karl Polanyi would thereby argue that the real distinction between economics and any other social science concerned with economic life is that a formalist economics dictates a picture of the economy derived from a utopian ideal on all empirical economies in history. Such an ideology, according to Polanyi, is not only outdated but also destructive in its promotion of self-regulating markets, simply because economies – past and present – are embedded and entangled in social relations and institutions (Gemici 2008).

The material approach, for which Polanyi finds inspiration in Aristotle, rejects the idea of choice induced by scarcity and insufficient means; choice may just as well arise from exuberance or "the intention ... to do the right thing." Polanyi explicitly states that only the substantive meaning of "economic" is useful for social science, which takes as its subject the study of "all the empirical economies of the past and present" (Polanyi 1944: 244). The formal meaning of "economic" is useful only for the study of the market economy. Thus, "economic" in its material sense refers to all interaction with nature and other people in the pursuit of livelihood and not to a particular type of behavior; therefore, the analysis of economic life should focus on this interaction (Gemici 2008: 21).

It is decisive and significant that there is a high degree of common agreement in methodology between Polanyi and post-Keynesianism and thus a common distance from neoclassical instrumentalism and individualism. As such, there is a common understanding between post-Keynesianism and Polanyi that both work in historical time in a non-ergodicity environment characterized by uncertainty.

POLANYI'S ANALYTICAL FRAMEWORK

What is special about Polanyi's analysis is, firstly, his characterization of the commodities land, labor, and money as fictitious because, in addition to their exchange value, they have a wider use value. Secondly, he examines what consequences these goods have for a self-regulated market and, finally, to what extent a self-regulated market can be embedded in the general society.

There are several examples of Polanyi being used for a new interpretation of the current crises via his definition of the three fictitious goods – land, money, and labor. Fraser (2014) argues that the concepts can match the ecological part of the crisis, the financialization of the economic crisis of 2007/2008, and increased difficulties of social reproduction.

These fictitious goods already exist as use value before they take the form of an exchange value, or it is produced as use value before it is appropriated and offered for sale. Above all, unlike a capitalist commodity, a fictitious commodity is not created in a profit-oriented labor process subject to the competitive pressure of market forces to rationalize its production and reduce the turnover time of invested capital.

Polanyi, as previously described, ignores the narrower, formal meaning of economics, and views the economic system in a more substantive sense. This means that specific forms of behavior such as reciprocity, redistribution, household or exchange, and social patterns are always present. Therefore, the implementation of a self-regulating market can be considered a fundamental and conscious transformation of organizational principles in society. For Polanyi, self-regulating markets, including competition as a fundamental principle, can be deliberately created and institutionalized. Self-regulation implies that all production is for sale on the market and that all income comes from such sales (Polanyi 1944: 75).

He does not regard the self-regulating market as natural, nor does he perceive competition as something desirable. Again, his view is substantivism: competition looks like "only one form among many of organizing the allocation of material goods." It is the movement from local non-competitive to internal competitive markets, created in the nineteenth century by the "artificial phenomenon of the machine" and culminating in the factory system (Polanyi 1944: 60). This required that all factors involved in production are always for sale and available, including labor, land, and money. The profit motive is particular to production for markets, and profit can be achieved if self-regulation is ensured through an interdependent competitive market (Polanyi 1944: 78).

In *The Great Transformation*, Polanyi discusses the institutionalization of what he calls a liberal utopia: the self-regulating market. He argues that the economic sphere was historically embedded in society and therefore subject to customs, norms, and moral beliefs. If the self-regulating market is to function, the undermining of past customs, norms, and moral beliefs is therefore necessary. "A self-regulating market requires nothing less than the institutional separation of society into an economic and a political sphere" (Polanyi 1944: 74). This institutional separation is also referred to as the disembeddedness of markets from society, as opposed to a market that is embedded in and regulated by social norms and institutions.

As part of his substantivism approach, Polanyi expresses the degree to which an economic activity is limited by non-economic institutions. It was his view that in non-market societies there are no purely economic institutions to which formal economic models can be applied: economic activities are embedded in non-economic kinship, religious and political institutions. In market societies, however, economic activities may have been rationalized, and economic action is thus detached from society and establishes its own logic, which can be captured in narrow economic modeling.

Subsequently, the term embeddedness was further developed by the economic sociologist Mark Granovetter, who argued that even in market societies, economic activity is not as detached from society as economic models would suggest (Granovetter 1985: 506). Embeddedness can also be assessed with the help of the concept the "double movement." As an example, workers and capitalists who, as major actors, engage on each side in two movements can thus represent respectively the key part of two rival movements. According to Polanyi's analysis, it can also be different social groups that actively participate in these movements. In general, workers tended to side with the countermovement against laissez-faire, while capitalists favored freedom and expansion of the market.

A Polanyian theoretical framework thus consists of both a special approach with demarcation of the condition of the fictitious goods but also a focus on how they form the basis of a self-regulated economy in extreme cases. However, this state of the economy can be challenged by different reactions in the form of countermovements.

THE SECOND GREAT EUROPEAN TRANSFORMATION

With *The Great Transformation*, Polanyi provides a thorough analysis of the collapse of the self-regulating market in the nineteenth century. With the intensified globalization since the 1970s, it seems that land, labor, and money are again increasingly detached from the rest of society.

The emergence of the free market paradigm was a political project that began with the crises of the late 1960s and 1970s – fully in line with Polanyi's description of the nineteenth-century liberal breakthrough – and culminated in the establishment of the EU's internal market and the implementation of a common currency, the euro, at the end of the century.

It transformed the subordinate role of the economic market to the post-war peace interest and ended up freeing the market more and more from politics and society. In Polanyi's work, the concept of fictitious goods and the associated dynamics of commodification are central. Although he, for good reasons,

Table 15.1 Political and institutional transformation in Europe

European transformation	The first: 1815–1914	The second: 1973–present day
Institutions	Self-regulating market The gold standard International peace Liberal constitutionalism	The inner market The euro (new gold standard) War in Europe Liberal constitutionalism
Political countermovement	New Deal, Marshall, Bretton Woods Welfare state	Fiscal rules, austerity

failed to predict a new wave of marketization, land, labor, and money are now commodified in a highly interconnected manner and on an unprecedented transnational scale.

Likewise, European economic integration with a minimalist social policy at EU level has been made possible by strong domestic labor market and social welfare institutions. The EU's market liberalization is embedded in institutions of social citizenship at the national level, which provides an opportunity to counteract the liberalization of the single market. But this construction has come under pressure. In addition to the challenges posed by the global economic crisis to the sustainability of the European welfare states, the jurisprudence of the European Court of Justice contributes to the internal market the fact that doubts are created about the sustainability of the so-called "embedded liberal agreement." Focusing on the role of the Court, particularly in its jurisprudence on the interplay between (EU) market freedoms and (national) labor law, undermines the ability of states to maintain their regulatory autonomy over labor or social law and thus accelerates the unraveling of the "embedded liberal trade."

The above can be used to make a first comparison between similarities and differences of Polanyi's analysis of the transformation in the nineteenth century and the ongoing transformation in more modern times, as illustrated in Table 15.1.

Based on Polanyi's methodology, it focuses on how several changes today have taken place for the fictitious goods money, labor, and land after the introduction of the internal market, as well as, by extension, examples of double movements. Below three illustrative examples are presented.

Money

When it comes to the commodification of money, Polanyi was remarkably prescient. But in the twenty-first century, financialization has reached new heights of vertigo far beyond anything he could have imagined. With the invention of derivatives and their metastasis, the commodification of money has floated so free from the materiality of social life that it has taken on a life of its own (Fraser 2014).

Polanyi's (1977) historical analysis calls for the rejection of the quantity theory because it treats money merely as the special commodity that happens to serve as numeraire. Although he does not develop the argument further, a credit-based view of modern money seems to be the next logical step in accounting for money in advanced capitalism. He could have taken inspiration from Keynes, who pointed out that even if central banks create a non-commodified unit of account, it is immediately brought into the logic of capitalist markets as a commodity sold at profit in the form of credit.

An incipient deregulation and liberalization of capital flows at global and European level in the 1970s and 1980s led to a rapid expansion of the EU's financial services sector as well as to its transformation from a bank-based system to a market-driven system (Frangakis 2014: 17).

Polanyi's claim about the fictitious nature of money deserves credibility today in the context of extensive central bank intervention in the economy. In the wake of the most recent episode of the global credit crunch in 2007/2008, financial companies had to be rescued from the undisturbed functioning of the market mechanism via the massive injection of central bank money into the money markets – as thoroughly analyzed by Hein (2016) and Sawyer (2022).

Contemporary monetary policy instruments demonstrate the continued relevance of Polanyi's notion of the fictitious nature and dual movement of money, namely the European Central Bank's unconventional monetary policy measures and its asset purchase programs, which capture the limits of the self-regulating market (Madsen 2022). The Bank as lender of last resort, via its program of quantitative easing, is a contemporary example of protection against the utopian nature of so-called benefits of an undisturbed market mechanism. Arguably, if left undisturbed, the market administration of purchasing power would be governed solely by periodic shortages or surpluses, which would have wiped out the eurozone's productive capacity. The crisis in the eurozone revealed an asymmetry in the monetary policy area, largely generated by the ban on monetary financing.

Labor

When it comes to labor, the emergence of actual labor markets ended traditional business relationships in families, clans, guilds, workshops, and other contexts that had provided trust, solidarity, and security. It transformed labor into a commodity that became salable regardless of many of these social relations. Filling the void and resulting uncertainty would have required government intervention in the market to re-establish trust, solidarity, and security. But that was exactly what the free market paradigm sought to avoid (Goldmann 2017).

Since the collapse of the Bretton Woods system and the liberalization of capital, it has been possible to ascertain that the labor force's share of the total income distribution has been decreasing. This is a phenomenon that has been observed both on a global and a European level (Frangakis 2014: 22).

The functional distribution of income is also the archetypal problem in political economy. This is what the classics fought over and what the neoclassics chose to ignore or dilute within the general framework of economic analysis. Furthermore, there are sharp inequalities in the distribution of personal income within the population of the EU as well as between its member states. Such inequalities undermine social cohesion, and they directly influence the extent and depth of poverty (Frangakis 2014: 24).

The financial sector contributes to put pressure on the labor income share through its overbearing presence in the economy and its implications for the allocation of resources between productive uses and financial and speculative uses. The International Labor Organization estimates that almost half of the decline in the income share of labor is due to the actions of the financial sector (Frangakis 2014: 25).

Wealth in both the United States and Europe has also been significantly increasing in relation to income. Piketty and Zucman (2014) find that in eight developed countries – the United States, Germany, the United Kingdom, Canada, Japan, France, Italy, and Australia – there has been a gradual increase in wealth-to-income ratios in recent decades, from around 200–300 percent in 1970 to 400–600 percent in 2010, indicating a return to levels of wealth-to-income ratios not seen since nineteenth-century Europe. The wealth-to-income ratio in Europe reached a peak in the late nineteenth century, thereafter falling largely because of the two World Wars in the first half of the twentieth century. In the 1950s it began to rise again, and since 1990 the wealth-to-income ratio in Europe has overtaken that of the United States (Frangakis 2014: 28).

The policy of distribution is very much in accordance with the Polanyian approach.

Land

When it comes to land there is only one purely fictional commodity: land. Nature was established historically and categorically prior to human institutions. Since land, water, and air unequivocally exist without human action or intent, the assignment of property rights to these elements is fictitious commodity improvements par excellence. The attribution of any aspect of ownership bundle (occupation, use, or sale) is therefore a fictitious commodity (Bonen and Coronado 2015).

Regarding land, Polanyi was also prescient as he in 1944 laid the foundations for an ecological critique of capitalism. He understood that nature is an indispensable prerequisite both for social life in general and for raw material production. He also understood that unrestrained use of nature is unsustainable, bound to damage both society and the economy. If land is reduced to a factor of production and exposed to unregulated market exchange, nature is destined to become a crisis node. At the same time, such treatment is the basis for provoking resistance and triggering countermovements to protect nature and human habitats from the ravages of the market. Polanyi also envisioned here a double movement, a two-sided struggle between environmentalists and free marketeers (Fraser 2012).

In the EU, agricultural policy and thus the use of land was one of the first common policy fields. Based on Article 39 of the Treaty of Rome in 1957, the intention was to increase the marketing of agricultural land by raising productivity via optimal utilization of the production factors. This led to price support, which gave rise to extra profits for larger farms and encouraged them to endlessly intensify production. This led to increasing support costs and consequently dumping on the world market. At the same time, market forces created pressure to industrialize processes, which entailed increasing pollution and loss of landscape heritage (Barthélemy and Nieddu 2007).

However, agricultural production in the EU extends further. The agro-food sector has become an arena for the double movement of global capitalism since the 1970s. The most important thing is the feed–livestock–meat complex, which experienced unprecedented economic growth but also raised social and environmental concerns about excessive meat production and consumption, as Europeans eat large amounts of meat and pork is their favorite variety.

Through large-scale imports of animal feed, the EU has expanded its access to land beyond its borders, thus expanding the worldwide agricultural frontier (Krausmann and Langthaler 2019). European pressure on overseas regions is mainly located in South America, primarily in Brazil and Argentina.

The accumulation of land, removed from rural communities and their environments, in the hands of the wealthy and powerful agricultural elite fueled various countermovements. In the 1990s, the displaced rural population formed the Landless Rural Workers' Movement, the largest social movement in Latin America.

A focus on prudent and sustainable use of land is strongly present in Polanyian thinking.

ECONOMICS FOR THE FUTURE: A POLANYIAN OUTLINE

A critical theory for the twenty-first century must be integrative, oriented towards understanding the current crisis. This can be done, among other things, by adopting Polanyi's idea of fictitious goods, to connect three major dimensions of the crisis: the ecological, the social-reproductive, and the financial (Fraser 2012).

What we can take from Polanyi is not so much his own answers, but the questions he poses. That challenge is multifaceted and should interest post-Keynesian economists. His contributions to the debates and substantivism and formalism remain relevant. Polanyi challenges us to understand economic systems from the point of view of the organization of production and distribution (substantivism), and to see them as historically highly differentiated phenomena, rather than assuming a series of minor variations in imperfect markets (formalism). Polanyi challenges us by asking what type of economic thinking actually applies, and also questions the assumption that reference to conventional economic theory can automatically provide adequate explanatory value.

Polanyi basically claims that there has been a conscious will throughout history to gradually commodify three factors of production – labor, money, and land. This transformation appears as a necessary prerequisite for the emergence of a "self-regulating" market (Postel and Sobel 2010), as the market must set a price for raw materials, the number of working hours, and productive assets financed with credit. The market economy thus needs these "fictitious goods" to establish its hegemony and ensure its endless expansion. For Polanyi, however, this transformation is unthinkable. Labor, money, and land are not commodities. These factors have never been produced to be sold.

His view is that only by assuming the material meaning of "economic" will we be able to provide the social sciences with the necessary categories for the study of all real economies of the past and present. For this reason, substantivists are particularly interested in studying economic institutions, i.e., the social structures that create the necessary framework for people to engage in activities such as production, distribution, and consumption.

For Polanyi, history is not subject to laws that drive it in certain directions. Better human attempts to understand historical experience are represented by theories for good or for worse. These theories shape responses to this experience, which then become part of the story. Because theories are formulated to understand historical experience, they must be evaluated within the context of that experience. An example could be the understanding of the rise and fall of nations and groups that may depend on whether their institutions are adapted to an underlying process of social change (Polanyi 1944: 27). The underlying process is often hidden and misunderstood by contemporaries.

Another way of understanding this is, following Polanyi, that it is not the market's failure to function according to the ideal of perfect competition that requires regulation, as neoclassical economics claims. Rather, the impact of market competition on social areas that are impaired by the market mechanism itself should be the primary area of regulatory effort. However, these regulatory efforts known from New Public Management are bound to fail under conditions of an institutional separation of political and economic affairs. Therefore, the regulation of markets can be examined in relation to the public sector and markets that develop together. It is crucial that the public sector not only deals with entrenched forms of market regulation, but also with the construction of markets through settlement procedures that promote the institutional and social conditions for market exchange. Therefore, it is a central Polanyian insight that regulation of markets is closely linked to the institutional features of market competition in society.

The commodification of labor is linked to the phenomenon of unemployment and, as Polanyi announced, can be traced back to the origins of capitalism. From a feminist perspective, it can even be made invisible to the eyes of the market, in cases where women's unemployment results in them working in their own homes instead. However, income from work is indispensable for the reproduction of families, and since housework is not valued, it forces women to sell their labor power, thereby also becoming a commodity on the labor market.

The commoditization of land has provoked its own speculation, such as removing land from farmers in the case of some Latin American countries. It also fueled urban land price speculation that has led to severe housing problems, rising costs of living in big cities, and fraud by real-estate companies. The other visible problem is the effects of environmental destruction. All environmental damage caused by the treatment of land, water, underground, air, and climate change was considered as subject to supply and demand. Furthermore, because they are not commodities, it is impossible to measure their true value with money.

The idea that environmental problems should be solved by government regulation changed in the 1970s against the background of fuel crises and environmentalists' warnings of an impending environmental collapse. Environmental issues, once largely treated as local political and regulatory failures, were recast as a form of quantified global aggregates. This has shifted normative understandings of causality from specific actors to a generalized "humanity" whose collective behavior has resulted in existential and rather intractable "global" crises. In parallel with the fact that the ecological and social consequences of globalization and growth have become more pressing and difficult to ignore, market thinking and financial valuation have increasingly found their way into environmental policies (Chiapello 2015).

As for the main international development institutions such as the International Monetary Fund, World Bank, and General Agreement on Tariffs and Trade/World Trade Organization, these are designed to enforce, not remedy, the market stratification that exists on a global scale. Until this changes, private growth in the international economy will continue to be the preferred policy solution for the richest states. The formalistic market mentality neglects the essential past and misreads much of the essential present. Having done so, it is of very limited use in efforts to imagine an alternative future. As in the past, we remain unprepared for the difficult choices that lie ahead. But instead of attributing this to our "outdated market mentality," perhaps it would be more accurate and more constructive to see our cultural attitudes as the product of a still-functioning market society.

A twenty-first-century critical theory must also connect the critique of commodification with the critique of dominance, going beyond Polanyi's idea of a double movement. Rodrik (2000), for example, has described a trilemma that states that democracy, national sovereignty, and global economic integration are mutually incompatible: we can combine two of the three, but never all three simultaneously. According to Rodrik, states embraced globalization and national autonomy in the late nineteenth century but sacrificed democratic decision making. In the post-Second World War period, states dealt with globalization via the Bretton Woods Agreement while embracing domestic democracy and national autonomy. The trilemma suggests that the reaction against greater globalization in the last few decades is rooted in a desire to regain democracy and national autonomy, even as it undermines economic integration.

As capital remains powerful in the economic sphere of capitalism, it becomes the stronghold of industrialists and capitalists, who form a minority in the political sphere as they are usually fewer in number. The democratic process ensures that workers, who are typically more numerous, control politics by building strong unions. If no tension is present, the conflict of interest remains latent. Once it breaks out, however, the system crashes. Due – in Polanyi's view – to the artificial and institutionalized separation of the economic and political spheres, the conflicting interests are no longer balanced by a compromise and turn into an intense conflict between the economic and political spheres; this is problematic because one needs the other to work.

Polanyi's critique, including the idea of fictitious goods, sought to expose contradictions of the "self-regulating market" model in the context of industrial capitalism. However, capitalism and the dynamics of value creation, as well as the shape, scale, and framework of environmental crises, have evolved greatly since the 1940s. Changes are reflected in the development of resource management, state–capital relations, and synergies between industrial and financial globalization. Market value is still created from nature through harmful industrial means of extraction, but also through technologies of economic extraction.

Polanyi arrives at the following question: what can be expected from the next movement? The direction the current system is moving toward is a form of socially coordinated capitalism, or toward "more of the same." Fraser (2014) shows that transformation of the basis of social life into fictitious goods has a strong echo in twenty-first-century society. The effects of this were already announced by Polanyi, but for future generations it deserves much attention, since the coming consequences of the second transformation are no less than those of the first transformation – quite the opposite.

A FINAL PERSPECTIVE

For good reasons, inspiration has been called for to renew the current economic thinking – especially after the financial crisis in 2007/2008. An attempt has been made here to summarize an exploratory study of Karl Polanyi's relevance, not least for post-Keynesian economic thinking.

There is basically a very good basis for this, as broadly the same economic methodology is used. Furthermore, Polanyi can provide several theoretical impulses and angles that can help develop a more comprehensive and critical theory about the crisis of the twenty-first century containing a summary perspective around ecology, financialization, and social reproduction.

The most interesting angle is Polanyi's focus on fictitious goods, i.e., those goods where a difference in use and exchange value can be immediately ascertained. A very central question is thus asked about how a supply function can even be provided for work, land, and money. This both opens new theoretical insights and focuses on the limitations of economic models.

Like Polanyi's analysis of the transformation of nineteenth-century Europe, the same happened to Europe with the introduction of the single market and a common currency. Among other things, this has resulted in a more extensive financialization, a falling wage share, and increasingly intensive land use.

It is important to protect democracy from the disruptive consequences of free markets, and this is only possible by expanding democracy to include markets in the form of decommodification of labor, land, and money.

REFERENCES

Alenda-Demoutiez, Juliette (2022) From economic growth to the human: Reviewing the history of development visions over time and moving forward, *Third World Quarterly*, 43:5, 1038–1055.

Barthélemy, Denis and Martino Nieddu (2007) Non-trade concerns in agricultural and environmental economics: How J. R. Commons and Karl Polanyi can help us, *Journal of Economic Issues*, 41:2, 519–527.

Bonen, Anthony and José Coronado (2015) Delineating the process of fictive commodification in advanced capitalism, Paper, New School for Social Research. https://newschool.academia.edu/AnthonyBonen/CurriculumVitae

Chiapello, Eve (2015) Financialisation of valuation, *Human Studies*, 38:1, 13–35.

Frangakis, Marica (2014) Inequality and financialisation: The case of the EU, RLS, 29 April. www.rosalux.de/publikation/id/7753/inequality-and-financialisation-the-case-of-the-eu

Fraser, Nancy (2012) Can society be commodities all the way down? Polanyian reflections on capitalist crisis, FMSHWP-2012-18, August.

Fraser, Nancy (2014) Can society be commodities all the way down? Post-Polanyian reflections on capitalist crisis, *Economy and Society*, 43:4, 541–558.

Gemici, Kurtulus (2008) Karl Polanyi and the antinomies of embeddedness, *Socio-Economic Review*, 6, 5–33.

Goldmann, Matthias (2017) The great recurrence: Karl Polanyi and the crises of the European Union, Max Planck Institute for Comparative Public Law and International Law Research Paper No. 2017-10. https://ssrn.com/abstract=2971073 or http://dx.doi.org/10.2139/ssrn.2971073

Granovetter, Mark (1985) Economic action and social structure: The problem of embeddedness, *American Journal of Sociology*, 91:3, 481–510.

Hein, Eckhard (2016) Causes and consequences of the financial crisis and the implications for a more resilient financial and economic system, IPE Working Papers 61/2016, Berlin School of Economics and Law, Institute for International Political Economy.

Krausmann, Fridolin and Ernst Langthaler (2019) Food regimes and their trade links: A socio-ecological perspective, *Ecological Economics*, 160:C, 87–95.

Lavoie, Marc (2010) Are we all Keynesians? *Brazilian Journal of Political Economy*, 30:2, 189–200.

Lavoie, Marc (2019) History and fundamentals of post-Keynesian macroeconomics, Lecture, FFM conference. www.youtube.com/watch?v=DEROFQIao4o

Machado, Nuno Miguel Cardoso (2011) Karl Polanyi and the New Economic Sociology: Notes on the concept of (dis)embeddedness, *Revista Crítica de Ciências Sociais*, 3.

Madsen, Mogens Ove (2022) Keynesian economics steering is back – end of liberal economic policy? In B. Greve (Ed.), *In a Turbulent Area*, Cheltenham, UK and Northampton, MA, USA Edward Elgar Publishing.

Piketty, Thomas and Gabriel Zucman (2014) Capital is back: Wealth-income ratios in rich countries 1700–2010. *Quarterly Journal of Economics*, 129:3, 1255–1310.

Polanyi, K. (1944) *The Great Transformation*, New York: Rinehart.

Polanyi, K. (1977) *The Livelihood of Man: Studies in Social Discontinuity*, New York: Academic Press.

Postel, Nicolas and Richard Sobel (2010) La RSE: nouvelle forme de dé-marchandisation du monde?, *Développement durable et territoires*, 1:3.

Rodrik, Dani (2000) How far will international economic integration go?, *Journal of Economic Perspectives*, 14:1, 177–186.

Sawyer, Malcolm (2022) *Financialization, Economic and Social Impacts*, Newcastle: Agenda Publishing.

Index